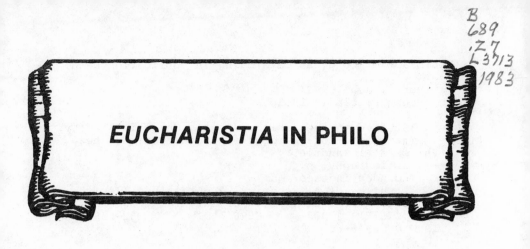

EUCHARISTIA IN PHILO

Jean LaPorte

Studies in the Bible and Early Christianity
Volume Three

The Edwin Mellen Press
New York and Toronto

Library of Congress Cataloging in Publication Data

LaPorte, Jean, 1924-
    Eucharistia in Philo.

    (Studies in the Bible and early Christianity ; v. 3)
    Translation of: La doctrine eucharistique chez
Philon d'Alexandrie.
    Bibliography: p.
    Includes indexes.
    1. Philo, of Alexandria. 2. Gratitude (Jewish
theology) I. Title. II. Series.
B689.Z7L3713 1983   296.7'2   82-25876
ISBN 0-88946-601-7

Studies in the Bible and Early Christianity
    ISBN 0-88946-913-X

The Edwin Mellen Press
P.O. Box 450
Lewiston, New York   14092

Printed in the United States of America

PREFACE

The publication of this English translation of La doctrine eucharistique chez Philon d'Alexandrie is due to the reception of the French original, and to the cooperation of many to whom I wish to acknowledge a debt of gratitude.

My book has been abundantly reviewed in Journals, and generally well accepted.[1] As a Philonic study, it shows the philological, liturgical, cosmological, and spiritual aspects of Philo's concept of eucharistia. Since its publication in 1972, except for studies relating the origins of the Christian Eucharist to Philo, nothing substantial has been added to the understanding of the Philonic eucharistia. These recent studies are mentioned as a complement to the Bibliography. They attest the importance of the study of eucharistia in Philo. The parallels between Philo and Palestinian Judaism refer to established scholarship, and serve a limited purpose within the study as a whole. But my book, as a Philonic study, does not pretend to be complete in this or other fields. During the ten years following the completion of my book, biblical scholarship has considerably increased. I have not attempted to incorporate this scholarship since it does not change the state of the question.

Acknowledging my debt of gratitude, first I want to renew my thanks to Cardinal Jean Daniélou, Mrs. Monique Alexandre, and Rev. Charles Kannengiesser, who not only honored this thesis on the day of its defense, but also contributed to its improvement by their suggestions. I am particularly indebted to Mrs. Alexandre for many philological remarks, for suggesting a stronger emphasis on pairs of opposite terms which is the key to the Philonic dialectics, and for the recommendation to give special treatment to the images of thanksgiving such as memory, loan, exchange and restitution a parallel to the term eucharistia and the other terms referring to praise, blessing and confession.

Finally, to Ms. Monique Cadic who prepared and published this book in the Beauchesne edition and permitted the English translation, to Prof. F. Ellen Weaver who revised the English translation, to Paul Meyendorff who edited the text and suggested many improvements, and especially to Prof. Herbert W. Richardson, Susan Reinbold, Marcia Moldowan and the staff of the Edwin Mellen Press, I am pleased to be myself eucharistos.

Jean LaPorte

Notre Dame, Indiana
20 June 1982

TABLE OF CONTENTS

PREFACE

INTRODUCTION

CHAPTER ONE   "EUCHARISTIA" AND OTHER EXPRESSIONS OF   1
                THANKSGIVING: A TERMINOLOGICAL ENQUIRY   7

  I.   The use of "eucharistein" outside the writings
     of Philo   8
     1.   In Greek, outside Judaism   8
     2.   In LXX and the *Letter of Aristeas*   16

  II.   The terms and rites expressing thanksgiving in
     the Bible   17
     1.   *Hll* (to praise)   17
     2.   *Kbd* (to glorify)   18
     3.   *Brk* (to bless)   19
     4.   *Hodah* (to praise)   20
     5.   *Todah* (praise)   22
     6.   *Neder* (vow)   24

  III.   The survival of biblical terms expressing
     thanksgiving in Philo   25
     1.   Hymns (*hymein*)   26
     2.   The honour paid to God (*timan*)   28
     3.   To bless God *(eulogein)*   30
     4.   The sacrifice of salvation with *todah*   31
     5.   Confession (*homologein, exomologeisthai*)   32

  IV.   The term *"eucharistein"* - *"eucharistia"* in Philo   36
     1.   *Charisterion*   36
     2.   *Eucharistiai*   37
     3.   *Eucharistia-acharistia, eucharistos-*
        acharistos   38
     4.   *Eucharistia* introduced by a preposition   39
     5.   The verb *Eucharistein*   39

  V.   Images with the connotation of thanksgiving
     in Philo   42
     1.   The memory of God and of His gifts   42
     2.   Reception, exchange, loan, restitution   44
     3.   Consecration and votive offering   45

CHAPTER TWO "EUCHARISTIA" AND LITURGY   49

   I.   *Eucharistia* and Benediction   50
         1. *Eucharistein* used in reference to the
            prayers at meals   53

  II. *Eucharistia* and *todah*   55
         1. Macarism or Beatitude   59

 III. *Eucharistia* and daily burnt-offerings   61

  IV. Burnt-offerings and vegetable offerings   63

   V. The meaning of the offering of the shew-bread
       in Judaism: comparison with Philo   68
         1. The meaning of incense offering and
            vegetable offering in Judaism:
            comparison with Philo   69

  VI. The eucharistic connotation of the first-
       fruits   70

 VII. *Eucharistia* and Jewish feasts   73
         1. The festival of every day   74
         2. The Sabbath and the Newmoon   75
         3. Passover, the Sheaf, the Shew-bread   77
         4. The feast of the Seven Weeks   81
         5. The feast of Tabernacles   85
         6. The feast of the Basket   88

VIII. Service of God and *eucharistia*   89
         1. Levitic priesthood and eucharistic
            mediation   90
         2. The sacrifice of prayer   93
         3. The service of God and the spiritual
            cult: Jewish positions compared to
            Philo's teaching   94

CHAPTER THREE   "EUCHARISTIA" AND COSMIC RELIGION   99

   I. Cosmic aspects in the forerunners of Philo   100
         1. The allegory of the "Physicists"   100
         2. Cosmic aspects of Wisdom of Solomon   102
         3. The *Letter of Aristeas*   103

II.   Cosmic thanksgiving in Philo   104
      1.   The world has a destiny of praise   106
      2.   Logos and high-priest   108
      3.   The furniture of the Tabernacle   111
      4.   The two altars, and sacrifices   113
      5.   The sacrifice of the Covenant of
           Abraham   115

III. The quest for a cosmic and anthropological
      philosophy in agreement with the principle
      of piety toward God   116
      1.   The philosophical "Tenets" of Philo   117
      2.   Criticism of the Greek philosophies in
           the language of biblical symbols   119
           a.   Cain, the Tower of Babel, Egypt   119
           b.   Those removed from the Assembly
                of God   120
           c.   The Chaldeans   123
      3.   Criticism of the particular philosophies
           in their own language   124
      4.   The rejection of materialism   125
      5.   The theology of the old Plato and of the
           young Aristotle   126
      6.   The maxim of Protagoras   131

IV.   Philonic teachings on the relations between
      God and the world   133

CHAPTER FOUR   "EUCHARISTIA" AND THE INTERIOR LIFE OF
               THE SOUL   139

I.   The beginnings of a theology of grace before
      Philo   141
      1.   Philo's contemporaries   141
      2.   Wisdom of Solomon   142
      3.   The *Letter of Aristeas*   143

II.   Aspects of grace, and our attitude toward
      grace, in symbols, allegories, and biblical
      laws, in Philo   144
      1.   The symbolism of grace   144
      2.   The allegories of virtue   147
      3.   The laws on the attitude to be taken
           toward grace   155

III. Parallels to these teachings in Greek
      philosophy and in Judaism   157
      1. God as a source of light   157
      2. God as Sower   160
      3. The three ways to acquire virtue: by
          learning, by nature, by asceticism   165

IV. The problem of merit   172
      1. In Philo   172
      2. The controversy on merit at the time
          of Philo   176

CONCLUSION   179

FOOTNOTES   187

ABBREVIATIONS   243

BIBLIOGRAPHY   245

INDICES   255

INTRODUCTION

The purpose of the present inquiry[1] is to trace and to explain as completely as possible Philo's notion of Eucharistia, a topic which has received little attention in the past. A few short studies have been published by F.J.A. Hort and J.O.F. Murray, "Eucharistia - Eucharistein."[2] Theodor Schermann, "'Eucharistia' und 'eucharistein' in ihrem Bedeutungvandel bis 200 n. Ch.,"[3] Paul Schubert, Form and Function of the Pauline Thanksgiving,[4] R.J. Ledogar, Acknowledgment, Praise-verbs in the Early Greek Anaphora.[5] These authors did not deal with the Philonic Eucharistia for its own sake, but only as one aspect of a larger study and in particular in relation to the Christian Eucharist. In the great studies on Philo, for instance, Emile Bréhier, Les idées philosophiques et religieuses de Philon d'Alexandrie,[6] Issak Heinemann, Philons griechische und judische Bildung,[7] Erwin R. Goodenough, By Light Light, The Mystic Gospel of Hellenistic Judaism,[8] Harry Wolfson, Philo,[9] we find almost nothing on Eucharistia. Wolfson grants it a few pages in a section on prayer.[10] Jean Danielou, in his Philon d'Alexandrie,[11] deals with the spiritual teachings of Philo and writes some suggestive pages on his theology of grace,[12] but, because of the limits he imposed on his own exposition, he can only offer suggestions for further research. Heinemann's study is very important in many respects because of its erudition, and because it seriously examines for the first time the data of Philo in the light of our knowledge of the Judaism of his time. But this study is very disappointing in regard to Eucharistia. In the first place Heinemann does not deal directly or sufficiently with it, and secondly, his whole understanding of Philo's spiritual teachings is coloured, if not vitiated, by his basic assumption that Philo is preaching Cynic Ethics and even relies on a "Cynic source," which he tries to reconstitute. Seen through this interpretation, the spirituality of Philo does not preserve very much of its own identity, or even of its Jewish nature. It is precisely what Heinemann overlooks, in particular, all the data on sacrifices and Jewish festivals, which is most important to this study. Scholars, for good reasons, have paid much attention to Philo's allegorical developments and have found in them cause for admiration or for scandal. All too often, however, their curiosity stopped there, and they did not discover, beyond Philo the allegorist, Philo the commentator on Jewish liturgy. In his book, The Jurisprudence of the Jewish Courts in Egypt,[13] E.R. Goodenough pointed out the importance of Philo as an expert of civil law. The present monograph does the same

1

for Philo's understanding of the liturgy, but its scope is
more limited, dealing only with Eucharistic aspects, which
he emphasizes.

It was a great surprise to discover the sacrificial
aspect of the Philonic Eucharistia, which was not, as supposed, limited to the notion of praise, nor bound to the
inconsistent framework of the allegories. Recent studies
such as those of Kurt Hruby, "Les heures de priere dans le
judaisme a l'epoque de Jesus,"[14] E. Lipinski, "Macarismes et
Psaumes de congratulation,"[15] R.K. Yerkes, Sacrifice in
Greek and Roman Religions and Early Judaism,[16] and particularly H. Cazelles, "L'Anaphore et l'Ancien Testament,"[17]
confirmed this new approach. The prayer of praise in Philo
is strongly eucharistic, but the eucharistic prayer itself
was already connected with the sacrifices of the Temple. In
Judaism, sacrifices and festivals were progressively imbued
with certain religious components. The Judaic liturgical
data, which are complex and sometimes obscure in their
meaning, include some Eucharistic aspects which are basic
and obvious. Thanksgiving is connected with agrarian rites
and refers to the Divine bestowal of the harvest. But it
also refers to the history of Israel, especially to the
Exodus and the Covenant. These two principles determine the
interpretation of the Ritual, whatever its detail. These
principles also determine the interpretation of the Philonic
Eucharistia. The book of A. Jaubert, La notion d'Alliance
dans le judaisme aux abords de l'ère chrétienne,[18] sheds
much light on the theology of the Covenant and, consequently, on the understanding of the notion of grace and of
the Ritual in both official and sectarian Judaism, in the
Judaism of the Diaspora, and particularly in that of Philo.
Her sections on the Priesthood of Israel, on spiritual
sacrifice, on the spirituality of Qumran, and her chapter on
Philo provide valuable insights.

The religious philosophy of Philo suggests two other
fields of investigation about Eucharistia. The first is the
Philonic vision of the world and of man, i.e., his cosmology
and anthropology. The second is his spirituality, i.e., his
conception of the life of the soul and of the development of
the particular virtues. E. Bréhier, E.R. Goodenough, H.A.
Wolfson, A.J. Festugière, La révélation d'Hermès
Trismégiste,[19] Jean Pépin, Théologie cosmique et théologie
chrétienne,[20] Jean Daniélou, and others present a very
complete study of these aspects, as well as of the sources
from which Philo could have drawn and of the influences
which acted upon him more or less directly. However, here
too the notion of Eucharistia was found to be a useful

criterion for understanding of Philo. In his eucharistic
vision of the great and the small cosmos, and the life of
virtue, he is truly original and reveals his fundamental
concern. As a consequence of his faith in God, everything
in the new field which his exceptional philosophical background had opened to him had to be referred to God. Thus
our inquiry led to our dealing with remote and proximate
sources of Philo, and to making comparisons. In the cosmological and anthropolgical section which deals with the
problem of the Chaldeans in Philo, Le Dieu cosmique of
A.J. Festugière was very helpful. It directed attention to
Plato and the lost treatise De philosophia of Aristotle,
rather than simply to the Stoics, as suggested earlier by E.
Brehier. Philo is struggling against Pantheism, opposing
the philosophy of a world without a Charioteer, or of a
world organized and quickened by a soul which is not ultimately transcendent to it. For this reason, according to
Philo, the believer must be purified by the ordeal of philosophical skepticism in order to reach the evidence of God.
Only thus can man affirm his faith in the transcendent God--
a faith expressed through confession and praise, both of
which are eminently eucharistic, since by restoring God to
the world and to man, one restores the world and man to God.

A.-J. Festugière and J. Pépin proved the influence of
the Young Aristotle on Philo of Alexandria and solved the
old problem, complicated by the accretions of many centuries
of philosophical and religious history, of the Demiurge of
Timaeus, by showing that the Father and Maker of Plato was a
mythical explanation of the origins of the world superimposed on a properly philosophical explanation by the
theory of the soul of the world. Following them, it was
possible to cope successfully with some apparent contradic-
tions in Philo, especially when he praises Aristotle for his
faith in God, but is never fully satisfied elsewhere with
his theology.

The proximate sources, the Letter of Aristeas, probably
the Wisdom of Solomon, and the Alexandrian Allegorists, show
a common interest in the cosmos and in the doctrine of its
creation by a transcendent God; but Philo moves far beyond
them when he develops his notion of the Cosmic Eucharistia
by the method of allegory. Old Jewish Prayers, particularly
the Hymns of Qumran, offer interesting parallels to the
Philonic notion of cosmic praise without indulging in
allegory.

The religious philosophy of Philo is not limited to the
problems of the structure of the world and of man, or to the

metaphysical question of their dependence on God.   It also
delves into the life of the soul and examines the birth and
development of virtue.   Knowledge, speech, and action are
involved in this process.   Philo's psychology is complex,
reflecting the contribution of several centuries and of
different schools.   The eucharistic aspect seems to determine the preoccupations of Philo himself and to provide a
way of bringing a kind of unity to the complexity of his
psychological theories.   In the first place, it serves to
explain how God can be the author of all that is best in
man--his thoughts, words, and good deeds, in a word, his
virtues--who is the crown of the created universe.
Secondly, it serves to refute the opposite attitude, self
love, which is the vice contrary to thanksgiving.
Theocentrism and anthropocentrism confront each other within
the soul itself, and Philo does not consider this conflict
as a mere refinement of thought, but as a matter of first
importance.   Protagoras and Cain are, among the Greeks and
in Scripture respectively, the protagonists of self-love;
while Abel with Juda are, among others, the witnesses to the
love for and confession of God.   Once more, the remedy is
thanksgiving, but this time not for the world and man, but
for the good accomplished in man.   To elaborate this, Philo
uses the symbolism of the persons and of the laws of
Scripture, particularly the laws on the first-fruits.   He
also uses an allegorical interpretation of the furniture of
the temple and of the incense offering, which refer to the
sacrifice of the soul as well as to that of the world.   The
remote sources, once more, are Plato and the De philosophia
of Aristotle, as well as the tradition of religious experience represented by the Hymn of Cleanthes.   The Letter of
Aristeas is a proximate source of particular importance,
because it contains a highly developed theology of grace.
Thanksgiving for the goods of the soul is found also in
Jewish prayers, particularly in the Hymns of Qumran.

        This inquiry into the Philonic theology of grace led to
an important discovery: Philo   seems to be very concerned
with the defense and the development of a theology of grace
in the context of the inner life, because a real danger
threatens those who are advanced in the way of virtue and
close to perfection.   This danger can be discerned only by
those who have reached this point and by the spiritual
writers who study the higher levels of religious life.   It
is particularly interesting to notice that both Philo, in
Egypt, and the spiritual masters of Qumran consider this
danger as very grave.   The texts of Qumran, cited in order
to show the way they address the problem of justification,
give witness to this concern.   And the same can be said of

Jewish prayers.   This literature reveals a certain distrust
of merit, and refuses to extol it as the cause of justification.   In other words, an ascetic should attribute the fruit
of his virtues, to God and not to himself.   He must, therefore, accept the idea of the operation of the grace of God
in the birth and development of his virtue.   He should not
assume that he is justified by his good deeds, i.e., by the
power of his will without the help of God.   This conclusion
is an extension of the theology of the Covenant to the inner
life.   To take pleasure in one's good deeds, or to consider
oneself as their only author without further distinction, is
to deny the necessity of God and to introduce impiety at the
summit of spiritual life, at the moment when perfection
itself seems close at hand.   With the gospel let us call
this perversion "Pharisaism," without presuming that it
represents the true position of the Pharisees.   As a remedy
to this perversion, Philo offers thanksgiving, since it is
the antidote to self-love.   Thus the importance of the
Philonic teaching on Eucharistia becomes clear, and it is
not surprising that it has impact on all his other teachings
and that it reappears on almost every page of his
commentaries when they deal with liturgical, ethical, or
psychological matters.

CHAPTER ONE

"EUCHARISTIA"

AND THE OTHER EXPRESSIONS OF THANKSGIVING

A TERMINOLOGY ENQUIRY

Our study begins with the consideration of the terms of the eucharistein family in Philo of Alexandria, the general meaning of which is "to give thanks". The use of these terms by Philo is very extensive. There are at least 150 references, including about 40 to the word eucharistia, and it is not possible to give the exact number of references in Questions on Genesis and Questions on Exodus, since these treatises survive mostly in an Armenian translation where the identification of the original Greek word is often questionable. But the investigation of the term eucharistein presupposes a series of preliminary inquiries.

First, we must know the history of this term. Eucharistein is a composed word, of recent origin like all the words with the prefixe eu-, which is found before Philo in concurrence with older constructions such as charin apodidonai in profane literature, in inscriptions and papyri, in LXX and in the Letter of Aristeas. The several connotations of this term in profane literature reappear in Philo, especially in connection with sacrifices and praise. The use of eucharistein in LXX is disappointing when we need a comparison with Philo, since this term is absent from the canonical books of Moses, and is found only in the last books of the Bible, which are translated into Greek or written directly in this language. Philo does not refer to these books, and he cites only Proverbs. After Philo, we find eucharistein in the New Testament, Josephus, Didache and the Fathers of the Church. Aquila uses eucharistia in his Greek version to translate todah.

In the canonical books, since Philo comments only on the Pentateuch, we must consider the Hebrew terms which LXX translates by ainein (to praise), homologein (to acknowledge), eulogein (to bless), doxazein (to glorify), hymnein (to praise in hymns). All these terms except doxazein reappear in Philo together with or associated to eucharistein.

7

Coming to Philo himself, we shall see how he uses these Greek terms especially eucharistein, in relation to the meaning of the Hebrew terms mentioned above. With a masterful possession of the Greek language, and with some innovations of his own, Philo employs the composition and the etymology of these terms in order to provide his teaching with a basis in biblical philology.[1]

Finally, Philo uses images to express thanksgiving. Among these images, first of all, are either the memory or the forgetting of God and of His blessings. Then there are the metaphors referring to the notions of reception, exchange, loan and restitution, and the group of images expressing the idea of consecration and votive offering. These images are essentially Mosaic laws, the literal meaning of which Philo does not contest, and which are very important in the life of the Israelites. The allegorical use of these laws simply extends their scope so that they become laws governing spiritual as well as temporal life.

These uses are typical of the general way he twists the literal meaning of most biblical texts where he finds the notion of thanksgiving. But symbolism and allegory divert attention from the literal meaning and from concrete people, things, and laws, only to focus it on the corresponding realities in the inner man. In this sense, the Philonic eucharistia appears to be chiefly spiritual. However, it would be wrong to limit it to this aspect, since eucharistia is not always a silent prayer, but finds its expression in words and in music. In addition, eucharistia belongs to the literal meaning of most of the laws on sacrifice.

I. THE USE OF "EUCHARISTEIN" OUTSIDE THE WRITINGS OF PHILO

1. In Greek, outside Judaism

The use of eucharistein and of terms with the same root has been studied more than once in the past. Regarding the Greek and Hellenistic literature excepting Philo, LXX, the New Testament, and early Christian literature, I have nothing to add, but we shall simply give a short account of the results, relying on the studies of Theodor Schermann (1910),[2] of Paul Schubert (1939),[3] of R.K. Yerkes (1963),[4] of Leon Halkin (1953)[5] and of R.J. Ledogar (1968),[6] Theodore Schermann limits his inquiry too narrowly to the terms eucharistia and eucharistein, but he pays much attention to their several forms and to their grammatical constructions. Paul Schubert extends his inquiry to the data of the papyri

and compares the epistolary formulae where these terms are
found to those of the Pauline Epistles. His study demonstrates that eucharistein was used in the Hellenistic times
with increasing frequency. R.J. Ledogar synthesizes the
results of this research. He rightly thinks that
eucharistein ought to be studied not in isolation, but
within a larger group of phrases with the same meaning and
containing the term charis. His purpose is to study the
history of the terms of praise (ainein, hymnein, homologein,
doxazein, eulogein, proskunein and their cognates) which,
together with eucharistein, appear in the prefaces of the
Christian anaphoras. R.K. Yerkes, in his study on
sacrifices and their terminology, widens the overly narrow
perspective of the eucharistein family. He also completes
our knowledge of the terms and rites of thanksgiving in
Scripture with a study of the vocabulary and customs of
thanksgiving among the Greeks. Leon Halkin contributes with
a parallel inquiry into thanksgiving among the Romans.

The eucharistein family is poorly represented in
classical literature, but its use increases in Hellenistic
times, after 300 B.C. The adjective eucharistos is found
once in Herodotus, three times in Xenophon.[7] The substantive eucharistia appears first in Hippocrates, if the section is genuine,[8] in a spurious writing of Demosthenes,[9] and
in Menander.[10] The meaning of the substantive in Menander
is "gratitude", and that of the adjective in Xenophon is
"pleasant" or "thankful".[11]

In Hellenistic times, eucharistein already appears with
all the constructions and meanings which it will have in the
future. Though not without several preliminary mutations of
meaning it becomes an expression of gratitude. The
Grammarians J. Pollux and Phrynicus define it as "being
benevolent", or "being grateful" (charin didonai), rather
than acknowledging a debt (charin eidenai).[12] The use of
the adjective eucharistos in inscriptions such as "the
thankful people" (ho demos eucharistos) also points to a
disposition of benevolence or gratitude.[13] We find the same
meaning in a construction such as eucharistein eis tina, to
show gratitude or benevolence towards someone in an inscription in honor of King Ptolemaeus.[14] In the first century,
with a dative complement or with the prepositions epi and
peri, the term eucharistein came actually to mean 'to thank'
and not just a disposition of benevolence or gratitude which
can please a benefactor.[15] Schermann discovers the meaning
of 'giving thanks' already in inscriptions dating to the end
of the third century B.C., but especially in the first
century B.C.[16] The post-Christian construction eucharistein

tina, or ti tini, "to thank someone for something,"
represents the conclusion of this development.[17]

In Hellenistic times the substantive eucharistia just
as the verb eucharistein, came to mean not only the disposition to be thankful, but also the expression of gratitude.
We find this meaning in Polybius, in the second century
B.C.[18] Schermann studies this verb in its several constructions, with a genitive objective and a genitive subjective,
with pros (tina), eis, charin, eneken.[19] He notes the form
eucharisterios in Polybius and Dionysius of Halicarnassus.[20]
In the latter, the reference is to eucharistic sacrifices
offered up to gods. P. Schubert observes that among other
instances of eucharistein found in inscriptions and papyri
in the Hellenistic times, there are references to thanksgiving to gods.[21]

R.K. Yerkes gives a rich description of the forms and
terms of thanksgiving among the Greeks. With him, we move
beyond the overly narrow limits of the term eucharistein itself, and we reach the other, generally older, expressions
and the rites and customs to which they refer. On the subject of vows and votive offerings among the Greeks, Yerkes
says:

> Vows were common in Greece both in
> the premigration days described by Homer
> and in the historical, strictly Greek
> days. The vow to sacrifice twelve
> heifers to Athene, if she would grant
> victory, is well known.[22] Agamemon
> vowed to present Teucer with a tripod,
> or two horses, or a concubine, if Zeus
> and Athene would allow him to conquer
> Ilium.[23] Before the battle of Marathon
> the Athenians made a vow to Artemis
> pledging, if they won, to sacrifice to
> her she-goats equal in number to the
> number of corpses of the slain enemy.
> They slew so many that the vow could not
> be discharged immediately; they
> accordingly divided their pledge into
> installments of five hundred per year
> and seem to have continued the payment
> for many decades.[24] Vows to perform
> acts for the gods abound throughout
> Greek legend and history. The pledge
> and performance of such vows must be
> regarded in the light of purchase price,

voluntarily offered by the worshiper,
for the coveted blessing. This trans-
action is familiarly known as do ut des
(I am giving in order that you may
give), or dabo ut des (I am giving in
order that you may give), or dabo ut des
(I shall give in order that you may
give). It will appear later in
interpretations of sacrifice.

Greek religions teem with sacred
gifts formally vowed or dedicated to the
gods.[25] To these is applied the general
Latin word vota (vowed, or dedicated
things). Some were in payment of
pledges; others were totally unpledged,
but spontaneously expressed appreciation
of blessings conferred. They consist of
gifts for the exclusive use of a god and
therefore banned from all secular use.
Articles of all sorts, from a temple to
a simple utensil or garment or wreath,
were offered to the gods, largely as
thank offerings for victory in battle,
for restoration from illness, for the
safe return from a voyage, for the safe
birth of a child, for success of an
undertaking and for innumerable minor
blessings. The temples were filled with
these offerings which were usually carefully listed.[26] The name applied to any
offering of this sort was anathema.
Such an offering might be made by a
private person or it might be publicly
voted by a city. The important element
in these gifts is not their devotion or
dedication, but the fact that they were
spontaneous acts of thanksgiving from
happy devotees who gladly gave the
richest offering in their power to
express their joy and thanksgiving.
Spontaneous thanksgiving is seen in the
application of the words charisterion or
eucharisterion, both meaning thanksgiving, to describe these gifts.[27],[28]

In his description of the sacrifices in the Iliad, R.K.
Yerkes notes that the first connotation of the word prayer
(euche, euchesthai) is not petition, but vow, and he gives

examples.   Prayers and   sacrifices are   performed before or
after men have received the desired blessing.   Yerkes
explains all the relevant terms in their original cultural
context:

> They must pray for omens before any
> serious undertaking,[29] or for oracles[30]
> or for guidance in   casting lots.[31]
> Prayer was a frequent accompaniment of
> oath[32] although we shall see another
> rite than the thusia used for many such
> instances. A dedication of a temple was
> a normal occasion of prayer and thanks.
> In the inscriptions we often read of
> prayers "for the safety and health of
> the council" or "of the people."[33]   Such
> rites were called by the name soteria,[34]
> a name we shall see appearing again
> under Jewish sacrifices.   Thusia and
> prayer were sometimes offered   at a
> marriage.[35]
>
> Frequent occasions of thusias and
> prayer were after success in an under-
> taking or achievement of purpose, when
> prayer took the form of thanksgiving and
> the ceremonial of the thusia was most
> elaborate.   It was inconceivable that
> one could ask a god for any kind of aid
> and not express profound appreciation
> after receiving it.   Our concept of
> thanksgiving is briefly to say, "Much
> obliged," when we do not forget it; the
> Greek concept was to offer a thusia.
>
> A well-known phrase for thanks-
> giving offerings was   thuein euchar-
> isteria.[36]   One method of showing great
> honour to prominent men and benefactors
> and to slain warriors was   to offer
> thusias for them.   They had not
> developed their thinking so far as to
> reason or argue upon just what was
> accomplished by such offerings.   They
> were happy and thankful; a thusia
> expressed that attitude.

The importance of formal acts of
thanksgiving, as expressions of appreciation for benefactions, increased with
the growth of city-state government. By
the third century B.C. they had become
quite conventional in Asia Minor and the
Aegean Islands. The technical term
eucharistia, which occurs in many
inscriptions, denotes a formal group act
of thanksgiving and appreciation. These
expressions of eucharistia were marked
by enthusiastic secular activity, such
as adoption of verbose resolutions by
the council of a city, or colourful processions or erection of commemorative
tablets in a temple.[37] The verb
eucharistein was used to denote these
acts,[38] and the council which decreed
the honours described itself as
eucharistos,[39] meaning appreciative or
thankful, and at least once by the
additional adjective mnemoneusa,[40]
meaning mindful. Formal thanksgivings
to god and man, as proper appreciation
of blessings, always had important consideration among the ancient Achaeans
and their successors, the Greeks. They
occupied a prominent place in the
religious and secular life which were so
interwoven as to be well-nigh indis-
tinguishable. The thusia was the most
adequate expression of thanksgiving.

Another group of expressions from
these secular inscriptions illustrates
the importance of thanksgiving in
ancient Greek life. The standard phrase
for "to return thanks" is charin (or
charitas) apodidonai. That this is considered a normal attitude is seen in an
inscription from Megalopolis, earlier
than 200 B.C., where public expressions
of appreciation to a benefactor are
described as dikaian apodidontes
charin[41] (returning right, or due,
thanks). That the gratitude should be
somehow commensurate with the benefaction is seen in such phrases as
charin axian,[42] charitas ... kat'

axian,[43] charitas axias[44] and charitas
kataxias[45] (worthy   thanks,   or   meet
thanks). The influence of these phrases
upon Greek thought led to their incorpo-
ration in   early Christian liturgies.[46]

R.J. Ledogar[47] makes a useful contribution when he
notes the connection between the eucharistein group and a
series of words composed with mneme and meaning memory
(mimneskomai, mneme, anamimnesko, anamnesis).   He finds
references to it in the Greeks, for instance in Polybius,[48]
Suicerus,[49] Sophocles,[50] and also in Philo.[51]   Gratitude,
in fact, consists of remembering gifts and benefactors, of
never forgetting them, and of keeping their memory present.
In Philo, a very important scriptural reference, Deut. 8:17-
18, adds new significance to this connection, which has
already been observed in the Greeks.

Leo Halkin[52] studies the ceremonial of thanksgiving in
Rome, citing the text. He distinguishes the "grateful
supplication" from "expiatory supplication" or "propitiatory
supplication":

> This form   of   supplication   is
> totally different from the latter two in
> its purpose. Here the concern is no
> longer to ask forgiveness or to beg help
> from the gods, but to give them solemn
> thanks for having granted the Roman
> legions victory over the enemy.   The
> ceremony is also quite different in
> character since, instead of terror or
> fear, we find boundless joy and well-
> deserved pride, and instead of tears and
> laments, loud rejoicing and triumphal
> singing. The form of prayer is no
> longer an obsecratio, but a gratulatio.
> During the days dedicated to such a
> ceremony, the people of Rome actually
> perform public celebrations of thanks-
> giving in honour to the gods. Here too,
> the   Senate   decides   authoritatively
> whether such celebrations should take
> place and how long they will last.   But
> in this case, the particular cooperation
> of priests is never required, even when
> sacrifices are included in the ceremony.
> [In ch. III, Halkin shows that] this
> ceremony of gratitude,   far   from

gradually disappearing during the first
century A.D., became more and more
important in the days of the Empire,
although it assumed quite a different
character.

Whatever their respective
characteristics in public worship, these
three forms of supplication share a
common feature which appears clearly in
the term itself. As we see from its
etymology, a supplicatio (or supplicium
in ancient Latin) was essentially a
religious rite which required the
worshipper to kneel humbly in the holy
place in the position of a supplicant.
By means of this prostration, he
publicly acknowledged the supreme
majesty of the gods and their sovereign
authority in the State. In addition,
this visible act of adoration was
regularly completed by visits to the
temples, recitation of prayers, and
offering of libations and sacrifices.

[For instance, there is an account
of the supplicatio following the victory
of Imbrinium by Fabius Rullianus over
the Samnites in 325 B.C.:⁵³] "Is it
right that Q. Fabius, who caused the
city to be found in rejoicing, victory,
supplications (supplicationibus) and
thanksgivings (gratulationibus), that he
because of whom the shrines of the gods
were opened, altars were smoking with
sacrifices and covered with ornament and
gifts, that this man should now be
naked, beaten with rods, in the presence
of the Roman people, in front of the
Capitol, of the castle, of these gods
on whom he did not vainly call in two
battles?"

The term used is supplicatio and, for this supplication, sacrifices of thanksgiving are offered. The general
meaning is expressed by the term gratulatio or, in Cicero,
by gratias agere.⁵⁴ We find parallels to this type of
thanksgiving celebration in Philo.

2. The LXX and the Letter of Aristeas

In LXX, if we limit ourselves to the instances of
eucharistein and its cognates, we find very few references,
and only in the last books, which were either directly
written in Greek or translated into Greek from the Hebrew.
We must explain the meaning of these terms very accurately.
For this purpose, we rely on the study of R.J. Ledogar.[55]
In Prov. 11:16, eucharistos means a "gracious" or "pleasing"
woman.   In Judith 8:25, the Hebrew of which is lost, the
meaning of eucharistein seems to be "to give thanks."   In
Sirach 37:11, eucharistia refers to God's "graciousness" or
"favourable disposition."   In II Mac. 1:11, eucharistein
depends on formulae from the Hellenistic epistolary style,
many instances of which are found in the papyri and in Paul,
where it means homage and gratitude offered to God.   In II
Mac. 10:7, the reading eucharistoun is not sure.   In III
Mac. 7:16, eucharistein signifies thanks to God for
deliverance.   In Esther 8:12d, eucharistia refers simply to
the disposition to gratitude. Finally, in Wisdom of Solomon
18:18:2, eucharistein rather seems to mean "to be grateful"
than "to give thanks."   Ledogar points out that the
eucharistein family does not enter Biblical literature as a
term of praise before the first century B.C., and it is not
used to translate a Hebrew or Syriac term of praise before
the first or even second century A.D.   In addition, it is
found only in the last and the most hellenized books of the
Bible, i.e., Wisdom of Solomon, the Greek additions to
Esther, and II and III Maccabees. In conclusion, we can see
that the uses of eucharistein in LXX show nothing new, and
simply witness to its increasing frequency just prior to and
at the beginning of the Christian era.   Let us add that no
correlation can be established between these references and
Philo, since he neither comments on nor quotes from any of
these books except for Proverbs.

In the Epistle of Aristeas, we find some interesting
references. Eucharistein itself appears only once,
expressing the king's gratitude toward the high-priest who
sent him the books of the Law, toward the messengers of the
high-priest who brought him the book, and toward God who
delivered the oracles.[56]   But other forms of the word appear
in relation to a sacrifice of thanksgiving, or in reference
to a gift offered to God in return for a greater benefit
received from Him (charisterion anathe, poieseis
charisteria, charisterion anatithentes).   We should also
mention another reference, even though the terms
eucharistein or charis are not contained in it - the
commentary on Deut. 7:18 and 10:21, where Aristeas explains

the thanksgiving for the various bodily and spiritual gifts based on the prescription of Deuteronomy to remember the wonders God has performed for the sake of man. In this section, there is even a reference to the offering of the first-fruits. Philo similarly develops on this precept of Deuteronomy using the terms of the family mneme, memory, in the same sense.

II. THE TERMS AND RITES EXPRESSING THANKSGIVING IN THE BIBLE

We turn now to the way in which thanksgiving is expressed and practised in Biblical tradition. Since the Hebrew has no exact term for thanksgiving, and eucharistein does not appear in the canonical Bible, we must turn to the terms and rites which are used for that purpose in the Old Testament. These terms are: 1) hll, to praise God, in the piel (hillel), with the substantive tehillah, praise; 2) brk, to bless, in the past participle form of qal (baruk), and piel (barek), with the substantive berakah, blessing; 3) kbd, to glorify, in the piel and hitpael, with the substantive kabod, glory; 4) ydh in the hiphil (hodah), to praise, and hitpael, with the substantive todah, praise and the sacrifice of praise. The cultic acts consist of hymns, blessings, praise, and sacrifices accompanied with todah, to which the terms mentioned above refer. Included also are vows, which generally involve a sacrifice, as well as the precepts of the Law concerning sacrifices and first-fruits, in so far as such a connotation is apparent in them.

There are a few recent inquiries which shed light on these different aspects: J.P. Audet,[57] J. Guillet,[58] K. Hruby,[59] Beyer[60] on benediction, J.M. Robinson,[61] G. Bornkamm,[62] Michel[63] on confession, S. Daniel[64] on sacrifice with todah, R.K. Yerkes[65] on sacrifices and vows, and Ledogar again, in a succinct manner, on all of them.[66]

1. Hll (to praise)

The verb hillel, the piel of hll, means "to praise." The context in which we are interested here is "praising God." This verb is frequent especially in the Psalms, where LXX usually translates it with ainein.[67] In classical Greek, ainein generally belongs to the vocabulary of poetry, meaning "to speak about," "to praise," "to approve." Attic prose prefers epainein, with its corresponding substantive epainos.

The substantive is tehillah, the prayer of praise,
adoration or thanksgiving addressed to God. LXX generally
translates this term with ainesis in the Psalms,[68] but it
sometimes substitutes other terms such as epainos,[69]
hymnos,[70] psalmos.[71] The noun ainesis does not appear in
Greek before LXX.[72]

Let us note that hillel and tehillah are terms
characteristic of the Psalter, which is the Prayer Book par
excellence. They refer to the praise of God, like the word
todah, which, however, appears more frequently. Various
terms within titles of psalms refer to the praise of God,
but, since they do not belong to the text, they do not of
themselves express the praise of God and, for this reason,
they are of less interest for us. S. Mowinkel[73] mentions
eight of these: sir, mizmor, sir hamma'aloth, miktam,
Maskol, siggayon, tehillah, tephillah. Mizmor, appearing in
fifty-seven titles, is the most frequent. LXX most often
uses psalmos, but we also find hymnos, ode, proseuche,
stelographia, ainesis and ainos, alleluia, either alone, or
together with another of these terms. In Philo, hymnos
usually refers to a psalm, but we also find asma and ode.

The kind of praise expressed by hillel and tehillah is
close to thanksgiving,[74] which is also a form of praise.
In addition, some psalms are termed "of thanksgiving," but
these point to a root other then hll.

2. Kbd (to glorify)

The problem raised by the interpretation of kabod
(glory) is made more difficult by the numerous meanings of
this word in the Bible.[75] LXX translates it with doxa,[76]
but not in its usual Greek meaning of "opinion." The
Biblical kabod and the doxa of LXX mean "wealth," "fame,"
and often "magnificence" or "splendor." To glorify God or
to tell His glory means to acknowledge His might, or to
praise Him, in a sense very close to that of hillel or of
todah, but with a connotation of kingly glory which befits
the majesty of God.[77] We find this meaning in Ps. 19:1:
"The heavens are telling the glory of God."[78]

Used in the piel, kbd means to glorify someone. It is
usually translated in LXX as doxazein,[79] and sometimes as
timan,[80] or even as eulogein.[81] Doxazein, however, appears
several times in Ex. 15, the Canticle of Moses, translating
expressions which do not contain kbd.[82]

Used with God as the object, κβφ means "to glorify God." In return, God glorifies man, according to I Samuel 2:30 - "those who honor me I will honor." Man can also glorify another man, especially the king, since glory is the attribute of kingship.[83]

Is it possible to say that 'to glorify God' and 'to give thanks to god' are close in their meaning? It is, insofar as to honour god means to praise God. Philo, who does not use doxa and doxazein to express praise of God, frequently uses timan-time in this sense.

3. Brk (to bless)

The two forms of brk with which we are concerned here are the past participle qal, baruk (blessed), and the piel berak (to bless). The noun berakah, blessing, does not enter this discussion, since it means a good granted by God, and not the return of this good to God in the form of blessing or praise, at least in the Bible. It is translated with eulogia.

Baruk (blessed) is regularly translated in LXX as eulogetos,[84] and sometimes by eulogemenos.[85] The verb in the piel is translated regularly as eulogein. The author of the blessing can be God. In this sense, to bless means "to confer a power" or "to grant a good." The author can also be a man, as when a man blesses another man, in particular his son or his subjects. It can also be used in an invocation, for instance, "God bless you!" The meaning which interests us here is the blessing by man either of God or of His name, where blessing means praise. The reason for praise is usually mentioned, generally based on God's gifts or on His sublime qualities. This is introduced by ki or aser (in Greek, oti, or hos). Usually, the blessing is very short, not exceeding one verse. The enumeration of God's virtues and gifts, however, can be greatly expanded and turn into a remembrance of His wonders, though this does not happen frequently and never occurs in the Psalms. Psalms often end with a short blessing.

In classical Greek, eulogein means "to speak well of somebody."[86] Only once does it appear in the biblical sense of being blessed by a god. Frequently, however, it has the sense of "praising God." There is no specific term and no particular act of benediction: eulogein means "to praise," not "to bless." Since the Jewish benediction evolved toward the notion of praise, the LXX translators could easily adopt

eulogein to express the idea of blessing. However, because
of its adoption by LXX, eulogein received the semantic
inheritance of berak - baruk, and should be interpreted in
LXX more in accordance with the semitic than with the
classical Greek background. In late Judaism, "to bless" God
became so completely synonymous with "to praise" God that it
became the designation for Jewish prayer.

According to K. Hruby,[87] and contrary to J.-P. Audet's
position, benediction is closely connected to worship. In
the Rabbinic tradition, the pre-eminent blessing is the
Aaronic blessing, recited in the Temple, and reserved to the
priest in the synagogue service. The prayer of the Eighteen
Benedictions, which is, with the Shema, the chief prayer of
the Jews, includes as its original core the three prayers
recited by the priests at the morning sacrifice.
Benedictions frame the Scriptural readings and the recitation of the Hallel Psalms. Benediction belonged also to
domestic liturgy: graces at meals; the sheva berakoth of
the Nuptial blessing; the blessings of the birkat gomel for
the benefits granted by God in personal life; and the
hundred blessings of daily life gathered by the Rabbis.[88]

J.-P. Audet, J. Guillet and K. Hruby explain that, in
Judaism, benediction was the most usual way to express
gratitude, both toward God and toward men. E.-J. Bickerman
also demonstrates this point well.[89],[90]

4. Hodah (to praise)

The root ydh in the hiphil gives hodah, which means "to
praise," "to acknowledge," "to give thanks." The verb
hodah, with which we begin, concerns us when its object is
God. In Psalms, LXX usually translates hodah with
exomologeisthai.[91],[92] In the other books, the usual translation is the same but we sometimes find ainein, hymnein and
eulogein.[93] LXX does not use exomologeisthai in the sense
of the confession of sins except in Daniel 9:4; 9:20 (LXX),
but rather terms such as exegeomai, gnorizo, exagoreo.[94]

Hodah is used either with a direct object, or with the
prepositions l-or al-, which the Greek translates simply
with a dative. As in the case of berak - baruk, the theme
of praise or confession is introduced by ki, and, in Greek,
by oti. Man is always the subject of hodah, and God, or the
name of God, is its object.

The verbs homologein and exomologein, and the
participles derived from them, are known in classical and
Hellenistic Greek. Homologein means "to say the same
thing," "to agree on something," or "to accept a reproach."
It also means "to certify a payment," "to agree on a
proposition," "to promise," "to approve." Sometimes, this
term also has a philosophical sense. For instance
homologia, in Plato, Crito 49E, means the basic agreement
which makes discussion possible between two persons. And
homologoumenos zen, in the Stoics, means "to live appro-
priately" or "according to nature."[95] This philosophical
aspect of homologein paved the way for the Philonic
deepening of the notion of confession. Note also that
secular Greek is ignorant both of exomologesis, which
appears in LXX, and of the use of exomologein in the sense
of praise, by which LXX translates hodah. LXX often uses
exomologeisthai but rarely homologein.

The Bible uses hodah and its Greek counterpart
exomologeisthai, more than other terms, in the sense of
praise or confession of God or of His name. When R.J.
Ledogar[96] explains the connection between the "name" and the
"memory" of God, he refers to Deut. 9:14, among other texts;
but the idea of the remembrance of God and of His providence
to Israel permeates the whole book of Deuteronomy and is
evident particularly in Deut. 8:17-18. It is found also in
the prayer of the Shema.[97]

The Bible also uses hodah for the confession of sins,[98]
though LXX avoids using exomologeisthai in this sense. G.
Bornkamm explains how hodah and its Greek counterpart
hexomologein, or the Latin confiteri, carry the twofold
meaning of the confession or praise of God and of the
confession of sins. Confession of sins before God is an
interior movement which causes a sinner to acknowledge God's
judgment. In the confession of his sin, moreover, the
sinner extends the idea of guilt and the acknowledgment of
divine revelation to all who surround him and, indeed, to
all men. In this sense, confession of sin appears as, first
of all, a confession of God and the result of a divine
revelation.[99]

James M. Robinson[100] does not pursue his study of the
"hodayot form" in the Bible, but he does show that this
formula is typical of the hymns of Qumran. These
characteristically use hodah as a term of praise in the
beginning of the hymn, mention the name of the Lord, and use
the preposition ki to introduce the reasons for praise,
i.e., the qualities of God or His gifts. He rightly

emphasizes the predominant use of hodah in the hymns of
Qumran, though the use of baruk with the same construction
also occurs. According to Robinson, Judaism later rejected
the "hodayot-form" in favour of the benediction, probably in
order to distinguish itself from Christianity. The
"hodayot-form" survived in the use of the Greek eucharistein
by the Christian who, for their part, refused to conform to
the Jewish mode of prayer. Such would be the reason for
which, in the beginning of the Christian era, the Jews
confined themselves more and more to the benediction, while
the Christians concurrently used eulogein and eucharistein,
finally favouring eucharistein. The chief reason for this
development, however, seems to be the growing fortune of
eucharistein in the Hellenistic period, and its influence on
Greek-speaking Judaism, even before the Christians could
think of adopting it. Philo witnesses to the fortune of
eucharistein among the Jews of the Diaspora, and he even
uses it in reference to the prayers at meals. We might add
that the reason for the use of the verb hodah and its
frequency in the hymns of Qumran is also that this verb is
most frequently used in the prayer of praise of Psalms, to
which the hymns of Qumran are closely related.

Since hodah means the acknowledgement of a gift of God,
or of the qualities of God, it thus comes to mean "to give
thanks." For "to give thanks" is not only to express one's
gratitude toward God, but, more basically, to confess the
qualities and the gifts of God.[101] But this can be done
even more properly by the sacrifice of salvation with todah.

5. Todah (praise)

As could be expected, many references to todah
seemingly reflect nothing but simple praise, often
accompanied by singing, music and joy, for the primary
meaning of todah, as a substantive of hodah, is praise. The
confession of God in fact turns into praise when the stress
is laid on the qualities and the mighty deeds of God. In
the sense of confession of praise, hodah is regularly translated by exomologeisthai, often under the substantive form
of en exomologesei.[102] This confession, insofar as it
recalls the qualities and mighty deeds of God, reflects the
injunctions of Deuteronomy to fulfill the duty of
remembering God (8:17-18). From praise, we easily come to
those who proclaim it, and todah comes to mean the function
of praising God, which belongs to the Levites, and to the
choirs of Levites, in the book of Nehemiah.[103],[104]

But todah acquires a specific meaning when it is
connected with the sacrifices of peace, or of salvation, as
we read in LXX and in Philo. Praise, here, becomes a part
of the sacrifice, and, in this sense, todah is no longer
translated by exomologesis, but by ainesis.[105] We read, for
instance, in Lev. 7:13 (LXX): epi thusia aineseos soteriou.
These three words regularly appear together, though
connected to one another in various ways.[106] Most of the
references to todah refer to the sacrifices of salvation
with praise, and we may suppose that some other references,
whose context is uncertain, also refer to these sacrifices,
especially in the context of public rejoicing. The fact
that todah is translated by exomologesis and not by ainesis
does not totally contradict this interpretation.

Mrs. S. Daniel provides ample information on the
selamim in the Hebrew Bible and on the way LXX translates
the vocabulary connected with them.[107] We borrow her
description and interpretation of these sacrifices.
According to Lev. 3 and 7, the Israelite offering a zebah
selamim, after laying his hand on the head of the victim,
must sacrifice it, or have it sacrificed, at the entrance to
the Tent. Then the priests pour the blood around the altar,
and burn the fat of the belly, the kidneys and the liver
upon the altar. They set apart the breast and the right
thigh for themselves, and the remainder of the victim is
delivered to the offerer, who, together with his relatives
and friends, may eat it according to the rules of ritual
purity. There seem to be three kinds of selamim - those
offered out of gratitude (todah), as the fulfillment of a
vow (neder), or completely freely (nedabah). According to
this view, all the selamim prescribed as an obligation by
the rules of worship could be considered as todah. The
collective selamim prescribed for the festivals (Lev. 23:18-
19; Num. 10:10) seem to be actual manifestations of the
people's gratitude for the gifts of God. Only the instances
of individual selamim prescribed by the Law, those which
must be offered by a nazir according to Num. 6:14, 17-18,
can represent a sacrifice of thanksgiving for the correct
fulfillment of a vow of penitence. S. Daniel next examines
the meaning and the different Greek translations of the term
selamim. LXX translates zebah selamim by thusia soteriou
(sacrifice of salvation) in Pentateuch. Later on, the
translators variously translate it by sacrifice of salvation, of plenitude, or of peace.[108]

The choice by LXX of the neutral substantive to
soterion derived from the adjective soterios, can be

compared to the use of this term for the sacrifices of
thanksgiving among the pagans.   S. Daniel says:

> The soteria of the Greeks were obviously
> sacrifices for "deliverance" from danger
> or sickness, and, as such, were almost
> always sacrifices of thanksgiving.
> Their meaning is thus more specific than
> that of the selamim, for the latter can-
> not probably be reduced simply to the
> category of sacrifices of gratitude,
> which would only be that of todah.[109]

Todah, or praise accompanying a sacrifice of salvation,
can be considered, according to H. Cazelles, as a thanksgiving, and Aquila translates it by eucharistia.   We shall
return to our discussion of todah as thanksgiving in our
chapter Eucharistia and Liturgy, where we explain the ideas
of J.-P. Audet, H. Cazelles and J. Jeremias concerning the
background of the Christian Eucharist in the religious life
of Judaism.

G. Bornkamm deals with the place of confession in
sacrifices.[110]   Confession, even when it is the confession
of sin, is a response to the manifestation of Divine might.
This meaning is more obvious when confession is connected
with a vow and with the sacrifice of thanksgiving offered
for its fulfilment.   The erection of a pillar can also be
considered as an eucharisterion by the Greeks.   We have seen
that LXX includes stelographia as a translation of miktam in
the titles of psalms (Ps. 16:1).   We shall find these forms
of confession or thanksgiving again in Philo.

6. Neder (vow)

The Hebrew term for vow is neder, and the verb,
occuring less frequently, is nadar (to vow, to promise).
LXX translates them by euche and euchomai respectively.

Like other nations, the Israelites made vows,
especially in order to strengthen their prayer when they
asked for great favours from God, such as healing, the
success of an enterprise, or protection in danger.   The
aspect of thanksgiving in vows, and in the sacrifice
promised to God within the vow, is too obvious to need
further evidence.   References to these terms, particularly
in Psalms, Proverbs, and Ecclesiastes, show that the
practice of making vows is quite common.[111]   Although no law

prescribed the offering of private sacrifices, except for
the nazir, the fulfilment of a vow was considered a sacred
duty, which a man should not neglect, and should fulfil as
soon as possible.[112] Prescriptions in Leviticus (27:1-8) on
the release from a vow through a gift of money, and in
Numbers (30) on the acceptance of the vows of a wife by her
husband, witness to the importance of vows in the life of
the Israelites. Certain references mention a sacrifice of
thanksgiving as promised in the vow.[113]

The most remarkable vow, and the only one for which the
Law gives detailed rules and prescribes sacrifices, is the
vow of the nazir (neder hannazir). The nazir consecrates
himself to God, promises to abstain from wine and fermented
drink, to keep his hair unshorn, and to avoid contact with a
corpse before the conclusion of his vow. Among the
sacrifices offered at the end, there is a sacrifice of
salvation with todah, i.e., a sacrifice of thanksgiving.[114]

Since, at first glance, the first-fruits and daily
sacrifices do not have an obviously eucharistic connotation,
and since a detailed discussion is necessary before drawing
this conclusion, it would be better to postpone this long
and delicate investigation to the chapter on Eucharistia and
Liturgy. The question, in any case, is more a matter of
interpretation than of terminology, as we can easily understand if we remember that, though the notion of thanksgiving
is present in the Bible, there is no specific term for it,
several terms being used for that purpose, each with its own
semantic history.

III. THE SURVIVAL OF BIBLICAL TERMS EXPRESSING THANKSGIVING
      IN PHILO

Before studying the various uses of eucharistein in
Philo, we must see his use of the Greek terms selected by
LXX to translate the Hebrew terms expressing thanksgiving in
the Bible. We shall consider briefly in Philo the terms
meaning 1) praise, in the sense of hillel and of tehillah:
these are chiefly hymnein and egkomiazein; 2) glory, in the
sense of kabod: the Philonic use of timan-time seems to be
the closest to this idea, since Philo does not use doxazein
and doxa in the sense of praise and of thanksgiving; 3)
benediction, in the sense of berak-baruk: the term in LXX
is eulogein; 4) the counterpart of hodah-todah in the sense
of praise and confession: LXX used two terms,
exomologeisthai-exomologesis and ainein-ainesis. The use of
ainein-ainesis is very limited and very specific in Philo,

and therefore presents no difficulty. But, if he rarely uses exomologeisthai in the sense of praise, he uses it often in the sense of confession, and he multiplies the terms meaning confession.

The other formulas through which he expresses thanks-giving are images, such as the memory of God and of His blessings, loans which must be acknowledged and repaid to the Divine owner, or votive offering which, through allegory, comes to mean spiritual and cosmic eucharistia. Since these images in Philo become a language of their own, we shall deal with them in a particular section, after we study his use of the term eucharistein.

1. Hymns (Hymnein)

Philo generally refers to Psalms by the term hymnos. This is certain in Plant. 29 for Ps. 94:9, in Conf. 39 for Ps. 30, in Conf. 52 for Ps. 79, in Mut. 115 for Ps. 23, in Plant. 39 for Ps. 36. Often hymnos seems to refer simply to psalms, but since the canticles of Scripture are also called hymns, as well as spontaneous or partly improvised composi-tions (Cont. 29; 80), it cannot be used categorically. A psalm can be called asma, for instance Ps. 23 in Agr. 50-51, a text where we also find the compound word hymnodia. On the other hand, a biblical canticle such as Ex. 15 can either be called asma (Leg. Al. II, 102; Ebr. 111), hymnos (Mos. I, 180; II, 256; Cont. 87), or ode (Sobr. 10). Songs of victory, other than Ex. 15, which are mentioned but not textually developed in the Bible, are either called hymnos, such as the song of Abraham after his victory over nine kings (Ebr. 106, cf. Gen. 14:22-23), or asma, such as the song following the victory of Phineas (Ebr. 115, cf. Num. 31:49-50). The song over the wells is called asma (Som. II, 271), and that of the basket is called both asma (Spec. Leg. II, 217, cf. Deut. 26:1-11) and ode (Virt. 95). Hymnos can also be associated with ton eucharistikon hymnon, for example in Som. II, 38. The verbs hymnein and adein are applied to the celebration of the praise of God through hymns and canticles, for instance in Leg. Al. II, 102; Ebr. 111. Philo frequently uses hymnos and hymnein.[115]

The praise expressed by these terms can be given by a man to another man (Jos. 246), to the false gods (Mos. II, 162), or to the true God (Jos. 253). Man is praised for his virtues (Jos. 246). Virtue itself is celebrated (Deter. 73; Spec. Leg. IV, 230). God is praised for His creation (Op. 4) or for His gifts (Spec. Leg. IV, 177). Philo becomes

lyrical in his praise of God for His special attention
toward two orphan girls, the daughters of Salpaad (Mos. II,
239, cf. Num. 27:1-11).

We must point out the connection made by Philo between
hymnos and eucharistia. The term eucharistia is associated
at least ten times with hymnos or its equivalents, for
instance in Ebr. 121, ton epinikion kai eucharistikon
hymnon, and in Plant. 135, tas eucharistous hymnodias.

This association between eucharistia and hymnos is not
superficial, but is rooted in Philo's very notion of the
praise of God. The Universe itself gives birth to praise in
order to give thanks to the God who created it so perfect.
Philo explains this idea (Plant. 126-133), which was also
found in Timaeus (29 a) and in Cleanthus' hymn to Zeus,
through the legend of the Muses told by Hesiod (Theogonia
50ff). He adds to it the notion of Memory, represented by
Mnemosyne, which suggests to men the duty of attributing to
God faithfully and simply the merit of His own works. The
continuation of the same text (134-136) introduces the
figure which, in the Bible, is the counterpart of the Muses,
i.e., Judah, the type of confession, as well as the type of
eucharistia and praise, which are three duties of man
deriving logically from one another. The praise of God for
the works of creation is also celebrated by Moses before his
death in his canticle (Virt. 73-75. cf. Deut. 32:1-43).

The gifts lavishly poured out by God upon men,
particularly upon Israel, by special providence call for the
expression of gratitude through hymns. We refer
particularly to the hymn of Ex. 15 which Moses and Miriam
sang on the seashore after they had divided the people of
Israel into two choirs, one of men, one of women (Mos. I,
180; II, 256). the Therapeutae sing it in their festal
vigils (Cont. 87), and the entire nation in the Pasch (Spec.
Leg. I, 145-149). Philo uses this image many times to
suggest thanksgiving for the victory over passions (Leg. Al.
II, 94-104; Agr. 79-83). The other hymns of victory found
in the Law of Moses express thanks in the same way, and also
lend themselves to symbolical interpretations.

Because of a lack of evidence, we cannot answer the
question as to why Philo interpreted certain psalms rather
than others in the sense of thanksgiving.

2. The honour paid to God (timan)

Philo does not use doxa-doxazein to mean the glory or glorification of God, but in its classical sense of opinion. He does use it once, though, in the sense of the glory of God (Spec. Leg. I, 45) when he seeks a Scriptural basis for his theory of the Divine powers. Philo expresses the idea of the shining splendour of God, the Divine kabod, by his notion of the Divine powers which represent the impact of God's shining forth on man, with a brightness proportional to each man's spiritual level. Here, however, we are not directly interested in glory as the shining forth of God, but in glory paid to God, i.e., in a form of the praise of God. To refer to the glory paid to God, Philo uses the pair time-timan. He does not use time-timan in quotations from Scripture, however, for which he would probably use the term doxa of LXX, but, in other contexts, he uses it often in phrases where doxa would be expected. He avoids using doxa-doxazein in the sense of "to glorify" or "to praise" God probably because the first sense of doxa in classical Greek is "opinion," and because the subsidiary meaning of "reputation" and "glory" has little religious value. The term time-timan, given its semantic past in secular Greek, fulfils the need of Philo quite well because of its large variety of meanings, from the price of an object in a store, or secular dignity to the moral appreciation of an action, a virtue, or a doctrine, to the honour paid to a person or to God.

Philo uses time in all its diverse forms: verbal, substantive, qualificative, adverbial, and sometimes with the prefixes en-, pro-, iso-, a-. He uses it frequently and in many different ways. We find all the secular usages: the price of an object (Jos. 178), a position of honour (Gig. 36), an honour conferred on somebody (Spec. Leg. I, 142), every kind of appreciation (Op. 17), the appreciation of an action or of a virtue (Spec. Leg. II, 160), the respect, or the honour, paid to a man (Legat. 153-154), and, finally, to God (Spec. Leg. IV, 178).

Philo very often refers to the honour paid to virtue by men,[116] and sometimes by God himself (Virt. 195; Mos. I, 328). Among men who deserve to be honoured, he mentions particularly parents,[117] priests,[118] and proselytes.[119]

The idea of honouring a praiseworthy action or a person worthy of respect for his moral qualities or his religious faith suggests a deeper meaning of the term time to Philo -- the implicit confession of the idea that every good comes from God and must serve to the glory of God. The religious connotation of this moral judgment appears in the respect usually paid to virtue (Sacr. 16), and in the brotherly regard which proselytes are entitled to enjoy: they share equal honour with the Israelites (isotimoi), because they honour the true God and have rejected the worship of false gods in spite of their ancestral tradition, and sometimes at the risk of their own life (Virt. 220-222; Spec. Leg. I, 52-54). Finally, priests ought to be honoured because they honour God. The tribe of Levi was granted the honour of the priesthood because they fought for the honour of God (Spec. Leg. III, 124-127; Mos. II, 166-175). The Phylarch Levi, who represents it, is introduced as the originator of the formula, "God, and God alone must I honour," since Moses did not ascribe to him a portion of the heritage with his brethren, but affirmed, "The Lord Himself is his portion" (Congr. 132-134, cf. Deut. 10:9).[120]

It is often useful to consider the negative counterpart of a term in Philo. For instance, in the case of time, we find the negative forms atimia, dishonour (Agr. 61), atimos, unworthy (Virt. 195), and atimazein, the refusal of the honour due, for instance, to parents (Ebr. 17). There are also positive forms which carry a negative connotation, because Philo always keeps in mind the reference of every good thing to God. It is thus possible to draw a graduated list of false glories from the negative value ascribed to bodily and external goods, which eliminates any sense of God (Spec. Leg. I, 25) and any interest in spiritual goods (Mut. 104), to the false gods of pagan idolatry (Spec. Leg. II, 165), or to the Universe, especially to the Heavens (Congr. 47-48; Dec. 61). The honour paid to divine powers is, in some regards, reprehensible (Som. I, 163; Abr. 119-120), and it is certainly wrong to honour the dyad, which is the symbol of the mixture of good and evil (Som. II, 69-70; Spec. Leg. I, 178-180).

This notion of honour, paid to God either directly or indirectly by an implicit reference to God, reveals a connection to eucharistia, which is the disposition to ascribe every good to God. But this connection appears also explicitly in a number of instances where Philo juxtaposes the two terms, as in Deus 7 (eucharistikos echein kai timetikos).[121] It remains true, however, that time primarily means the glory or honour paid to God, and only implicitly praise and thanksgiving. The same is true of the verb therapeuein, in spite of its association with the notion of priesthood, with the Levitical ideals and with the Therapeutae. It properly means "to serve God through

worship" and not to praise, to honour, or to give thanks to
God.[122]

3. To bless God (eulogein)

Whereas LXX makes frequent use of eulogein in the sense
of "to bless," Philo rarely does so, and only in those
places where he refers to Biblical blessings. We must first
examine the forms under which this term appears. We find,
on the one hand, eulogein, with eulogia, eulogos,
eulogetos,[123] eulogemenos, on the other hand, eulogistein,
with eulogistia and eulogistos.

The use of eulogein by Philo needs to be investigated
carefully, and we must not suppose that it means everywhere
"benediction." In classical Greek,[124] eulogein appears in
the sense of speaking well of somebody, and eulogia means in
this context "praise" or "plausible" affirmation."
Eulogistein means "to reason with prudence," eulogistia
means "a good reasoning," and eulogistos means "well
calculated." Eulogein also means "to bless," but this
meaning is almost entirely restricted to the LXX. All these
meanings reappear in Philo. Of course, the only meaning of
eulogein and its cognates with which we are concerned here
is "to bless God," because this is the only one where
eulogein has the sense of praise or thanksgiving.

When eulogein, eulogetos, eulogemenos, eulogia refer to
the benediction conferred by God upon men, or by men on
other men, this refers to a gift from God, and not to a
blessing of God by men. There is another noteworthy use--
the blessing over food. To refer to God blessing bread and
water, Philo uses eulogein, because he considers them as a
gift of God.[125] But when Philo speaks of the prayer a man
should say before a meal, or at the beginning and end of any
good deed, he uses eucharistein because, in this context,
the prayer is addressed by man to God.[126]

The difficulty encountered in a study of eulogein in
Philo stems not only from a lack of precision on the side of
the reader about the exact meaning of the term, but also
from the fact that Philo sometimes plays on words. He
starts from a biblical blessing and, from the biblical
meaning of the benediction, he passes to the sense of praise
found in profane Greek, or even, playing on the etymology of
the word, to the sense of "fine speaking." For instance,
the third gift of God to Abraham, eulogia, according to Gen.
12:2-3, comes to mean "I will endow thee with excellent

reason and speech" (epaineton logon), or excellent reasoning (Migr. 70-71).[127]

The few references to the blessing of God by man are the following. Shem is the type of the Sage, citizen of the world and worshipper of God, because we read in Gen. 9:26, "Blessed (eulogetos) is the Lord, the God of Shem." Philo sees a grace in the fact that Shem is related to "God" rather than to the "Lord." In return for this grace, Shem must bless and praise God (eulogein kai epainein). This blessing in return (ameibesthai) suggests the idea of eucharistia, which consists in returning to God His own gifts (Sobr. 51-58). The second instance is the blessing addressed by the servant of Abraham to God, for His favour to Abraham in the choice of Rebecca (Q.G. IV, 114, cf. Gen. 24:26; cf. Q.G. IV, 118, cf. Gen. 24:31, where Philo, following LXX, ascribes to Laban, "Blessed (be) the Lord"). The third instance refers to the attributes of Judah (Plant. 135; Som. II, 38, cf. Gen. 49:8). Among these we find benediction, and Judah appears as the type of the mind which blesses God.[128] In this type, benediction is associated with confession and eucharistia.

4. The sacrifice of salvation with todah (ainein-ainesis)

First, we must distinguish between ainein and epainein. The second term is frequent in Philo and appears under the following forms, epainein, epainetos, to epaineton. It means praise, which derives from the usual meaning of the term in classical Greek rather than from LXX, which makes little use of it. Its parallel is the pagan term egkomiazein-egkomion, which means praise, eulogy, panegyrics. Eulogies and panegyrics, are found among the acts of personal worship, which the eucharistic spirit, personified by Judah, performs before God (Som. II, 38). In this sense, they are related to eucharistia (cf. Spec. Leg. I, 224).

The Philonic use of ainein is very limited and very specific. Whereas in LXX, particularly in Psalms, ainein is the usual translation of hillel (to praise), in Philo this term disappears almost completely. We find it in association with Judah (ainesis, Leg. Al. III, 26; ainetos, Plant. 126; 135), probably because of his name, "which includes everything understood in the name of ainesis" (Spec. Leg. I, 224). Here also, Philo seems to conform to the Greek usage, which confines ainein to the vocabulary of poetry.

As in LXX, <u>ainein</u> refers to the <u>todah</u> associated with the sacrifice of salvation. The praise accompanying this sacrifice is also called <u>ainesis</u> (<u>Spec. Leg.</u> I, 224), and includes macarisms, votive sacrifices, and "the other forms of eucharistiai" (<u>Spec. Leg.</u> I, 225).[129] Finally, the sacrifice of salvation with praise is, in its entirety, interpreted as a way to return to God His own gifts eagerly and without delay (<u>Spec. Leg.</u> I, 225, <u>metadosis</u>).

5. Confession (<u>homologein</u>, <u>exomologeisthai</u>)

We note, first of all, that Philo, unlike LXX, frequently uses <u>homologein</u> and seldom uses <u>exomologeisthai</u>, thus following the classical Greek practice. Second, <u>exomologeisthai</u> appears only in the sections where Philo speaks of Judah, and where it characterizes this biblical figure.

a) Exomologeisthai

Let us first deal with <u>exomologeisthai</u>, which is the same as to deal with Judah.[130] We noted that LXX usually translates <u>hodah</u> by <u>exomologeisthai</u>, thus paving the way for the Philonic equation, Judah = <u>exomologesis</u>, i.e., Confession. But LXX does not take advantage of the two biblical references where the Hebrew plays on the common origin of the words <u>hodah</u> (to praise), and Judah. In Gen. 29:35, Leah gives thanks to God (<u>exomologeisthai</u>) and, for this reason, she calls her son Judah. In Gen. 49:8, when Jacob blesses Judah saying, "Judah, thy brethren shall praise thee," the Hebrew associates <u>hodah</u> and Judah again, but LXX translates "to praise" by <u>ainein</u>. Philo takes full advantage of the play of words found in the two Hebrew references, and uses it to enrich the LXX term <u>exomologeisthai</u>. Therefore, Judah becomes the type of the Confessor of God, <u>ho exomologoumenos</u>.[131]

It is interesting to know what kind of confession Judah figures, and what its object is. First of all, he is the type of the Confessor because his mother "confessed" when she gave him birth. We must turn to the action of Leah, because her own confession of God and her naming her son "Confessor" are the only basis on which Philo builds his figure of Judah.

Judah, therefore, is the type of confession whose object is the Lord (to kyrio, <u>Plant.</u> 134-136), or God (<u>Leg. Al.</u> II, 95-96; cf. <u>Congr.</u> 125: pros ton theon homologiai).

But Judah does not properly mean confession of the existence, or of the name, of God, or even that of His sovereign authority. With Judah, we are no longer on the level of conversion, among proselytes, atheists, apostates, and the servants of all kinds of false deities. We are on the level of spiritual life and of those more advanced in perfection. The object of confession is the idea that God, and not man, is the source of all good things, especially the goods of the soul. This is what we find in all the other texts about Judah.[132]

Two decisive events in the life of Judah witness to this meaning. First, at his birth, Leah brought forth the perfect fruit, Confession, a fruit which can be compared to Isaac, innate grace (Som. I, 37; cf. Q.G. IV, 123). The object of this confession is the idea that God, and not man, is the source of all spiritual good (Leg. Al. I, 79-84; II, 95-96). We have seen this already. In this passage, Philo develops the contrast between Judah and Issachar. Judah is the perfect man who acknowledges the operation in himself of the grace of God, whereas Issachar is the hard-working ascetic who fights on his own for the acquisition of virtue. Jacob does not need to pray for Judah, because Leah, having received him, can receive nothing better among the gifts of God. Philo also contrasts Judah with Dan, whose name (krisis) suggests the distinction between temporal and eternal blessings, which are indiscriminately desired by his mother Billah, the "insatiable one." This distinction certainly requires the help of God (Leg. Al. II, 95-96). The texts mentioned above refer to Gen. 29:35. The second event is Judah's acknowledgment that Tamar is justified, since he has not given her to any mortal (Gen. 38:26). Here again, Judah is a Confessor: he acknowledges that Tamar is pregnant with a Divine seed, and he does not pretend to be the father, because God alone is the father of spiritual goods (Mut. 136; Congr. 125).

The advantage of being praised among his brethren, together with the blessing reserved to him by Jacob (Gen. 49:8), can therefore be ascribed to Judah as a privileged portion of heritage. Philo enumerates these various kinds of praise and places them under the general title of ainesis (praise) (Spec. Leg. I, 224), or of eucharistia (Som. II, 38). The elements of praise are variously grouped under the name of Judah and of the guild named after him (cf. Ebr. 94; Plant. 135).

The association of the figure of Judah with eucharistia is already obvious from what we have just explained, but it

can also be based on the term itself. If exomologeisthai
(Confession) is connected with Judah because of the association in LXX, the same can be said of eucharistein, though,
here, Philo may be responsible for it. We observed the
presence of eucharistiai among the various kinds of praise
(Spec. Leg. I, 224). We shall find these forms of praise
again as the characteristics of the eucharistic spirit
represented by Judah (Som. II, 38) of the soul blessing God,
which is also represented by Judah (Plant. 135). As Judah
is called "Confessor," he is also honoured with the title of
the "Eucharistic man" (Plant. 136). He is the head of the
guild, known after his name, which raises the hymn of
thanksgiving (Ebr. 94). He confesses "eucharistically"
(exomologeitai eucharistikos, Leg. Al., I, 80). God gives
him thankfulness (to euchariston, ibid. 82). Finally, the
colour of the gem representing him on the logeion of the
high-priest is the ruby, figure of the soul warmed with
eucharistia and pouring forth to God the enthusiasm of a
noble drunkenness, perhaps within the context of a sacrifice
of thanksgiving (ibid. 84).

In Philo, eucharistein tends to replace exomologeisthai
in the different meanings of hodah, as noted by J. Robinson,
who points out the importance of the play of words on the
name of Judah in Philo. J. Robinson shows[133] that, though
Philo uses exomologeisthai, he inclines to substitute
eucharistein for it, i.e., the Greek term which in his time
better reflected the meaning of hodah in the common
language. In the choice of his own vocabulary, indeed,
Philo seems to yield to the usage of his time, which
favoured eucharistein.

b) Homologein

Since the use of exomologeisthai is rather rare in
Philo, we can suspect the use of other terms to refer to
confession in its place. In fact, his vocabulary in relation to confession is very rich, if we accept the idea that
every form of affirmation may connote confession.

The first term which comes to mind is the verb
homologein, which means "to agree," "to promise," "to
acknowledge," together with the substantive homologia, which
means "agreement," "promise," or homologesis, acknowledgment. This term is very frequent in Philo, where it sometimes comes with the prefixes an-, pros-, syn-, and ex-, the
last one producing exomologeisthai, with which we dealt
above.

Either God or man can be the author of acknowledgment, promise, and assent. For instance, God praises Noah without recognizing his previous merit (Leg. Al. III, 77). God promises to guide Israel (Moses, I, 86): He confirms that actually He takes nothing for Himself, when He takes without being in need Himself (Her. 123). An affirmation which comes from God, from Moses, or from Scripture assumes its full strength. Coming from man, it can simply be profane and without any religious connotation (Flac. 18),[134] or it can also be very serious, becoming a moral or religious commitment, or a profession of faith. For instance, Laban acknowledges that he kept his daughters, the senses, prisoners of perceptible objects (Leg. Al. III, 21); Rachel and the weaker souls acknowledge that they cannot rise above the visible goods (Ebr. 56); we must admit that male thoughts of virtue come from God (Sacr. 106). Confession of sins is expressed through homologein and exomologeisthai (Leg. Al. II, 78; Praem. 163, Leg. Al. III, 198).

The most interesting instances are the confession of God considered as a profession of faith. For example, Joseph confesses that he is "God's" (Migr. 22); Greeks and Barbarians unanimously acknowledge the supreme Father of gods and men (Spec. Leg. II, 165). Abraham is the author of several confessions of faith expressed by the verb homologein (Ebr. 105-107, cf. Gen. 14:22-23; Her. 108, cf. Gen. 15:9; Mut. 57-58, cf. Gen. 17:3; Cher. 106-107, cf. Gen. 18:1-15). Let us add the two antithetic confessions (homologia) of Abel and Cain (Sacr. 2-3).

We should also point out the importance of the term pisteuein in the vocabulary of confession of faith, particularly in connection with Abraham, who is the type of faith. Faith adds to confession the strength coming from Divine credibility, which itself reflects the stability of the faithful (pistos) God. Philo sometimes even bases his reasoning on the contrast pistos-apistos represented in the same Abraham (Her. 93).

Philo frequently uses the opposition of gignosko-apogignosko in order to explain Abraham's conversion to faith through renunciation of the self (Som. I, 60, cf. Leg. Al. III, 48). A similar play of words is found in the use of exomologein in relation to Judah (Leg. Al., I, 82), and with the couple lethe-mneme: to forget the self paves the way for the memory of God, and vice-versa (Som. II, 232).

We must also note the use of terms meaning "to say" or "to know," for instance, nomizein, legein, gnorizein. Their context can confer the connotation of confession on them.[135]

In this regard, the most important among the verbs of opinion are dokein and doxazein, with the substantives dogma and doxa.[136] For instance, Cain and Abel represent two opposite dogmas: self-love (philautia), and the love for God (to philotheon), because Cain means possession, whereas Abel, because of his name, refers every thing to God (Sacr. 2-3; Deter. 32). To refer everything to God is the principle of thanksgiving, provided we, like Abel, know how the offering must be divided. We should not ascribe the merit to ourself, as did Cain,[137] nor should we ascribe to God all things without distinction--evil as well as good - as did Seth.[138]

IV. THE TERM "EUCHARISTEIN"-"EUCHARISTIA" IN PHILO

While also frequently using the other words built on charis, especially charisterion, Philo uses eucharistein most often. We must now examine the various uses of this term in Philo. We shall consider, first, the particular use of eucharistia, generally in its plural form, in the sense of a sacrificial offering of thanksgiving. Then, we shall come to the virtue of eucharistia, and to its opposite, acharistia. The adjectives eucharistos-acharistos correspond to this pair, and the same coupling is found in the adverbs. We find the form eucharistikos in both adjective and adverb. The substantive eucharistia is sometimes introduced by a preposition which confers a eucharistic purpose upon the action. The uses of the verb eucharistein, in particular, enables us to observe the action, the author, the addressee, the object, and the method of thanksgiving, and therefore to know its exact meaning. In addition, Philo provides us with the text of several formulas of thanksgiving, which, though spontaneous and improvised, both reveal a style of personal thanksgiving and allow us to speculate about the style of the ordinary prayer of thanksgiving, both individual and communal.

1. Charisterion

Philo offers no less than 17 references to charisterion, and there would probably be more if we could be sure of the Greek words underlying the Armenian translation of Questions on Genesis and On Exodus. This term

appears in its substantive form, in the adjectival form
charisterios, and even with the prefix eu-(eucharisterios,
Legat. 355-356; Cont. 87; Mos. II, 147-152). It refers to
the victim of a sacrifice of thanksgiving, for instance when
sacrifices are offered by pagans and Jews for the recovery
of Emperor Gaius (Legat. 355-356), or when Moses offers up
sacrifices for victory and fulfills vows (Mos. I, 219, cf.
Ex. 17:15), or when Abraham is preparing to sacrifice his
son Isaac (Deus 4). In this sense, charisterion can be used
alone as a substantive, or it can be added to modify thusia
or another term meaning offering (Ebr. 128-129). The adjective charisterios is used to specify the quality of a hymn,
thereby giving it the connotation of a eucharistic offering
or of a sacrifice of thanksgiving (Cont. 87; Mos. I, 253).
Finally, Charisterios can mean kindness and liberality, as
when God extends His beneficent powers (charisterious) upon
the wise Abraham (Ebr. 105-107).

2. Eucharistiai

Philo uses eucharistia, usually in the plural, in
reference to an offering or to a sacrifice of thanksgiving.
He is the first witness to the use of this term in the
plural,[139] which occurs in at least twelve instances. Thus
we find the eucharistic offerings (tas eucharistias)
performed according to the seasons of the year (Spec. Leg.
II, 175). In the singular, eucharistia can also have this
meaning, for example, the eucharistia offered upon the altar
when victims are sacrificed (Spec. Leg. I, 275). In both
the singular (Spec. Leg. I, 210-211) and the plural (Mos.
II, 42), the eucharistic offering can mean a verbal thanksgiving only, as for instance, in Mos. II, 42, since it was
impossible to offer sacrifices on the island of Pharos as in
the temple of Jerusalem.[140] We find this meaning again in
the case where the worshipper who offers himself up to God
in a spiritual sacrifice (thusia) completes his offering
with hymns and eucharistiai addressed to his Benefactor and
Saviour (Spec. Leg. I, 273). The eucharistia and honour
paid to God at the beginning of every pure deed (Q.G. IV,
130), or at a meal (Spec. Leg. II, 175), are also expressed
through words and actions. The eucharistiai appear to be
simple actions and words of human gratitude when Moses shows
his gratitude towards his adoptive parents (Mos. I, 33).

3. Eucharistia-acharistia, eucharistos-acharistos

Eucharistia and acharistia are two opposite dispositions of the soul. The reference is usually to gratitude,
or ingratitude, towards men or towards God. Thus Gaius was
supposed to hear through Flaccus about the gratitude of the
Jews (Flac. 99-100), and his praise inspired by gratitude
would resound throughout the world if he were to spare the
temple of Jerusalem (Legat. 284). The fire on the altar
symbolizes the continuity and unity of the eucharistia
(Spec. Leg. I, 285-286). The soul warmed by giving thanks
to God, pours itself out before God in manifestations of a
sober drunkenness (Leg. Al. I, 84). In these cases and
others, eucharistia, i.e., the eucharistic disposition of
the soul, manifests itself through words, actions and
offerings, and properly becomes "thanksgiving." The
eucharistic disposition appears independent from these
manifestations when contrasted with the opposite disposition. For instance, the eucharistic soul (psyche
eucharistos) is opposed to acharistia (Virt. 165).
Acharistia, which implies the absence of manifestations of
thanksgiving, appears more exactly as a simple disposition
or negative attitude, such as the acharistia which comes
from forgetting the gifts of God (Sacr. 52-58).[141]
Eucharistia can also be silent and totally interior to the
soul (Ebr. 94). However, though Philo tends to interiorize
eucharistia, we cannot say that he minimizes its exterior
manifestation since he considers the latter as quite
natural.[142]

Eucharistia can not only be an attitude of the soul or
an occasional disposition, but also a virtue. Philo
considers eucharistia as the holiest of virtues (Plant.
126). Eucharistia must also be interpreted as a virtue in
Mos. II, 207 (euchariston diathesin), Virt. 72-75
(diatheseos eucharistou), Spec. Leg. II, 208-209
(eucharistoi gignontai to ethos).

The adjectives eucharistos-acharistos (or
eucharistikos-acharistikos) can modify persons, dispositions, or actions (deeds and words),[143] and the same is true
of the adverbs built on them. For instance, the reward of
the eucharistic mind (to eucharistiko) is the very act of
giving thanks (to eucharistein) (Plant. 136; Virt. 165).
Philo however abstains from referring collectively to the
eucharistic minds, as he does for the ungrateful (hoi
acharistoi, Legat. 60; Deus 48; 73; Jos. 99; Her. 302).

We also find the use of the adjective as a substantive
in the neutral form with to. It either means eucharistic
offering or a eucharistic disposition. For example, the
thanksgiving of such a soul receives immortality and is
inscribed in the records of God (steliteuetai para theo,
Mos. II, 108). The act of giving thanks (to euchariston),
when God reveals it to Abraham, is the work of God and not
of men. In this case, the term can also refer to the object
of the eucharist, Isaac, who in fact represents the
eucharistic disposition of the soul which empties itself out
in order to leave the place open to God (Leg. Al. I, 82).

4. Eucharistia introduced by a preposition

The use of a preposition with eucharistia can suggest
that the action has an eucharistic meaning or purpose.[144]
For instance, the sheaf is given in thanks for the fertility
and abundance which the (Jewish) nation and the whole human
race are enjoying (Spec. Leg. II, 171). We also find eis,
eis eucharistias hypomnesin (Spec. Leg. II, 147), hyper
(Spec. Leg. I, 169), kat (Her. 15), eneka (Spec. Leg. IV,
98), pros (Migr. 25; Sacr. 63), symbolon (Mos. II, 101) used
in combination with eucharistia in order to express the
eucharistic purpose of an action.

5. The verb eucharistein

The verb eucharistein expresses the very action of
giving thanks. Its subject is a great man, such as Abraham
(Mut. 186), or the high-priest in his function (Spec. Leg.
II, 168); or it is a group, such as the Jews of Alexandria
after the fall of Flaccus (Flac. 99-100), a nation (Spec.
Leg. II, 168), any individual (Mut. 222), any creature (Her.
226), the world itself and all its parts (Her. 199-200). It
can also be the Muses (Plant. 130), the Heavens and the
choir of the stars (Virt. 75).[145]

The object of thanksgiving, when it is mentioned,
appears in the dative form. It can be a man (Flac. 99-100)
or God (Mos. II, 42). When the object is not mentioned, we
must often suppose God (Plant. 130). The motive for the
prayer of thanksgiving is a work or a gift of God. It is
introduced by hyper, for instance, when thanks are given to
God for the heavens and for mortal natures (Her. 226), by
peri (Sacr. 74), or epi (Spec. Leg. I, 283), by a
participle, for instance when God delivered the Jews at the
fall of Flaccus (Flac. 121), or by oti (Spec. Leg. III, 6;

Deus 7). The motive can be also a quality of God, put in apposition, such as when God is called the Teacher and Guide (Congr. 114; Spec. Leg. II, 204), Maker and Father (Her. 199-200), or Benefactor and Saviour (Plant. 130; Q.E. I, 2; Deus 48).

Attention should also be paid to the manner of giving thanks, namely, the moral conditions required in the sub- ject, the method or division of thanksgiving, and the posi- tion of the body during this form of prayer. The moral requirements are represented by the purity required in the victims brought to the altar (Spec. Leg. I, 167). No one can give thanks correctly if he is unworthy (Deus 7-9), or if he thinks himself able to buy God through bribery with rich offerings (Q.E. II, 50; Plant. 107-108; Spec. Leg. I, 280-284). The method consists of the proper division, represented by the knife with which the priest divides the sacrifice (Spec. Leg. I, 210-211). First, one should not ascribe to oneself the gifts of God, either by forgetfulness or by acquisition, even if one happens to possess them as if they were the fruit of his effort (Sacr. 52-60). Also one should not suppose that God is the cause of any evil (Q.G. I, 78; Leg. Al. I, 48-52; II, 78). Then, the thanksgiving must be divided logically, from the general to the particular, in the evocation of the works and gifts of God, without, however, entering the detail of the description (Sacr. 74ff, cf. Lev. 2:14; Spec. Leg. I, 210-211; Congr. 92-95; Q.G. I, 64; Ebr. 105-108). Every one must give thanks, even those of mediocre virtue, "according to the power of his hands" (Numb. 6:21) and according to the value of the gifts in his possession (Mut. 216-227, cf. Gen. 17:18; Gen. 27:38; Numb. 6:21). It is necessary to criticize one's own motives for giving thanks so as to choose the best among them, since to give thanks out of love for God is better than to do so out of self-interest (Spec. Leg. I, 283). One must also give thanks spontaneously and without delay (Q.G. I, 64),[146] offering up to God the best motion of the soul rather than the first in time (Sacr. 52- 58, cf. Deut. 8:12-18; 23:21). One should not neglect to give thanks immediately for an unexpected gift, a Divine inspiration, for instance (Virt. 165; Som. II, 268). Thanks should be rendered for all kinds of goods, both material and spiritual, as the law on the first fruits suggest.

Thanks can be given by means of buildings, by oblation and sacrifices, but especially by words of praise (Plant. 126). We cannot place too much emphasis on the importance of words of praise, and it is essential that we ascribe to each word of the following quote its own and full meaning:

> Because we know that, in all that has
> to do with shewing honour to God, one
> work only is incumbent upon us, namely
> thanksgiving, let us always and every-
> where make this our task, using voice
> and skillful pen. Let us never tire of
> composing eulogies in prose and poetry,
> so that, with or without musical
> accompaniment, in whatever function the
> voice may exercise, be it eloquent
> speech or song, high honour may be paid
> both to the world and to its Creator --
> the former, as it is said (Timaeus 29a),
> the most perfect of creatures, the
> latter the best of causes (Plant. 131).

We can conclude from this that Philo, in this sense,
considers the whole of his homiletic and exegetical work as
a thanksgiving, since it consists in discovering and
celebrating God's deeds and words (cf. Som. II, 38).

This text also shows that, if Philo knows of silent and
interior thanksgiving and even grants it a preeminence (Ebr.
94; Mos. II, 106-107), he also highly recommends its
exteriorization by all the means possible to man, and
particularly by loud speaking. Among the bodily aspects of
this form of prayer, there is the standing position, the
raising up of the hands (Ebr. 105), and choral singing (Mos.
I, 180; II, 255-257; Ebr. 119-121; Cont. 87). Of course,
thanksgiving is performed with joy (Leg. Al. I, 84; Spec.
Leg. II, 155-156) and with spontaneity (Q.G. II, 50; Spec.
Leg. II, 182; Sacr. 65).

As examples of prayer of thanksgiving found in Philo,
we can mention the meditation ascribed to Abraham, where
there is a combination of confession and thanksgiving with
their respective terms (Her. 24-39), the thanksgiving of the
Jews of Alexandria after the fall of Flaccus (Flac. 121-
124),[147] and the last thanksgiving of Moses (Virt. 72-76).
We must also consider as examples of thanksgiving simple and
spontaneous prayers which appear as exclamations, sometimes
in the very middle of a sentence, such as "Thank God,"
"Thanks be to God" (Charis to theo, Leg. Al. II, 60; cf.
Leg. Al. III, 40; Spec. Leg. III, 5), or "Many thanks to the
Creator, that He did not grant the power of words to Balaam
as a sword into the hands of a madman!" (Cher. 32).

The meaning of eucharistia-eucharistein must therefore
be determined by the context. It is often a disposition to

and expression of gratitude, but also the praise of the
Divine Creator and Benefactor. It is also connected with
the sacrifice of thanksgiving, where eucharistia refers to
the eucharistic offering or sacrifice.

V. IMAGES WITH THE CONNOTATION OF THANKSGIVING IN PHILO

The images which Philo uses to express thanksgiving can
be divided into three groups: first, the memory - or
forgetfulness - of God and of His gifts; second, exchange,
loan, and restitution, which imply the notion of a good
which should be acknowledged as belonging to God; third,
consecration and votive offering. Philo does not invent
these formulas, although he extends their meaning through
allegory to include the objects of interior life. These
are, actually, laws borrowed from Deuteronomy, Exodus, and
Numbers. Sometimes they are illustrated by examples found
in Genesis, but, more often, by those found in ordinary
life.

1. The memory of God and of His gifts

Memory as a Biblical image of thanksgiving, and its
counterpart, the warning against forgetting God, which
causes man to ascribe to himself what belongs to God,
derives from the law of Deuteronomy 11:18:

> Take heed lest you forget the Lord your
> God, by not keeping his commandments and
> his ordinances and his statutes, which I
> command you this day: lest, when you
> have eaten and are full, and have built
> goodly houses and live in them, and when
> your herds and flocks multiply, and your
> silver and gold is multiplied, and all
> that you have is multiplied, then your
> heart be lifted up, and you forget the
> Lord your God, who brought you out of
> the land of Egypt, out of the house of
> bondage ... Beware lest you say in your
> heart, "My power and the might of my
> hand have gotten me this wealth." You
> shall remember the Lord your God, for it
> is he who gives you power to get wealth;
> that he may confirm his covenant which
> he swore to your fathers, as at this
> day.

The image of memory and forgetfulness of God appears frequently in Philo. This image is connected with the idea of thanksgiving, and often with the term eucharistia. The chief text is Sacr. 54-57, where Philo depicts several types of ungrateful people. Those who forget God and His gifts are simply ungrateful, but those who ascribe to themselves the merit of their good deeds also sin by forgetting that it is the mighty hand of God which gave them the power to perform these deeds. Both types disobey the law of Deut. 8:11-18.[148]

We find many applications of this text in Philo, both literally and allegorically. For instance, in Virt. 163-165, the offering of the first-fruits serves to remind us of God. The eucharistic connotation is formally added to it by the introduction of the verb eucharistein. The application of the law of Deut 8:11-18 is very developed literally and allegorically. In Spec. Leg. II, 171, the offering of the sheaf (Lev. 23:1-9) is interpreted in the same sense of remembering God, and its eucharistic purpose is specified (ep' eucharistia... theou mneme). The same can be said about the offering of the first loaf (Spec. Leg. I, 132-133) and about the fasting ordered to commemorate the preservation from starvation in the present generation (Spec. Leg. II, 203). We can add to these texts Migr. 56, where Philo says that the greatness of the nation is due to its invocation of God, because the beginning and end of every noble work is the unceasing remembrance of God and the reference to His covenant (cf. Deut. 4:6-7). Elsewhere (Cont. 26) we read that the Therapeutae keep the memory of God alive even in their dreams, whereas the impious refuse to God even the most common of all tributes, that of remembering Him (Cont. 62). The memory of the commandments of God appears in connection with the laws of Lev. 11:3-8 and Deut. 14:6. In Spec. Leg. IV, 107 and Post. 149, the ruminants are compared to memory, and Philo derives the necessity of meditation on the word of God from this allegory.[149]

The most interesting development of the idea of memory is Plant. 126-131, where Philo uses the figure of the Muses and their mother, the virgin Mnemosyne (Memory), in order to teach us that the mere recounting of the works of God in praise, without embellishment, is the purest fruit of the virtue of eucharistia, which is introduced here as the most eminent virtue.

2. Reception, exchange, loan, restitution

A series of images express the idea that we must acknowledge God's ownership of our many possessions. Acknowledgment that all in our possession comes from God, that we are simply caretakers of His property, that even what we exchange with Him belongs to Him, affirms His dominion over all our possessions. The presence of the term eucharistein, or of other terms connected with the notion of thanksgiving, such as aparchesthai (to give the first-fruits) confirms the eucharistic meaning of these images.

The images are connected to a number of laws to which Philo refers in the context: loans (Ex. 22:6-7); levies of all kinds: first-born (Ex. 13:11-16), first-fruits (Numb. 28:29), first loaf (Numb. 15:17-21), fruits of the fourth year (Lev. 19:24; cf. Virt. 159; Abr. 13; Plant. 117), tithes (Lev. 27:30-33), shekel (Ex. 30:11-16; cf. Q.G. IV, 110; 118); the obligation for every adult to come before God with an offering (Ex. 23:14-19); the basket (Deut. 26:1-11); the dedication of the Levites to God as a ransom for the first-born of Israel (Numb. 3:41). We must add Numb. 28:2, which introduces the regulations about festivals, and Ex. 21:1-11, on the slave who prefers bondage to freedom.

The notion of the loan,[150] which man should not keep for himself but return to its owner, according to Ex. 22:6-7, figures in a very rich text (Her. 100-124),[151] where we also find references to other laws and other images interpreted in the same sense of thanksgiving. There is the reference to the sacred loan (104-105) of the soul, the senses, and speech, which man must acknowledge as a gift of God and return to Him through the symbols of the heifer, ram, and goat (Gen. 15:9).

There are also the laws on levies (103, cf. Ex. 25:1-2), laws on the first-born (117, cf. Ex. 13:1-2), laws on the Levites taken as ransom for the first-born of Israel (124, cf. Numb. 3:12). This text is a commentary on Gen. 15:8-9, where, to the question of Abraham, "Master, by what shall I know that I shall inherit?", God answers, "Take for me ... a heifer, a ram, and a goat," etc. Philo reads, "Take for me" (labe moi). This phrase suggests to him the idea that the objects represented by these animals are the gift and possession of God, which Abraham should treat only as a sacred loan which must be returned to its Divine owner (apodosis, ameibesthai, 104), and of which he is the guardian (parakatatithemai, 104-105). Philo returns to the same idea (113-114) when he interprets Ex. 25:1-2, "Speak

(Moses) to the sons of Israel and take for me beginnings
(labe moi aparchas). Philo specifies that Moses is not to
take for himself, but for God, and he derives from this law
the idea that beginnings, represented by the first-fruits
(117, cf. Ex. 13:1-2), and ends (120, cf. Numb. 31:28ff)
both belong to God--in other terms, the totality of creation, and especially the operation of good in the soul.
Therefore, man must keep (phylattein) these goods worthily
and acknowledge he received them from God (homologesei
lambanein, 123). The idea of thanksgiving is obvious when
Philo explains the return (apodosis) of the gift of God as a
means of exchanging grace for grace (charin chariti,
104).[152]

It would also be useful to look into the other
references to ameibesthai (to give in exchange), apodidonai,
and antiparechein (to return), phylattein, diaphylattein,
diaterein (to keep). Let us mention Plant. 130, Sobr. 58,
and Spec. Leg. I, 224, where ameibesthai clearly points to
thanksgiving toward the Benefactor and is combined with the
term eucharistia.

We can also mention the frequent use by Philo of two
laws: Numb. 28:2[153] and Ex. 21:5-6. Philo refers to the
former in order to recall that everything belongs to God:
he refers to the latter in order to stigmatize the attitude
of the man who, by saying "my master, my wife, my children,"
etc., announces his rejection of the freedom received from
God in relation to the mind and senses. Let us note,
furthermore, Philo's interpretation of the song over the
basket (Spec. Leg. II, 219, cf. Deut. 26:1-11): the
Israelite is presenting what he in fact receives (komizein-
lambanein). Finally, an investigation of the term 'not to
find' would lead to similar results. For instance, Noah is
the figure of the man "who finds," when he "found grace"
(Gen. 5:8). Philo interprets this text in the following
sense: Noah "found that everything is grace" and manifested
thereby his eucharistic disposition amidst an ungrateful
generation.

3. Consecration and votive offering[154]

As we did for the preceding images, we must first
determine the laws which Philo applies through symbolism to
the contents of the inner life. These laws are those on
anathema and vows: Lev. 27:28 (anathema); Numb. 30 and
Deut. 23:22-23 (vows); Numb. 6:1-22 (the Great Vow, as Philo
calls it). Let us also add the prohibition to erect a

pillar beside the altar, which, according to Deut. 16:21-22,
would be an offense to God, in contradistinction with the
pillar erected in honour of God, for instance by Jacob (Gen.
31:13). The associated terms in the context are anathema
(anathema, anatithemi), consecration (hieroo, anieroo,
katieroo), and vow (euche, euchesthai).

Philo grants them a eucharistic meaning, and sometimes
combines them with eucharistia or another term with a
similar meaning. For instance, in Mos. I, 252, when the
Israelites invade the land of Canaan, they dedicate to God
as first-fruits the first cities which they take, thereby
turning the whole country into an anathema to God. The
terms used are anatithemi, anathema, anieroo, and the
eucharistic formula, tas charisterious homologias epeteloun
(they made eucharistic confessions).

Let us examine Som. I, 241-256, which contains all the
terms and references relevant to the laws mentioned above.
Philo discusses the apparent contradiction between Deut.
16:22, the interdiction to erect a pillar, and Gen. 31:13,
where Jacob erects a pillar. He interprets the "to thyself"
of Deut. 16:22 ("And thou shalt not erect a pillar [for
thyself], which the Lord your God hates") in the sense of
the exaltation of man before God, which is characteristic of
the fool and of the impious. Jacob, on the contrary,
erected a pillar "unto God" (Gen. 31:13, "Thou anointedst
unto Me a pillar"). Philo then gives examples: a nazir
dedicates himself to God (Numb. 6), and Hannah gives her son
Samuel to God (I Sam. 1:11). In this text, Philo proposes
the dedication to God of the goods of the soul and of the
soul itself. We notice an interesting development of the
same idea: the entire heaven and the universe are dedicated
to God (anathema theou), therefore the Sage, who is a
citizen of the world, must also dedicate himself to God and
not erect a pillar "to himself." The opposite of the pious
dedication of a pillar is illustrated in the case of Lot's
wife, who was turned into a pillar (Gen. 19:26) because she
averted her eye from virtue in order to behold lower goods.
In spite of the absence of the term eucharistia, the whole
section is permeated by the idea of eucharistia. Let us
mention the characteristic terms: pillar (stele), anathema
(anathema), consecration (anieroo), the inscription on a
pillar, and vow (euche).

The section on the Nazir (Spec. Leg. I, 247-254) is
also very rich. We find the same terms, and the idea of

thanksgiving is not only spread through the entire development, but explicit in the sacrifices offered at the fulfillment of the vow (252).

We have seen in a text examined above (Her. 100-124)
that intelligence, speech, and senses were considered as a
loan entrusted to man by God. They too are an anathema, and
they should be dedicated to God (Her. 108). We must also
dedicate the arts and sciences (Her. 114-116), beginnings
and ends (Her. 117), and the self (Her. 110) to God. We
find the same doctrine in the image of dedication in Her.
73, which Philo interprets in the sense of renunciation of
self - the faculties of the soul and body - which consecration signifies. Philo conceives of renunciation as an
interior flight from self. This text has many parallels
(Migr. 184-195; Sacr. 58; Cher. 106-109).

Human life must be dedicated to God (Dec. 108). Man
must consecrate to God the best of himself, i.e., the good
movements of his soul (Sacr. 109, anathema, anieroo). In
professional life, as we have seen, the sciences and arts
must be dedicated to the service of God (Her. 114-116). In
public life, festivals are God's, and, because of their
sacred nature, they should not degenerate into profane
entertainment (Spec. Leg. II, 51). Terms belonging to
dedication, consecration, and vow appear many times in
association with sacrifices. But, because of his inclination to cosmic speculation, Philo considers the Universe
itself as an anathema consecrated to God (Her. 200). He
draws parallels between the consecration and anathema of the
world, the heavens, and the soul of the wise man, who is the
citizen of the world. We saw it in Som. II, 243: we shall
find it again in Spec. Leg. I, 286-287, where the fire on
the altar becomes a symbol of the eucharistic soul of the
wise man.

CHAPTER TWO

EUCHARISTIA AND LITURGY

The present chapter[1] considers 1) the liturgical aspects of Philo's eucharistia, 2) his notion of spiritual sacrifice, and 3) draws a comparison between Philo and the Judaism of his time. The following chapters will deal with the Philonic eucharistia as related to the Cosmic religion of Hellenism, which Philo calls the Chaldean doctrine, and with the importance of eucharistia in the life of the soul. The present chapter is particularly difficult for several reasons: in the past, the liturgical aspect in Philo has been treated only sporadically, incompletely, and sometimes prejudicially. Moreover, the exact meaning of the rites and liturgical terms in the Judaism of the time of Philo is far from simple and clear, especially in regard to thanksgiving. The many discussions about the origins of the Christian Eucharist helped to raise the question of the Jewish eucharistia, but often with the result of increasing the confusion because the particular approach of scholars tended to bias the issue.[2] We must, therefore, compare both the Philonic and the Palestinian eucharistia with the benediction and with the todah, which is the praise connected with those sacrifices of communion which, today, are usually called sacrifices of plenitude, but which Philo called sacrifices "of salvation." For J.-P. Audet, the origins of the Christian Eucharist are to be found in the "Benediction," which he considers as a literary form. H. Cazelles, on the contrary, points to the todah. In this second hypothesis, eucharistia is essentially sacrificial. What do we find on this subject in Philo? Only a detailed inquiry can tell us. Concerning the relation between eucharistia and benediction, we may rely on our own inquiry of the Philonic use of eulogein and on our findings about the Philonic use of eucharistein for the prayer at meals.[3] K. Hruby called our attention to the eucharistic prayers connected with the daily sacrifices in the Temple. It is interesting to discover that Philo grants these sacrifices a eucharistic meaning. Once revealed, the eucharistic aspect proves to be rewarding.[4] Both in Philo and at the Temple of Jerusalem, we discover eucharistic meanings. These are more obvious in Philo, but they are certainly present also in the Temple, where they appear in the sacrifices of communion, in the burnt-offerings, in the cereal-offerings which accompany sacrifices, in the shew-bread, and in the first-fruits. An inquiry into calendar festivals reveals eucharistic aspects in the meaning of festal liturgy both in Philo and in

49

Palestinian Judaism.   Once more,   these eucharistic aspects
are more clearly manifested in Philo.   This inquiry, in
addition, enables us to insist upon our affirmation of a
sacrificial character in the Philonic eucharistia: instead
of vanishing into the vague notion of praise common to the
different   Hellenistic   cultural   families,   Philonic
eucharistia appears to be rooted in the sacrificial liturgy
of the Temple.   These distinctions,   together with the fact
that Philo does not tell us anything about the contents of
the synagogue prayer, to which we would be tempted to refer
his eucharistia, help us to see more clearly the place of
spiritual sacrifice in Philo.   Philo presents interesting
materials with his notion of the Levitic ideals of the service of God, and he particularly introduces the Therapeutae
as witnesses to hymnic prayer.   Since he does not comment on
the book of Psalms and does not cite the so-called psalms of
thanksgiving, the comparison with Judaism can be made only
on the basis of the spiritual sacrifice which is attested to
in Judaism and appears particularly in the literature of
Qumran.   The parallel between Qumran and the Therapeutae of
Philo would be far more rewarding if we were sure that Philo
had good knowledge of the Essenes, and that his Therapeutae
were actually connected with the people of Qumran.

I. EUCHARISTIA AND BENEDICTION

     J.-P. Audet explains his theory of the identity between
eucharistia and benediction in his   article,   "Esquisse
historique du genre littéraire de la 'bénédiction' juive et
de l''eucharistie' chrétienne,"[5] and in his book, La
Didachè, Instructions des Apôtres.[6] He presents the
"Benediction" as a literary form of its own, the Jewish
berakah.   The origins of the Benediction, he says, are not
sacral, i.e., they do not belong to the world of worship--
the service of the Temple and sacrifices.   The earliest
examples are meaningful in this regard: in Gen. 24:26-27,
the servant of Abraham bows down and adores Yahweh, saying,
"Blessed be Yahweh, the God of my master Abraham, who has
not forsaken his steadfast love and his faithfulness toward
my master.   As for me, the Lord has led me in the way to the
house of my master's kinsmen." Two literary elements of the
Benediction appear in this reference: first, an exclama-
tion, "Blessed be Yahweh;" second, the motive, in a relative
clause, "who has not forsaken his steadfast love and his
faithfulness toward my master."   The sentiment of gratitude
is implicit, not expressed other than through the benediction.   In the case of the benediction pronounced by Jethro,
when he rejoices for the good things done by Yahweh to

Israel when He delivered it from the hands of the Egyptians
(Ex. 18:9-12), the proclamation of the name of God calls for
a "confession of faith." Therefore, the Benediction
develops in the direction of praise (cf. the eulogein family
and its parallels) and confession (the exomologeisthai
family). The literary form of the Benediction, once
absorbed into the sphere of worship, underwent some changes.
There, it tended toward a declamatory style and a hymnic
form. The motive for benediction is more developed and is
borrowed from the common treasury of the "mighty deeds of
God." Titles ascribed to God are more diversified. Precise
rules in the Mishnah determine the literary form of the
Benediction.

More recent examples of the Benediction include the
psalms of thanksgiving, the benediction of Amidah, the
hodayot of Qumran. We might also mention the short blessings pronounced by the faithful in all circumstances, represented by the "hundred benedictions" of daily life gathered
from the Talmud. In turn, terms from the eucharistein
family entered the biblical vocabulary and became associated
with the preceding families in the expression of praise.
The first examples of this appear in the Greek biblical
books or complements, where they express thanksgiving for
the gifts of God.

Coming to Philo, J.-P. Audet notes from the first that,
with this writer, continuity with the literary forms is
almost broken. References to the eucharistein family multi-
ply, and consequently the association between this family
and the two former ones, which began in the recent Greek
texts or versions, was strengthened. At the same time,
there is the development of a semantic balance of
eucharistein-eucharistia favoring the use of the term to
express gratitude.[7] The Philonic experience, he adds, is
very significant at this point, since it paved the way for
similar changes which were to occur elsewhere and on a quite
different scale. He is referring to the success of the
notion of thanksgiving in Christianity, and to the distortion which it imposed on the original notion of the
Eucharist as an expression of praise. To confirm his position, he takes advantage of the fact that ancient
Alexandrian translations of the berakah prefer eulogein to
eucharistein, even while noting the growing fortune of the
notion of thanksgiving. The meaning of the term
eucharistein, in his opinion, is generally to be determined
from that of the two other semantic groups (eulogein,
exomologeisthai), and not the reverse, as lexicographers,
because of routine, take for granted. Finally, on the basis

of this analysis and these conclusions, he believes he can
translate the term <u>eucharistia</u> in the <u>Didache</u> as "benediction".[8]

The theory of J.-P. Audet was well received, although
it also met with some criticism. R. J. Ledogar writes on
doxology, which he considers as the basis of the formulas of
Christian benediction:

> This berakah-doxology is something quite
> different from the "literary genre"
> which Père J. P. Audet calls a
> "Benediction" and considers as the fore-
> runner of the Christian Eucharistic
> Prayer. Among other things, it does not
> generally contain the "anamnesis" of the
> "mirabilia Dei," which he considers an
> essential feature. Audet's analysis
> does not respect the boundaries which
> distinguish prose from poetry, as well
> as other literary forms in the Old and
> New Testaments, but selects from each of
> them only that which fits the pattern he
> describes. This is legitimate and
> useful for the sake of isolating the
> trends that will eventually crystallize
> into the fixed berakah of the Talmudic
> period, but it does not justify fitting
> all the praise formulae of the first
> century into a single mould. And, most
> important, it does not justify translat-
> ing <u>eucharistein</u> as "to bless."[9]

H. Cazelles also rejects the identification proposed by
Audet between <u>berakah</u> and the Christian <u>eucharistia</u>.[10]

This discussion shows that we must not incautiously
consider the so-called "terms of praise" as mere inter-
changeable synonyms. But the thesis of the literary form of
the Jewish Benediction offered by J.-P. Audet is also too
narrow in its scope, since it improperly includes in the
same concept other forms of praise or thanksgiving which
possess an identity of their own. Specifically, the term
and the notion of <u>eucharistia</u> reflect a complex reality,
consisting of different elements whose sacrificial aspect
has been brought to light. These elements cannot be reduced
only to the Benediction, and the <u>eucharistia</u> should not be
considered as a different way to translate the Benediction
because of the contamination through the current Hellenistic

usage.   We must maintain, though, that J.-P. Audet is right
to consider the Benediction   as a way to give   thanks, since
it is   the   most   traditional   method   of   thanksgiving in
Judaism. The articles of A. Guillet and of K. Hruby confirm
this view.

We have seen   the place of the Benediction   in Philo--a
very small one, limited   to the sections where he   quotes a
Biblical blessing.   We have   also noticed how _eulogein_, the
proper term for Benediction, takes on the sense of praise or
of thanksgiving.   Examples of this are very few, because of
this   limitation   and   because   Philo   uses   the   term
eucharistein   to give thanks. Had he left us more materials
about   the   prayers of   the Synagogue   or   about spontaneous
prayer, we   probably would find more references   to _eulogein_
in this   sense.

1. _Eucharistein_ used in reference to the prayers at   ·
   meals

In spite of   his limited   use of   _eulogein_,   Philo does
provide interesting information about the prayers   at meals.
These, on the one   hand, consist   of blessings, but,   on the
other hand, convey   the idea of thanksgiving, or   the prayer
of   "Graces," in addition to praise.   Significantly in this
context,   Philo   discards   the   term   _eulogein_   and   uses
eucharistein.   The New Testament witnesses to this change in
the narratives of the Last Supper.[11]   Let us examine Philo's
references to the prayers at meals.

In Q.G. IV, 130,[12] Philo   comments on   the   gesture of
Abraham's servant, who bows down to the Lord before presenting Rebecca   and   her mother   with their   presents   and dis-
cussing the affair of   marriage.   "For it is proper," Philo
says, "to give   thanks   and   honour to God   (_eucharistian kai
timen_) at the beginning of every pure deed." This statement
has no direct relation to the table, but it presents   a general   precept about a particular action.   Reference to   the
meal is found in Spec. Leg. II, 175, where Philo, commenting
on the sheaf of   barley offered as first-fruits, says: "It
would be . . . unlawful to enjoy and partake of any   form of
food for which thanks had not been offered in the proper and
rightful manner."   Here, the term _eucharistein_ appears in a
text where we   would expect _eulogein_, the Benediction.   The
reason   may well be   that the   use of   _eucharistein_ for the
prayers at meals   is much earlier than is   commonly assumed,
and   that Philo is   showing his   usual reticence in   the use
of   _eulogein_.   Another text   sheds additional   light on the

meaning of eulogein (to bless) in relation to the the
prayers at meals: Q.E. II, 18, about Ex. 23:25b,

"I will bless (eulogeso) thy bread and thy water, and I
will turn away illness from thee." Here, we note that Philo
agrees with the Hebrew and does not follow LXX by not
mentioning the wine, but this may be due merely to an
ascetic scruple, or because wine is not essential to life.
He writes:

> It teaches us a most worthwhile lesson
> and one that is in order, showing that
> neither bread nor water gives nourish-
> ment by itself alone, but that there are
> times when they do more harm than good,
> (namely) if the divine Logos does not
> graciously bestow upon them his helpful
> powers. For this reason, he (Moses)
> says, "I will bless thy bread and thy
> water" as if they were not sufficient to
> give nourishment by themselves alone
> without the loving friendship and care
> of God.

Procopius paraphrases, me tou theou dynamin opheletiken dia
tes eulogias parechontos (unless God grant through His
blessing a power assisting the water and bread). If the
term eulogia of Procopius is authentic, we possess two
pieces of evidence (the first one being eulogeso) for the
idea that the divine blessing has an effect on the bread and
wine, making them profitable for the human body. Therefore,
what is true in the case of food is also true in the case of
the sensibles and the intelligibles, which God not only
sends like rain upon our mind and senses, but also makes
assimilable to them (Leg. Al. I, 25-27). Thus, the
eucharistia, used above in reference to the prayers at
meals, finds its relevance: man gives thanks to God for the
gift of food and its assimilation since God provided it and,
by His blessing, made it profitable for man. I have found
no evidence in Philo for man's blessing God or the table
with the term eulogein or eulogia; but the use of
eucharistein to designate the prayers at meals is well
attested.

There are other instances of the use of eucharistia in
connection with the table. In Q.E. II, 72, commenting on
Ex. 25:30, "Thou shalt place upon the table bread before Me
continually," Philo suggests that "continually" means that
the gift of food is continual and uninterrupted, while

"before" means that it is pleasing and agreeable to God both
to be gracious and to receive gratitude (eucharistian probably corresponds to charizesthai).

The idea of "repaying" God reappears in connection with
the table in Q.E. II, 69, which comments on Ex. 25:23, about
the table of pure gold.   Philo enlarges on the meaning of
the table, which suggests communion and exchange.   "The
table," he writes, "indicates a kind of communion among
those who receive a common share of salt and sacrifices.
For this leads to loving one's fellow for his own sake."
Here, Philo seems to refer to the sacrifices of communion.
Speaking of the love among the parts of the world made from
the same substance, he adds, "for one who is about to eat
and to be made glad by the Father, (Who is) the begetter of
these (foods), is taught from above to return the benefit as
if to brothers by the same father and mother."   There is no
reason to see in this text a thanksgiving addressed to God,
unless we follow the Armenian glossist who takes this
sentence to mean the gratitude of the elements of the world
toward the Divine powers.[13]

We may add to the above references Jos. 196, where
Joseph invites his brethren to partake of his salt and
board, which are the symbols of genuine friendship (ibid.
110), and frg. 20,[14] where the sacred table (trapezes
hieras) is distinguished from the table of the false gods.
At this sacred table, Philo says, it is not becoming to
behave like youngsters who gorge themselves to the point of
unconsciousness.

We can conclude that even if Philo actually used
eulogein when he said, "Graces" at meals, about which we are
not certain, he considered this prayer as eucharistia and
called it thus.   With more reservation, we can suppose that
he used eucharistein in the very formula of this prayer.

II.   EUCHARISTIA AND TODAH

Henri Cazelles attacks the position of J.-P. Audet,
which up to then seemed to be generally accepted.[15]
Cazelles maintains that the question is whether the
Christian Eucharist represents formulas which, via the prayers of Synagogal type, actually go back to an earlier type
of prayers connected to the sacrifices of the Temple.
Rather than concentrating on the liturgy of the Pharisees
(the Synagogue), which is non-sacrificial, we should inquire

whether there is in the background an earlier Jewish
liturgy, which disappeared together with the ruin of the
Liturgy of the Saducees.

Cazelles finds in Philo, in connection with
eucharistia, several obvious references to the todah.[16] We
mention them together with his remarks in the following
paragraphs:

In Spec. Leg. I, 224, Philo speaks of euchais thusiais and
other eucharistiais. He closely associates eucharistia with
the cult in Vita Mosis II, 101, in connection with the altar
of incense. Elsewhere, when Philo speaks of tes
eucharistias thusias (Spec. Leg. I 297), we can hardly
escape recognizing a counterpart of the zebah todah of Lev.
7:12-15. Similarly, in Leg. Al. I, 84, where the man who is
giving thanks to God is permeated with fire and is drunk
with a sober drunkenness, we recognize an allusion to
sacrifices and to the libations which accompany them. In
Sacr. 62, eucharistia is connected with the Passover
sacrifice. In Spec. Leg. I, 169, again, Philo mentions the
two lambs offered daily referring to Numb. 28:3ff, and sees
an eucharistia in this offering. The biblical text does not
mention a berakah or even a hymn, but an offering of fine
flour mixed with oil: this is precisely what characterizes
the todah sacrifice in Lev. 7:12-15. The Philonic
eucharistia is sacrificial and points to the todah of the
Old Testament. It is rooted in the sacrificial synthesis of
Leviticus.

This sacrifice is very ancient: it is already mentioned in the eighth century B.C. in the writings of the
Prophet Amos (4:5). But the practice of todah flourished in
Israel after the return from the Exile and the reconstruction of the Temple. There are at least twelve references to
todah in the Psalter, especially in the last psalms. Apparently, the title of Psalm 100 is to be interpreted as pointing to its use for this type of sacrifice of communion
accompanied by hymns. The priestly synthesis of Pentateuch,
however, progressively reduced its importance. Leviticus
emphasized burnt-offerings and the sacrifices for sin, rele-
gating the sacrifice of communion to a minor role. The
restrictions of the Pentateuch influenced the Essenes and
Pharisees. The community of Qumran preserved hymnology with
the hodot, but the Rule of the Congregation does not refer
to such songs in its description of a cultic meal. The Rule
of the Community knows only of the levy of the lips, of the
hallel and psalmody, not of todah. The destruction of the
Temple was to put an end to the role of todah in the Jewish

community.   But todah was welcomed in the Christian community, for which the true Temple was the body of Christ.

Philo describes the sacrifices of communion in the context of the types of sacrifices defined in Leviticus.   The
chief reference is Spec. Leg. I, 212-252, to which we must
add Spec. Leg. I, 251-252, which deals with the presence of
a sacrifice of salvation in the threefold sacrifice marking
the end of the Great Vow.   The other references--Leg. Al.
III, 133; Sacr. 136; Post. 123; Spec. Leg. I, 123;   145 give
moral or allegorical exegeses about the lobe of the liver,
the fat, the blood, and the shoulder and breast of the victim, but tell us nothing more about the sacrifice of salvation.   Moreover, since sacrifices could only be offered in
the Temple of Jerusalem, we can assume that Philo had little
personal experience of them.   He does speak of his pilgrim-
age to Jerusalem and of the friendships made in such circumstances (Providence 64; Spec. Leg. I, 70), but in these
references, which are very laconic, he tells us nothing
about what he did in the precincts of the Temple.   However,
what he does say in his long description in Spec. Leg. I,
212-225, is very interesting, at least in sections 220-225.
The prescription to eat the victim on the same day presupposes that the offerer and his folk share in a sacred banquet.   God, not man, is the host who welcomes and entertains
the company, since, because of the sacrifice the victim is
His.   But the last part of this section (224-225), Cazelles
points out, deals directly with the todah.   The reference is
to what Philo calls the sacrifice of praise, which is a part
of the sacrifice of salvation as a whole (tes de tou
soteriou thusias en eidei perilambanetai he legomene tes
aineseos).   Philo borrows the expression used by LXX to
translate the Hebrew zebah todah selamin (the sacrifice of
communion with praise).   The man who enjoys a life of peace
inwardly and outwardly, Philo comments, must requite God his
pilot "with hymns and benedictions and prayers and sacrifices and the other expressions of gratitude as religion
demands.   All these together are called praise."[17]   We must
see this   section in all its importance.   The todah
(aineseos) does not mean here simply praise, understood
apart from the sacrificial context.   Neither can the over-
simplified notion of praise be assimilated to the other
forms of cult mentioned here, including the eucharistiai,
since to do so would be to empty them, as well as this particular form of praise, of their original content.   Such a
conclusion would imply that Philo retains only a vague
notion of praise out of all these forms of worship, a notion
from which the biblical data is missing and which we could
expect from any Hellenistic mind.   Actually, we are dealing

with a well-determined form of cult, with a long and rich
tradition, a cult which the biblical references given more
generously in Cazelles's article illustrate and explain. In
the todah of the sacrifice of communion which is continued
in the sacred banquet, there is a place for hymns, macarisms, and vows. The sacrifices seem to point to offerings
of victims: the "other eucharistiai," apparently, do not
simply summarize what has been said before, but refer to
offerings of thanksgiving whatever be their nature, even if
they are only verbal sacrifices, as the plural of the word
eucharistia indicates.

Can we go farther, or at least find other references?
In Philo's descriptions, the banquets of the Ancients which
followed sacrifices (Plant. 161-163), although general in
their character, seem to reflect the biblical rather than
the pagan practice:

> For our forefathers inaugurated every
> noble business with sacrifices duly
> offered, deeming that an auspicious
> result would by this means be ensured.
> However urgently the crisis might call
> for immediate action, they never failed
> to tarry to pray and offer sacrifices
> before and, deeming that what is rapid
> is not always superior to what is slow.
> . . . Knowing, then, that, like other
> things, the use and enjoyment of wine
> needs great care, they took strong drink
> neither in great quantity nor at all
> times, but in such order and season as
> was befitting. For after having first
> prayed and presented sacrifices and
> implored the favour of the Diety, when
> they had cleansed their bodies by ablu-
> tions and their souls by streams of holy
> ordinances and instructions in the right
> way, radiant and gladsome they turned to
> relaxation and enjoyment, in many cases
> not after returning home, but remaining
> in the temples in which they had sacri-
> ficed in order that both the recollec-
> tion of their sacrifices and their
> reverence for the place might lead them
> to celebrate a festivity in actual truth
> most holy, sinning neither in word nor
> deed. You must know that it was from
> this, so it is said, that 'getting drunk'

> (methuein) got its name, because it was
> the custom of the men of earlier times,
> to indulge in wine after sacrificing
> (meta : after ; thuein : sacrificing).
> Now with whom, I ask , would the mode of
> using strong drink just described be
> more in keeping than with wise men, with
> whose character the act which precedes
> the drunkedness, namely the act of
> sacrificing, is also in perfect
> accord?[18]

Indeed, this etymology of methuein goes back to
Aristotle, according to Atheneas,[19] but the presence of wine
corresponds to Numb. 15:7, and purifications were required
in the Temple of Jerusalem. Moreover, the reference to the
shrines in the plural corresponds very well to the biblical
examples which refer to a period preceding the unification
of the cult at the Temple of Jerusalem.

Cazelles mentions other references in Philo (ibid.
pp. 16-17), especially Spec. Leg. I, 169, where the Passover
lamb, daily burnt-offerings, and the complementary sacrifices offered on Sabbath days and on festivals are given a
eucharistic meaning, as are the incense-offering in Leg. Al.
I, 84. Here again, according to Cazelles, we find todah,
without any reference to berakah. We think that Cazelles is
right, if our conclusion about the use of eulogein (to
bless) by Philo in the limited context of the biblical benedictions is true. However, it is difficult to extend the
notion of the sacrifice of salvation to other forms of
sacrifices in Philo. If the latter actually include todah,
we face another problem, which would be very interesting for
the eucharistic interpretation of todah in Philo.

1. Macarism or Beatitude

The idea of studying macarism separately from praise
and benediction can be contested. We do it because macarism
has its own terms, even though these usually associated with
"hymns," "eucharistiai," "honour" (time) paid to God,
"festivals," "praise" (ainesis'), and "confession"
(exomologesis) itself. Properly belonging to macarism are
the terms of the families of makarios and of eudaimonia.

Macarisms, or the formulas proclaiming God as happy,
stem from the notion that only God is happy, that He alone
enjoys absolute happiness (Sacr. 40), that He is transcen-

dentally happy (Legat. 5; Plant. 35). As a consequence, happiness and festivals are His only (Spec. Leg. II, 53). He is, indeed, free from every evil: He is the absolute of Good and the source of all good things which He bestows like rain on heaven and earth (ibid. 53). Those who love the solitude which is dear to God will be the first to assimilate His blessed and happy nature (Agr. 87).

Let us mention several examples of macarism. In Agr. 80, the mind in its perfection, as figured by the choir of men led by Moses, and sense-perception made pure and clean, as figured by the choir of women led by Miriam (Ex. 15:1-20), render to God hymns and macarisms (hymnous kai eudaimonismous), for it is fitting to harmonize our intellect and sense-perception in giving thanks and honour (eucharistia kai time) to our unique Savior. In similar fashion, Her. 110 prescribes the repayment to God of the loan of intellect, speech, and sense-perception. The loan of speech is repaid through panegyrics, hymns, and macarisms (cf. Spec. Leg. II, 7; 199). Macarisms, together with the other forms of praise, are ascribed to Judah in Som. II, 38.

We did not find the benediction (eulogein) among the terms associated with macarism. Moreover, the grouping of all these terms around the figure of Judah in the last reference points rather to hodah (to praise) than to barak (to bless). Macarism therefore consists in proclaiming the happiness of God and invites us to partake of His happiness. It presupposes confession; and it is already homage and praise. As praise, it is close to eucharistia, especially when it includes the notion of participating in the happiness of God or benefitting of His grace. Sometimes, we find it in formal association with thanksgiving.

E. Lipinski wrote a study on macarism in the Psalms, which led us to the idea of making the same inquiry into Philo.[20] Lipinski distinguishes between macarism and benediction, and raises macarism to the rank of a literary form, as Audet has done for the benediction. Macarism, or beatitude, he says, which is opposed to imprecation as benediction is opposed to curse, is not, like benediction, a formula of speech, which at the same time means something and effects it. It is rather a kind of congratulation, and it presupposes a happiness which is either already realized or in the process of being realized. It readily assumes the form of an exhortation, since it implicitly invites the listeners to join the category of the "Blessed." Macarism is found especially in hymnic writings, such as in

<u>Deuteronomy</u> 33:2-5; 26-29, and in the book of Psalms: there
are 45 instances in the Massoretic text, including 26 in
Psalms. The earliest macarisms are in the form of collective or national congratulations, but, later on, individual
cases and the cultic context predominate--macarisms of this
kind are for the purpose of congratulating those who trust
in Yahweh and turn to Him for help. The occasion is often a
ceremony of thanksgiving for healing, performed in the
Temple itself or in the Synagogue. Let us remember the
connection between macarism and thanksgiving, as well as the
liturgical context where it is found.

We must note, however, that Lipinski mentions only
macarisms which have man as their object: the nation, the
righteous, or an individual who received a grace from God.
Philo knows of this type of macarism, but he seems to
reserve it for the wise man. But, in Philo, macarism generally has God for its object and proclaims God as happy. It
is in this sense particularly that macarism means praise and
<u>eucharistia</u>. It is close to benediction in meaning, but on
<u>terminological</u> grounds, we see the need for distinguishing
it from benediction as well as from praise and <u>eucharistia</u>.

III. EUCHARISTIA AND DAILY BURNT-OFFERINGS

Kurt Hruby[21] studied the question of the daily sacrifices, of the prayer of the priests at the time of Tamid in
the morning, and of the prayer recited three times a day
(according to <u>Ber</u>. IV 1).[22]   The daily sacrifices are prescribed by Numb. 28:2-8; Ex. 29:31-42. But it is not clear
whether both the morning and evening sacrifices included a
lamb as a burnt-offering, or whether a lamb was offered in
the morning, and a simple vegetable oblation in the evening.
The persistence of distinct terms for the morning and evening sacrifices seems to favor the second opinion as reflecting the ancient usage. Philo mentions two burnt-offerings,
but he relies on Numb. 28:2-8, rather than on the custom of
his own time (<u>Spec. Leg</u>. I, 169).

The prayer of the priests at the time of the morning
Tamid was recited in the "cut-stones room" after the immolation of the lamb destined for the burnt-offering. This
prayer included a blessing, the Decalogue, and finally three
blessings over the people. K. Hruby tries to identify these
blessings among the Eighteen Benedictions. The morning
prayer of the lay people took place later, after the combus-
tion of the parts of the burnt offering, during the incense
offering. Priests and Levites bowed in adoration, and then

blessed the people.   Delegates from each circumscription of
the nation assisted at the daily sacrifices.   Kruby determines the time and duration of these sacrifices.[23]

In L'action de graces dans la liturgie juive,[24] Kruby,
as expected, since he is dealing with Synagogal prayer, sees
berakah as the nerve of every Jewish prayer.   Benediction
being, in the Jewish sense of the term, praise addressed to
God for any act or grace whatsoever, implies a   solemn proclamation of God as the cause of every good thing, as well
as the idea of thanksgiving.   Kruby quotes a page of Elbogen
on berakah, from which we derive the idea that berakah came
to mean praise, therefore becoming the designation for the
prayer of praise and thanksgiving.   Moreover, it is always
hymnic in character, and it is patterned after the many
prayers of praise found in Psalms.

The author adds an interesting terminological remark
which confirms the eucharistic meaning carried by the three
chief roots of the terms called "of praise."   On this
point, he affirms his agreement with R. J. Ledogar: "We
observe," he says, throughout the development of biblical
and post-biblical   literature, a slow   but progressive
differentiation between certain practically synonymous terms
of praise, such as b-rkh, h-ll, y-d-h (in the Hif'il
hodah), which the Greek versions translate by eulogein,
exomologeisthai, eucharistein.   This evolution continues
until Rabbinic times, where hodah increasingly assumes the
sense of 'thanksgiving.'"[25]

Kruby proposes to study particularly the hodayah, or
the thanksgiving prayer of the Eighteen Benedictions.   He
proves its high antiquity, and thinks he reaches the same
conclusion as Louis Finkelstein:

> since the hodayah was found in the daily
> Synagogue service immediately after the
> 'abodah, and since it had the same place
> in the priestly service of Yom-Kippur,
> it seems probable that the two were
> associated in the same way in the daily
> service of the Temple.[26]

He tries, then, to analyse the original contents of
this prayer.   There are two Talmudic versions, the
Palestinian (17th eulogy) and the Babylonian (18th eulogy).
The version given in the Sulzberger Codex of the Seder
'Amran Gaon presents relatively few variants from the
Babylonian version.   He concudes that, because the priestly

prayer is essentially the prayer of a community,[27] hodayah
can be considered as a prayer of general thanksgiving.

For our purposes, the most interesting conclusion which
we can derive from these two studies by K. Hruby is, first,
the presence of hodayah in the primitive layer of the
Synagogal prayer, as well as in the liturgy of the Temple in
connection with the daily sacrifices, and, second, its
eucharistic meaning. If we add to this the eucharistic
meaning of the daily incense offering, whatever the discre-
pancies in Philo's[28] description of the way these rites were
performed, Hruby was certainly right when he perceived a
eucharistic connotation in the daily burnt-offerings and
incense-offering.

IV. BURNT-OFFERINGS AND VEGETABLE OFFERINGS[29]

From the daily burnt-offerings of two lambs or young
goats prescribed by Lev. 1, we come logically to the burnt-
offerings offered each sabbath, at new moon, and at the
various festivals, as well as to the burnt-offerings presented by the faithful as votive offerings. Let us begin
with the latter. The emperor himself supported, out of his
own treasury, daily burnt-offerings (Legat. 156-158; 291).
Philo criticizes the offerings of hecatombs by the rich who
believe that by so doing they can buy the good will of the
Deity. Their belief is superstitious, having nothing in
common with enlightened piety (Cher. 94; Deter. 102-103; cf.
Plato, Laws, X, 905b). God, who does not accept the offering of the harlot (Spec. Leg. I, 280-284), will certainly
not welcome the offering of riches acquired through
iniquity, whoever be the offerer (Spec. Leg. I, 278-279).
Philo insists on the importance of the disposition of the
soul, on interior sacrifice as the most valuable in the eyes
of God (Som. II, 177; Sacr. 74). God is pleased with the
sacrifice of a few ears of roasted wheat (Q.E. II,99) or of
a few grains of incense (Spec. Leg. II, 276-277). Actually,
He needs nothing at all, and when He prescribes sacrifices,
His only purpose is to train us in piety (Her. 123). He is
pleased with the sacrifice of the poor, even if they have
very little to give, and even if they bring to the Temple
nothing but the good dispositions of their soul: In the
eyes of God, they have sacrificed correctly (Spec. Leg. II,
271-272). The fire on the altar, which burns continuously,
unites all sacrifices and ensures the equality of the sacrifice of the poor with that of the rich (Spec. Leg. I, 285-
286).

All these considerations seem to apply to burnt-
offerings rather than to the other kinds of votive offerings. Sacrifices for sin probably required some secrecy,
and sacrifices of salvation were followed by a banquet with
a certain number of guests. But we know that the latter
were disappearing at the time of Philo. At the same time,
burnt-offerings were endowed with an expiatory value which
conferred upon them a more general meaning.[30] We can assume
their number as very large because the hides of the victims
represented a large part of the income of the priests (Spec.
Leg. I, 151).[31]   Burnt-offerings therefore acquired a great
significance in the sacrificial liturgy of the Temple of
Jerusalem.[32]

The original and essential meaning of burnt-offerings
was, however, thanksgiving, as R. de Vaux explains
succinctly:

> A burnt-offering is basically homage
> expressed through a gift. In this
> sense, it is the type of the perfect
> sacrifice, of the homage paid to God
> through a total gift, the qorban, i.e.,
> the "offering" par excellence, Lev. I,
> passim; a power of atonement was finally
> ascribed to the rite of blood in the
> burnt-offering, Lev.1:4, as in all
> sacrifices (Lev. 17:11).[33]

H. Cazelles says the same:

> In Israel, burnt-offering seems to have
> always been practiced, and to have held
> the primary place in the Book of Judges.
> It is offered as eucharistia when the
> presence of God is manifested. It is a
> prayer of thanksgiving in answer to a
> Divine favor, and the angel of Yahweh
> carries it to heaven ('alah for the
> Hebrews who call this sacrifice 'olah)
> in the smoke, thus uniting the believer
> with his God. Burnt-offering has expia-
> tory power in Lev. 1, but this element
> is not present in the ancient burnt-
> offerings.[34]

This eucharistic connotation of the burnt-offering is
clearly and firmly taught by Philo. He points to it in the
references given above, as well as in the following ones.

The flame on the altar for instance, is eucharistic (Spec.
Leg. I, 285), as is the offering of the good dispositions of
the soul, which is greater than the most costly offerings
(Spec. Leg. I, 271-272). The altar on which the offerings
are burned generally represents thanksgiving for the fruits
of the earth (Q.E. II, 100-102), bloody sacrifices serve as
thanksgivings for our flesh, and the incense-offering represent thanksgiving for our dominant part, the rational
spirit-force within us which was shaped according to the
archetypal form of the divine image (Spec. Leg. I, 169-171).
The burnt-offerings performed daily (Spec. Leg. I, 169), on
sabbath-days (ibid. 170-171), on new moons (ibid. pp. 177
and 180), and at the other festivals (ibid. 181-189),
whether associated with other sacrifices or not, preserve
their connotation of thanksgiving defined in Spec. Leg. I,
171. Moreover, the division of a burnt-offering, common to
all sacrifices, with the difference that in this case the
severed parts of the victim are burnt upon the altar, suggests to Philo a similar division of the prayer of thanksgiving according to the several motives for which we should
praise God: for Himself, for His powers and perfections,
for His qualities as Creator, for His providence, then for
the various parts of the Universe, of mankind, and of the
individual (Spec. Leg. I, 208-211). It is possible, indeed,
to see in this idea of the division of thanksgiving an
influence of the Stoics with their Divider Logos.[35] But we
cannot contest that Philo begins his reasoning from the
notion of the biblical burnt-offering, which is endowed with
eucharistic meaning. He then continues in the same line:
the development of the eucharistic meaning of burnt-offering
invites us to become aware, more fully and in greater
detail, of our motives for thanksgiving.

    Let us consider the vegetable offering. It can be the
shew bread deposited on the sanctuary table together with
incense and perhaps salt, which is renewed on every sabbath-
day (Lev. 24:5-9).[36] It can also be the offering which
accompanies a sacrifice of communion as well as a burnt-
offering (Numb. 15:1-12, cf. Ex.29:40; Lev. 23:17).
Finally, it can be the daily offering of fine flour--a tenth
of an ephah half in the morning and half in the evening--
performed by Aaron and his sons on the day of their anoint-
ing (Lev. 6:12-15) and perhaps subsequently performed as a
daily sacrifice. It does not however include the first
loaf, which is destined for the priests (Numb. 15:18-20),
nor the unleavened or leavened loaves which are interpreted
as first-fruits, offered during some festivals. Except in
the first case, where the loaves are given to the priests
after being displayed, the vegetable offering is burned on

the altar and can thus be considered as a burnt-offering.
In fact, the vegetable offering appears as a complement to a
burnt-offering and to a sacrifice of communion. Let us note
that, in a sacrifice of communion, only a part of the
vegetable offering is burned on the altar, while the
remainder is given to the priests (Lev. 2:8-9). To the
category of vegetable offerings, we must add the ears of
roasted wheat or the wheat loaf, a portion of which are
burned by the priest upon the altar after the addition of
oil and incense. In this instance we have an offering of
first-fruits, a part of which is treated as a burnt-offering
(Lev. 2:14-16).

Philo accords a eucharistic connotation to vegetable
offerings.

The shew bread, in Philo, has a eucharistic meaning.
While, in Spec. Leg. I, 172-176 and II, 161, Philo considers
the shew bread as pointing to temperance and frugality
because of the absence of leaven, in Mos. II, 104, he
includes it in a eucharistic development, concluding with
the suggestion that the true offering is that of the soul
which is friendly with God. In Q.E. II, 71-72, the eucharistic connotation is even more clear. Not only do the ves-
sels and tools laid upon the table for the incense offering,
as well as the libation, suggest the eucharistia of a soul
dedicated to God, but the loaves continually offered before
God mean that the divine gift of food is uninterrupted
because - as suggested by the phrase "before God" - God
likes to give lavishly and to be repaid with gratitude.

The vegetable offering accompanied the burnt-offering
and the sacrifice of communion. Commenting on the law of
the tenth of an ephah of fine flour, Philo notes in Congr.
102 that the number 10 characterizes God and the cult we owe
to Him: the tithes must therefore be dedicated to God as a
eucharistic offering (Congr. 93). In Q.E. II, 102, Philo
answers our question in a more decisive way:

> The altar (of bronze) is an altar of
> bloody offerings, for men give thanks
> both by sacrificing victims and (by
> making) offerings of first-fruits; and
> they offer new (portions) of grain
> together with fine flour, and offerings
> of wine with oil, in which the fine
> flour is dipped and mixed, along with a
> basket of fruit.

Since vegetable offerings accompany burnt-offerings, they have a eucharistic connotation (Spec. Leg. I, 171).[37] Moreover, since the sacrifice of salvation, accompanied by praise, includes eucharistic offerings (Spec. Leg. I, 224), we can conclude that the vegetable offering associated with it also has a eucharistic meaning. This conclusion is confirmed by Spec. Leg. I, 185, where the faithful, giving thanks because God has delivered them from the threat of evils, carry loaves to the altar and, after holding them up to heaven with outstretched arms, distribute them, together with the flesh of the sacrifice of salvation, to the priests, in order to honor them in a manner appropriate to their sacred office.

The vegetable offering made by the priest is also eucharistic, since it is interpreted as their first-fruits, and we know that first-fruits have a eucharistic connotation (Spec. Leg. I, 152). Leviticus (6:13) mentions this offering only at the ordination of Aaron and his sons. From this, Rabbinical tradition derives the prescription requiring an ordinary priest to make such an offering on the day he begins his function, and for the high-priest to do so daily. Philo presents it as the priestly offering (Spec. Leg. I, 255-256), probably because, while the high-priest provided it, it was offered by the priests on duty.[38] The fact that it is an offering consumed by fire, and that it is assimilated to the burnt-offering of his own hair by the author of the Great-Vow (the man who offers up to God the sacrifice of his own person as first-fruits in acknowledgement of the sovereignty of God over him) reinforces the connotation of thanksgiving in the case of the offering of fine flour by a priest in his own name.

There is still another form of vegetable offering--the ears of roasted wheat offered as first-fruits according to Lev. 2:14. The first-fruits are offered to God first, and then delivered by God to the priests. They are thus not entirely burned on the altar, but a portion is levied and thrown into the fire. Such is the form of the offering of first-fruits in the form of ears of roasted wheat or of baked loaves made of ground wheat. Philo comments at length upon this prescription of Lev. 2:14. Commenting on its literal meaning, he notes that God does not prescribe a costly offering, but is pleased with a dish of barley (Spec. Leg. I, 271), and grants the same value to a small quantity of roasted wheat as to hecatombs, for He considers only the dispositions of the soul, the thanksgving of a man living reasonably and honestly (Q.E. II, 99). But the longest commentary is found in Sacr. 76-87, where Philo sees in this

prescription a complete method of thanksgiving. He comments
on the four terms which he reads in LXX, Lev. 2:14: ean de
prospheres thusian protogennematon to kyrio, nea pephrugmena
chidra erikta to kyrio. The term nea (new) suggests the
good thoughts which are to be offered to God as first-
fruits; pephrugmena (roasted) refers to virtue proved by
the exercise of reason as gold is proved by fire: chidra
(divided) points to the way athletes are trained to chew
their food so as to assimilate it better. So must we also
'chew' or meditate the thoughts with which we are presented,
in order to assimilate them more perfectly by the exercise
of reflection. If we obey this prescription, the offering
of the first-fruits of the soul to God as a sacrifice will
be the most perfect offering.

V.   THE MEANING OF THE OFFERING OF SHEW BREAD IN JUDAISM;
COMPARISON WITH PHILO[39]

A. Pelletier is the author of an article on shew bread
in the Supplément du Dictionnaire de la Bible. He explains
its meaning in relation to Lev. 24:5-9:

> The characteristic terms "in memory of"
> "permanently" and "as a covenant for
> ever," make of this offering the sign of
> a reciprocal faithfulness between Yahweh
> and His people. It is expressed, on
> Israel's side, by the offering to Yahweh
> of the dishes of His table. In return,
> Yahweh welcomes to His table the entire
> people of Israel, represented by their
> priests. On both sides these prescrip-
> tions, in principle, eliminate any kind
> of failure.[40]

Pelletier then discusses the interpretations given by Philo,
Josephus and Christian theology, with good reason
criticizing their allegorism. We shall deal later with the
cosmological and anthropological symbolism, endowed with a
eucharistic connotation, attached to this offering by
Philo.[41] Our purpose here is only to add to Pelletier's
inventory a reference to Philo which confirms his
interpretation--Q.E. II, 69, where the table suggests a kind
of communion among those who partake of the salt and
sacrifices. This observation points to a sacrifice of communion with todah, including a eucharistic aspect, but we

should not press this point in the text more than is reasonable. Let us add that the presence of incense in the offering of shew bread also confers upon it its own symbolism,
that of praise and sacrifice, so that the table becomes, as
it were, a kind of altar on which first-fruits are offered.
Philo, however, never calls the table an "altar," although
he relies on these two items of liturgical furniture for his
notion of the soul as an altar.

1. The meaning of the incense offering and vegetable
   offering in Judaism: comparison with Philo

Among the general forms of offering, we also find that
of incense.   In Philo, this offering is a figure of the
eucharistia of cosmic praise and the eucharistia of the soul
itself consisting of thoughts and virtues.   Does Judaism
ascribe a similar meaning to the offering of incense?   With
reason, we immediately think of Ps. 141:2: "Let my prayer
be counted as incense before thee, and the lifting up of my
hands as an evening sacrifice."   Edouard Cothenet, in his
article on the kinds of perfume in the Bible and their
cultic use, examines the meaning of this offering, which is
linked with many kinds of sacrifice and is also a specific
rite in the daily liturgy.[42] If the incense offering of
Yom-Kippur is granted a power of atonement, its primary purpose is the more general appeasement of the Deity.   It is a
sacrifice properly speaking, depending on the priestly dignity.   The daily incense-offering belongs in principle to
the high-priest, but an ordinary priest is called to substitute for him if he is absent.   This offering is clearly
understood as a symbol of prayer.

Its combination with a vegetable offering (Lev. 2:1-3)
helps to clarify its meaning.   According to E. Cothenet,
"the handful of fine flour and oil (minhah), plus all the
incense, everything the priest will send up as smoke at the
altar as a memorial ('azkarah)--food consumed as a perfume
of appeasement for Yahweh--is a rite whose title ('azkarah)
is taken from the first words of the accompanying prayer.
Two psalms with the title "for the commemoration" (Ps. 38
and 70) were to accompany this sacrifice." Is. 66:3a clari-
fies an interesting point: Following the parallelism, he
who performs a memorial of incense is like the man who
blesses an idol.   Therefore the 'azkarah is essentially the
benediction of the Deity during the burning of incense.   By
extension, the word 'azkarah also designates the incense
which is burned.   E. Cothenet refers to H. Cazelles,[43] who
interprets the vegetable offering in this manner:

> This offering of fine flour is called
> 'azkarah probably because of the opening
> words of the prayer accompanying the
> sacrifice, "I will recall . . ."

H. Cazelles mentions a similar prayer and rite in Deut.
26:1ff, which implies (Cazelles says) a prayer of this kind,
in which the greatness of God is celebrated. But (Cazelles
continues) "we have here a form of sacrifice of communion,
whereas the sacrifice of Leviticus is rather an imitation of
the burnt-offering."[44]

VI. THE EUCHARISTIC CONNOTATION OF THE FIRST-FRUITS

Are the offerings of the first-born and of the first-
fruits interpreted in the sense of an offering of thanksgiving in Judaism as they are by Philo? The treatise
Bikkurim[45] deals with first-fruits, specifically describing
the procession of the bearers of the first-fruits entering
Jerusalem in rejoicing, accompanied by the sounds of the
flute, and welcomed by the highest officials of the Temple
(Bik. 3:1-4). This note of joy and the connection made by
Bik. 3:6 between the offering of the first-fruits and the
basket ceremony including the accompanying prayer (Deut.
26:1-11) invite us to recognize a theme of thanksgiving, at
least in a general sense, in the offering of the first-
fruits. The sections on the first-fruits (Ex. 23:19, 34:26;
Lev. 19:24; 23:9-11; 15-17; Numb. 18:12-18; Deut. 26: 1-11,)
however, do not give precise indications about the reasons
for which they are offered, and modern authors are vague on
this point. John L. McKenzie, however says:

> The motivation of offering the first-
> fruits is not expressed; and while it
> may be a thanks offering for the annual
> harvest, this does not appear in the
> text. It was perhaps conceived as
> sacred in the same sense in which the
> first-born was sacred. The only
> explicit motivation which accompanies
> their offering is the Credo of Deut.
> 26:3-10, in which the offerer professes
> his thanks for the deliverance from
> Egypt and settlement in Canaan.[46]

The reason for the offering of the first-born of Israel
is the destruction of the first-born of the Egyptians during
the Exodus (Ex. 13:14-16). This interpretation is probably

more recent than the practice of this offering. The
original idea was probably that the first-born is sacred to
Yahweh because he opened the way by which life comes
forth.[47]

Thus, the only motives expressed in the texts depend on
the so-called "historicizing" interpretation of worship,
i.e., on the projection of the events of the Exodus on
earlier religious practices. These are partly inherited
from the Canaanites, and the new interpretations confer a
new meaning on these practices, as we shall see in the section on festivals.[48]

Let us note that Philo interprets the first-fruits in a
sacrificial sense when he combines the terms aparche, thusia
and kathiero in Virt. 159 and Spec. Leg. I, 255. In the
first reference, the verb aparchesthai means to offer first-
fruits on the altar. As a consequence, Philo comes to consider the victims and the vegetable offerings destined for
a sacrifice (thusia) as first-fruits (aparche) when he says
that the first-fruits are to be divided between the sacrifices and the priests (Spec. Leg. IV, 98). Philo makes much
use of the term aparche, particularly when he thus calls the
portion ascribed to the priest in a sacrifice, as for
instance in Spec. Leg. I, 117-130, where the aparchai not
only seem to be the first-fruits, but include everything
that comes to the priest from the altar.[49]

Philo interprets the offering of the first-born and of
the first-fruits in a eucharistic sense. He emphasizes
first, the seriousness with which his countrymen obey these
laws,[50] and their importance in the life of the Jewish
Palestinian community and of the Diaspora. Every Israelite
above twenty years of age is subject to the law of the
first-fruits, as well as to a tax for the maintenance of the
cult in the Temple of Jerusalem, the "ransom money" (lutra),
which the donors bring with cheerful zeal. For those who
live too far there are banks where they may deposit their
offerings, and delegates are appointed to carry this money
to Jerusalem (Spec. Leg. I, 76-78). Commenting on the law
about the offering of the first loaf, Philo tells us that,
though deprived of a land of their own, the priests who
share the eucharistic offerings with God are happy, because
the nation is numerous and the first-fruits are plentiful,
so that the poorest among the priests is well-to-do (Spec.
Leg. I, 132-133). He continues the theme of the prosperity
of the priests when he deals with the laws on the first-
fruits of the harvest, the first-born of cattle, and the
didrachma of the redemption of the first-born. The priests,

he says, are treated like kings, and, since the first-fruits
offered in thanksgiving are delivered to God, the priests
are not ashamed to receive them from God Himself as a salary
(Spec. Leg. I, 134-152). As for the temple attendants, they
receive the tithes, but they do not avail themselves of
these tithes until they themselves have rendered one tenth
of them as first-fruits (aparchesthai) to the priests (Spec.
Leg. I, 156). The same topic of the income of the priests
is brought up again in Spec. Leg. II, 215-222 (the portion
of the victim which is alloted to them); and Virt. 95 (the
baskets are full of the products of the autumnal season).
Three times a year, every male in Israel must appear before
God, not with empty hands, but loaded with the first-fruits
of every living thing in which there is no blemish
(Q.E. II,7).

Next, Philo stresses the moral aspects and the allegorical meaning of the first-fruits. They are a lesson in
piety. Trained to offer the first-fruits of even the most
common food, particularly the first loaf, the faithful do
not fail to remember God (Spec. Leg. I, 132). The offerings
of the first-born, even though they are redeemed and the
Levites have been substituted for them, affects every Jew in
his own person, and the tithes affect him in his income
(Spec. Leg. I, 156). Even Levites give the tithes of their
income to the priests, and the author of the Great Vow dedicated his own person to God (Spec. Leg. I, 247-249).

The term eucharistia is often associated with the
offering of the first-fruits, as seen, for instance, in the
case of the tithes. Philo (Congr. 96) says that tithes
ought to be paid (dekatas aparchesthai) "from everything
that passes through under the shepherd's staff" (Lev. 27:30-
32), and for which we must give thanks (eucharisteon).[51]

Through symbolism, Philo extends the application of the
laws on the first-born and the first-fruits to include the
domain of the soul. The first-fruits come to figure the
first motions of the soul in worth rather than in time,
which a eucharistic mind hastens to offer to God without
delay. These are also the good deeds inspired by the particular virtues (Sacr. 73-76; cf. 102; 106-114; 114-138).
Allegorically, the first-fruits represent the body, the
senses, the mind and its faculties, virtue--all of which we
must offer and return to God, because they belong to Him
(Congr. 96-98; Mut. 191-192; Som. II, 76; 272; Mos. II,
137).

VII. EUCHARISTIA AND JEWISH FEASTS

We come now to the study of thanksgiving in the feasts of the Jewish calendar. The celebration of these feasts includes sacrifices, particularly burnt-offerings, and the offering of first-fruits, whose eucharistic meaning is now known to us. Each feast, however, presents some specific aspects which may add to our knowledge of the Philonic eucharistia. We shall therefore compare what we know, or suppose, about the importance of thanksgiving in the feasts of Palestinian Judaism to the statements of Philo. Two preliminary remarks are necessary. First, Philo focuses on the biblical text rather than on the practice of his own time in Jerusalem, a practice he knows more or less accurately, though sometimes more so than scholars presume. Second, Philo writes for apologetic and ascetic reasons, reasons which, however, blend very well in his thought. We shall not therefore find in Philo the type of exegesis or history which we find in, or expect from, historians and exegetes today. As an apologist, Philo tries to present the moral and liturgical life according to the Law of Moses as the fitting answer to the requirements of the Hellenistic ideal of ascetical life. Moreover, because of the very existence of this ideal, with which he is well acquainted, he searches Scripture sincerely, diligently selecting any item or symbol which can illustrate or clarify his ascetical doctrine. In this search, he does not work in isolation, as a man who would deliberately distort the data of Scripture in order to fit them into his individual doctrine. He belongs to the Alexandrian exegetical and ascetical tradition represented by the Therapeutae and others. More generally, he follows the tradition of the authors of biblical wisdom literature, who sometimes go beyond the literary genre of maxims and proverbs and reflect on the great biblical heroes or on the liturgy.

These comments are intended to respond in a general way to Isaak Heinemann, who speaking of the interpretation of festivals, accuses Philo of depending more on Cynicism than on Judaism. Heinemann even thinks he can reconstruct a "Cynical source" which Philo would have used in his interpretation of festivals.[52] Actually, the Cynicism of this source is questionable, and it could very well be understood as Stoic, and Philo simply reflects the ideas common to the ascetical milieu of the Hellenistic world. But, far more important from our perspective, Heinemann fails to see the exact meaning which Philo ascribes to each of the Jewish feasts, and he does not grant sufficient importance to Philo's eucharistic interpretation.

Let us therefore, consider the feasts of the Jewish calendar one after the other in order to determine the place of thanksgiving in each of them. Philo writes a general commentary on festivals in <u>Spec. Leg.</u> II, 42-222, and a commentary on Ex. 12 (Passover) in <u>Q.E.</u> I. He also mentions festivals in many other places.

Philo distinguishes ten festivals, grouped into three large units: the time of Passover, of Pentecost, and the month of the Fall equinox. He does not mention the recent feasts of the Dedication and of Purim (<u>Spec. Leg.</u> II, 41).

1. The festival of every day

The first festival is that of every day (<u>Spec. Leg.</u> II, 42-56). This is the feast of the wise man, a citizen of the world, who everywhere, among the Jews (for instance, the Essenes and the Therapeutae) as well as among the Greeks and barbarians, lives "according to nature," or obeys the law of the Universe, which for him is reflected in moral law and in the acquisition of virtue. This man is the enemy of pleasure and vice, and rejoices in virtue. He alone enjoys happiness, for the wicked cannot attain it. Actually, God alone is happy, but the wise man shares in His joy by participation, like Sarah, who "laughed" and became the mother of Isaac, "laughter" (Gen. 18:11-15).

We must acknowledge that there is nothing about a festival of every day in Judaism, and here Heinemann is right when he says that Philo borrows this entire section from the Cynics.[53] We can mention Diogenes the Cynic as the author of the maxim. "Should not a man of worth consider every day a festival?"[54] F. H. Colson[55] suggests another reason for the insertion of this festival within a biblical context: the notion of a daily festival comes from Numb. 28 and 29. In 28:2, we read (LXX), "Take heed to offer me in my feasts, my offerings," etc., followed by the list of the daily sacrifices. This list begins with the daily sacrifices and continues in the same order as in this book, with the sole exception that the sheaf is not mentioned. Philo uses the indication suggested by Numbers to support the doctrine that only the wise man can keep a feast (cf. <u>Spec. Leg.</u> II, 42): he does elsewhere (<u>Sacr.</u> 111).

Nothing, however, seems to bring out the eucharistic connotation of this festival, but we can deduce it in two different ways: first, because joy is eucharistic in itself, being represented by Isaac who is the type of

thanksgiving (Sacr. 111); second, because Numb. 28:2 is one
of the chief texts upon which Philo relies for his notion of
eucharistia, which is to repay God with His own gifts (Deus
6-9; Cher. 84; Sacr. 74; Leg. Al. III, 196).

2. The Sabbath and the Newmoon

The second festival is the Sabbath day. Philo speaks
at length on the meaning of this feast, which is marked by
the number seven and by the obligation of rest. He connects
with it the seventh and the fiftieth year, which are ruled
by the same principle. For this reason, his commentary is
very long (Spec. Leg. II, 56-140). The only elements relevant to eucharistia are considerations on the Sabbath as the
commemoration of the creation of the world (Spec. Leg. II,
59) and the idea that the world created in six days is manifested on that day as perfect in all its parts. Philo might
have continued with a reasoning similar to that of Plant.
127 ff, on the creation of the Muses for the celebration of
God's eucharistic praise, which is implicitly contained in
the perfection of His works. The connection between the
Sabbath and the creation of the world offers a eucharistic
aspect of this nature in Mos. I, 207, and especially in Mos.
II, 209-212. The Sabbath day is destined for philosophy,
which we must understand in its deepest meaning--
contemplation leading to the confession of God. Philo,
however, does not mention eucharistia in this section. In
order to find a eucharistic meaning in his understanding of
the Sabbath, we must turn to the sacrifices and see that on
the Sabbath day the number of burnt-offerings is doubled,
and that the shew bread is renewed on the table of the sanctuary. All of these are performed in connection with the
commemoration of the creation of the world and are endowed
with a eucharistic meaning, even confirmed by the presence
of incense (Spec. Leg. I, 168-176).[56]

The same reasoning can apply to the festival of the
Newmoon, which corresponds to the third feast, because on
that day the number of burnt-offerings reaches ten, a
perfect number, and because the number seven, suggested by
the seven lambs, rules the lunar month which includes four
quarters of seven days respectively. The two calves and the
ram are connected to the month, and the vegetable offerings
are connected to the influence of the moon and of the
seasons on the fertility of the soil (Spec. Leg. I, 177-
179). It is interesting to note that the eucharistic aspect
of the Sabbath and of the Newmoon depends on the sacrifices
which are offered rather than on the singing of hymns, as we

might expect. The reason is that Philo, while noting that
in the practice of the synagogue the leisure time of the
Sabbath day is spent on philosophy, comments on the Sabbath
liturgy of the Temple; and he thus directs his attention
towards the sacrificial eucharistia connected with burnt-
offerings and the vegetable offerings which accompany them,
and towards the shew bread with the offering of incense.

Heinemann emphasizes the Pythagorean, Stoic and Cynical
aspects of Philo's thought on numbers, on the origin of the
world, on rest and on effort, and his considerations on
slavery.[57] But he says nothing of the very particular character of Philo's philosophy, which is, as we shall see,[58]
ruled by his faith in a transcendent God and by his notion
of eucharistia.   Nor does he say anything about the meaning
of the sacrifices offered on Sabbath days and Newmoons.

Let us inquire now as to the meaning of the Sabbath in
Palestinian Judaism.   Is it possible to ascribe a eucharistic meaning to it? The obligation to rest is well attested,
as are the humanitarian and sacred character of this day.
The same can be said of the connection between the Sabbath
and the repose of God after the creation of the world.   R.
de Vaux writes:

> Its distinctive trait lies in the fact
> that it is a day made holy because of
> its relation to the God of the Covenant;
> more, it is an element in that Covenant.
> Other religions had a day which was
> ταβξ; in Israel, this became a day "con-
> secrated to Yahweh," a tithe on time,
> just as the first-born of the flock and
> the first-fruits of the harvest were a
> tithe on the work of the other days.
> This is why a clause about the sabbath
> appears in the various pacts inaugurat-
> ing the Covenant in the original pact at
> Sinai.[59]

Modern writers prefer to consider the Sabbath apart from the
liturgy of the Temple, and not in the Temple itself or in
the light of the Temple liturgy. Philo, therefore, calls
attention to the sacrificial aspect of the Sabbath, which is
perhaps neglected in our time.

3. Passover, the Sheaf, the Shew bread

The fourth festival is Passover; the fifth is the Sheaf; and the sixth is the feast of Unleavened bread, according to Spec. Leg. II, 41. They are grouped in one span of time, following one another without interruption, but Philo distinguishes them clearly and grants each of them its own, particular meaning. He deals with these three feasts in Spec. Leg. II, 145-175.

The Philonic Passover includes many elements of thanksgiving. Let us mention, first, the ten burnt-offerings on each of the seven days of the feast of Unleavened Bread, as many as for the Newmoon. We know the eucharistic meaning of these sacrifices. The Passover, properly speaking, consists of the sacrifice of the Paschal lamb. On this occasion, once a year, the whole people, old and young alike, are raised to the dignity of the priesthood (Spec. Leg. II, 145; Mos. II, 224); or rather, they exercise a priesthood which basically belongs to them before being entrusted to the priests who minister in the Temple (Q.E. I, 10). Philo reminds us of the reason for this general sacrifice (Spec. Leg. II, 146-149): this feast is a reminder and a thanksgiving for that great migration from Egypt made by more than two million men and women in obedience to the oracles revealed to them. This practice, which on that occasion was the result of a spontaneous and instinctive emotion, was sanctioned once a year by a law which reminds them of their duty to give thanks. On this day, every home is invested with the character and dignity of a temple. The guests assembled for the banquet have been cleansed by purificatory lustrations. They eat moderately and recite prayers and hymns according to the custom handed down by their fathers (Q.E. I, 2).

Philo does not indicate whether the Passover lamb should be sacrificed in the precincts of the Temple, as was the practice in his time, or anywhere in Palestine or in the world, since he comments on texts which describe the events of the Exodus and, ficticiously or not, represent an action preceding the construction of the Temple and even of the Tabernacle. However, in Q.E. I, 2, we read that everyone must purify his soul and his body during the days preceding the Passover, so as not to step on the pavement of the Temple of God with unwashed feet: this presupposes that the immolation took place at the Temple and not elsewhere. Philo adds an allegorical interpretation of Passover as the passage of the soul out of the bondage of the body and of

the passions (Spec. Leg. II, 147; Q.E. I,3; 4; 11). However, the memorial and thanksgiving for the salvation of the
first-born of Israel and for the migration from Egypt seem
to rank first in importance (Q.E. I, 7; 10; 12; 13; 14).
Later on, in Q.E. I, 11ff., Philo develops his ascetical
thought on Passover as a symbol of purification and of progress, for sheep represent progress, and the word sheep,
probaton, derives from the verb probaino, to progress.
Such a consideration by an ascetical writer is not unexpected. We learn that, if every house becomes a temple with
an altar at Passover, the same is true allegorically of the
soul (Q.E. I, 12).   We must pass from the visible to the
invisible (Q.E. I, 11); we must make haste, that is, return
without delay to the simplicity of life by reducing the
length of meals (Q.E. I, 14); we must eat bitter herbs and
unleavened bread, that is, curb the excess of the senses and
reject the leaven of pride, and, finally, we must keep our
loins girded and our staff in hand, that is, master the passions and rely on a strong discipline of life.   The
Destroyer is the evil spirit, whose native presence in the
soul is destructive, whereas the good spirit, its twin
brother, has a salutary influence, and achieves the Paschal
victory over the evil one (Q.E. I, 23).   Philo connects the
thanksgiving for this victory with the triumphal hymn which
the men sing under the leadership of Moses, and the women
under that of his sister Miriam, after the Crossing of the
Red Sea (Agr. 79-83; Ebr. 104-121).

Heinemann, who is interested almost exclusively in the
"Cynical" or ascetical aspects (in the sense of the Greek
doctrines) of the statements of Philo on festivals, sees
only the interpretation of Passover as diabateria, or crossing of the soul from the bondage of the passions.[60] And the
other authors who deal with Philo interpret it in the same
sense.

To what extent was Passover interpreted in Palestinian
Judaism as an action of thanksgiving? R. de Vaux determines
the religious meaning of Passover as follows:

> All this historical evolution must be
> taken into account in order to discover
> the religious significance of the
> Passover sacrifice: after the settle-
> ment, Passover and the feast of
> Unleavened Bread commemorated the liber-
> ation of the people coming out of Egypt
> under Yahweh's guidance. Passover was a
> "memorial," zikkaron (Ex. 12:14), as

also was the feast of Unleavened Bread
(Ex. 13:9). But the liturgy actualizes
this memorial of the past and makes it a
present event. In explaining Passover
to his son the Israelite had to say:
"It is because of what Yahweh did for
me, when I came out of Egypt"
(Ex. 13:8), and the Mishnah develops
this aspect at the end of the tractate
on Passover: "It is because we have the
duty of thanking, honoring, praising,
magnifying, exalting, and elevating Him
who performed all these wonders upon us
and upon our fathers, and who brought us
from slavery into liberty."[61]

The feast of Unleavened Bread, which lasts for seven
days, is commented on in Spec. Leg. II, 150-161. Philo
(150-158) notes that the unleavened bread can be considered
in relation to the migration of the nation and in relation
to the order of nature. By the former, he means the
national event commemorated at the feast of Passover, for
which he has already recommended thanksgiving: By the
second, he means the springtime of creation, when prosperity
reigned without the restriction imposed by sin, and when men
lived with simplicity and frugality. Here, Philo speaks as
an ascetic writer, as he did when he interpreted Passover as
the liberation from passions. He emphasizes the eucharistic
character of this week, which commemorates the good things
of Creation:

The feast is held for seven days to mark
the precedence and honour which the number seven holds in the universe, so that
nothing which leads to cheerfulness and,
public mirth, and thankfulness
(eucharistian) toward God should be
estranged from the sacred number seven,
which He intended to be the source and
fountain for men of all good things
(Spec. Leg. II, 156).

Heinemann, as before, sees only Philo's development of
the ascetical aspect and the memory of the springtime of the
world, ideas which, not without reason, he ascribes to the
Cynics.[62] But he fails to see precisely what is Philo's
original contribution, as compared to that of the Cynics and
other Greeks, which manifests his Jewish approach to these
ideas--the character of the feast of Unleavened Bread as a

thanksgiving for the good things of Creation and as a eucharistic commemoration of the migration of Israel. R. de
Vaux recognizes the eucharistic character of the feast of
Unleavened bread. It was an ancient agrarian festival,
later combined with Passover, when the latter came to be
celebrated in Jerusalem, because the two feasts were celebrated at the same period of the year and included a common
rite, that of the unleavened bread. Consequently, the feast
of the Unleavened Bread was connected to the event of the
migration from Egypt, and its meaning came to be identified
with that of the feast of Passover, in which it was
included.⁶³ We have explained above that, as R. de Vaux
discovered this meaning was both commemorative and
eucharistic.⁶⁴ Philo is therefore within the tradition of
Judaism. Moreover, he is certainly right to distinguish
between these two feasts more clearly than was probably done
by his contemporaries.

The feast of the Sheaf (Lev. 23:9-14) comes at the same
time of the year, following the first day of this composite
festival. Philo consecrates a long and important section to
it (Spec. Leg. II, 162-176). The ceremony consists of
offering a sheaf of barley at the altar as first-fruits of
the harvest of the new year. This sheaf is offered in the
name of the Jewish nation, but also in the name of the whole
human race (Spec. Leg. II, 162). Philo makes this point
when he introduces the Jewish nation as the priest of all
mankind. Through their obedience to the law of Moses, or,
rather, to the law of nature, the Jews enjoy the priesthood
conferred on those who conform to this law. He specifies
that this is the high-priesthood more exactly than the
priesthood. The reason for this distinction is probably
that priests exercise a more specific function, closer to
positive law in liturgical matters, whereas the high-priest,
far above the priests, exercises a more general cultic function, according to the paradigm of the Divine Logos or of
the perfect Man. Philo, then, shows that all nations, the
Jewish nation in particular, must give thanks for the good
things which Nature conferred upon their respective coun-
tries, especially for the fertility of the land. Finally,
he explains the reason for offering a sheaf of barley, and
not of wheat, although wheat is superior to barley. Thanks,
he says, is also to be offered for the inferior grains which
we use. Moreover, wheat is not yet fully mature at this
time of year. Therefore, the sheaf of barley is a thanksgiving for all the crops.

Heinemann sees once more, and not without reason, the
Cynical source where Philo finds his considerations on the

gifts of Nature to the various nations and his idea of a
universal priesthood of the Jewish nation.[65]   He is wrong,
according to F. L. Colson,[66] to wonder at the idea that this
universal priesthood of the Jewish race is connected with
the comparatively insignificant rite of the Sheaf.   For the
Sheaf, Colson continues, is in fact the first fruit of the
whole harvest; and Philo does not deduce the notion of the
universal priesthood from this rite, but affirms it on the
basis of the obedience of Israel to divine law, and on
Israel's unique monotheism.   Elsewhere, Colson adds, Philo
says that it is the high-priest, and not the Jewish nation,
who prays for the world (Spec. Leg. I, 97).   Annie Jaubert
supports the idea of the priesthood of the people of Israel
among the nations.[67]   In the same work[68] she presents
Philo's teaching on this point, explaining:

> Israel is therefore the priestly nation,
> the priest-nation.   Upon this common
> affirmation of the Jewish tradition
> Philo confers a special stress by empha-
> sizing the universal character of the
> priesthood of Israel. He thus offers a
> remarkable development of the theology
> of the role of Israel among the nations.
> The salvation brought by Israel was con-
> sidered as a light reflected upon the
> nations.   Philo adds to it the function
> of Israel as a world-intercessor, as the
> universal priest, a role for which there
> were some preparations in the Hebrew
> Bible.[69]

Concerning the Testaments of the Twelve Patriarchs, she
notes a greater acceptance of foreigners in certain Jewish
circles influenced by the Essenes.[70]

4. The Feast of the Seven Weeks

The seventh festival, according to Spec. Leg. II, 41 is
the feast of Weeks, or Pentecost.   Philo dedicates the section of Spec. Leg. II, 176-187, to it, and there is a parallel passage in Spec. Leg. I, 183-185, which particularly
mentions the presence of burnt-offerings.   This would
suffice to prove the existence of a eucharistic aspect in
this feast.   Two lambs are added to the burnt-offerings:
these are not destroyed by fire but are given to the
priests, together with the loaves, as their recompense.
Therefore, in addition to burnt-offerings, we find a

sacrifice of salvation (amnous . . . ous epikalei soterious,
Spec. Leg. II, 183-184). This sacrifice of salvation has a
eucharistic purpose, because it is offered for the good
harvest which divine providence protected from natural or
other disasters.[71] Let us return to Spec. Leg. II, 176-187.
Philo begins with considerations on numbers, which connect
the feast of Weeks with the world and with the divine monad.
Then, he state that this feast is called the "feast of the
first-fruits" (he . . . heorte protogennematon). At this
feast there is an exceptional offering of two leavened
loaves, because these loaves are given to the priests, and
leavened bread is more palatable than unleavened. This is a
token gift which manifests thanks to God, who bestows His
favours abundantly and continually. The choice of the
wheat, the best of all cereals, suggests that the thanks
given through this offering includes the other forms of
food, just as the prince represents the city. The number of
loaves suggests thanks given for the past and for the
future, because the gratitude also applies to the good
things hoped for from God. Finally, the use of leavened
bread supposes the thanks given for this excellent form of
food, and for the joy of the soul which it represents.

     There is still another very interesting text dealing
with the feast of the Weeks, the treatise On Contemplative
Life, which describes the meals and the prayer vigil of the
Therapeutae for the feast of Weeks. This beautiful treatise, in addition, raises unanswerable questions about the
frequency of this feast, whether it is annual and corresponds to Pentecost, or whether it occurs periodically during the year. In the second hypothesis, their pentecostal
meals could be compared to those of the Chaburoth 2, especially because these groups of pious Jews also have a common
meal every Sabbath day (Cont. 30-36).[72] There is no mention
of an offering of first-fruits at this celebration. In any
case, what could such an offering mean at a feast of
Pentecost celebrated more than once a year? The guests eat
moderately and sing hymns. There is also food for the
souls, for the president lectures on a section of Scripture
which he interprets allegorically, and questions are raised
by listeners. Finally, a sacred vigil characterizes these
Pentecostal meals. The vigil consists of hymns and dances
performed by two choirs, one of men, the other of women,
later united into a single choir after the pure wine of
divine love has raised them to the proper level of sacred
enthusiasm. By this dance they commemorate the chief event
of the history of Israel, the salvation from Egypt; and they
sing the hymn of thanksgiving of the Israelites after the
Crossing of the Red Sea (eucharisterious hymnous eis ton

sotera theon) (Cont. 87). Let us note the connection
between the Pentecost of the Therapeutae and Passover:
their common hymn is Ex. 15. But nothing here reflects an
agrarian feast, where first-fruits are offered, or even the
granting of the Law to Moses, which the Jewish tradition
commemorates at Pentecost. Everything derives from
Passover. Should we speak of a "Pentecostal" spirituality
into which the feast of the first-fruits, commemorating the
coming to Canaan, merges and becomes a single mystery with
the celebration of Passover, as suggested by V.
Nikiprowetzky?[73] The answer would be affirmative if it were
true that the Therapeutae celebrate the festal vigil only
once a year, precisely at the feast of Weeks. But, if this
feast occurs periodically during the year nothing justifies
this assimilation. There is no reference to the first-
fruits, nor to a future, material prosperity of eschatological character.

Heinemann notes the fact that Philo does not connect
the feast of Weeks with the granting of the Law or to the
Covenant of Mt. Sinai, as the Book of Jubilees does, and as
was commonly done in first century Palestine.[74] He passes
next to Philo's speculations on numbers, to his considerations on unleavened and leavened bread, as a sign of joy,
and a sign of toil. In both cases, there are certainly
Jewish sources, but it is difficult to know how great a part
they play in a text obviously marked, according to
Heinemann, by Cynical teachings. Heinemann pays no attention to the eucharistic aspect of this feast in Philo.

In Judaism, the feast of Pentecost is both the feast of
first-fruits, which confers upon it a eucharistic meaning,
and the feast of Weeks, which establishes a relation with
the Pasch. Its connection with the ancient feast of
Unleavened Bread only confirms its original agrarian meaning, and the time-span between the first sheaf and the end
of harvest justifies the seven weeks. But the seven weeks
are also related to the Pasch, which commemorates the Exodus
from Egypt and the Crossing of the Red Sea. For these reasons, the feast of Weeks came to commemorate the granting of
the Law and the Covenant on Mt. Sinai.

R. de Vaux explains the evolution of the feast of Weeks
in its second stage, the so-called "historicizing" period:

> Like the Passover, the feast of Weeks
> was eventually related to the history of
> salvation, but this connection was made
> at a far later date. Ex. 19:1 says that

the Israelites reached Sinai in the
third month after they had left Egypt:
and since they had left Egypt in the
middle of the first month, the feast of
Weeks became the feast commemorating the
Covenant at Sinai. II Chronicles 15:10,
mentions that under Asa a religious
feast was held in the third month to
renew the Covenant, but it does not
expressly state that this was the feast
of Weeks. The first time the connection
is openly mentioned is in the Book of
Jubilees, which puts all the covenants
it can discover in the Old Testament
(from Noah to Sinai) on the day of the
feast of Weeks. The Qumran sect, too,
which called itself the community of the
New Covenant, celebrated the renewal
of the Covenant on the feast of Weeks,
and this was the most important feast in
its calendar. Among orthodox Jews, however, the feast of Weeks always remained
of secondary importance. It is omitted
from the calendar of Ezekiel 45:18-25,
and (apart from liturgical texts) it is
mentioned only in late books of the Old
Testament, and only in connection with
something else (II Mac. 12:31-32 and
Tob. 2:1). The Mishnah gives a complete
treatise to all the annual feasts except
this one, and the idea that it commemorated the day on which the Law was given
on Sinai was not accepted by the rabbis
until the second century of our era.[75]

Philo considers Pentecost, as we have seen above, only
as the feast of the first-fruits. And if, among the
Therapeutae as among the Essenes, which is not certain,
Pentecost commemorates the covenant between God and Israel,
the actual commemoration is the same as that of Passover.
The feast of Weeks is, therefore, in Philo, a feast of
thanksgiving for the harvest: the Pentecost of the
Therapeutae, on the other hand, is a eucharistic celebration
of the salvation of Israel at the Exodus from Egypt. Both
themes are, of course, expanded through allegory so as to be
accomodated to the needs of ascetical and spiritual life as
perceived by Philo and his fellow exegetes in Egypt.

5. The Feast of Tabernacles

The eighth feast, according to Spec. Leg. II, 41, is the day opening the Sacred month; the ninth is the Fast; and the tenth is Tabernacles. The three are celebrated during the days accompanying the autumnal equinox. Philo dedicates to them a section of Spec. Leg. I, 186-189.

The day which inaugurates the Sacred Month (hieromenias) is also called the feast of Trumpets. Philo recognizes in the sound of the trumpet the commemoration of the trumpet which sounded on Mt. Sinai at the promulgation of the Law, a most important event for both the Jewish nation and for all humanity. It is interesting to note that this interpretation permits Philo to associate the commemoration of Sinai with the feast of the autumnal equinox rather than with the feast of Pentecost. The fact that the Jews must live in cabins (Philo says "tents" skenais, Spec. Leg. II, 207) is also a reminder of the camps of the ancestors during their long migration throught the desert.

Trumpets and tents suggest to Philo the idea of thanksgiving. The trumpet, an instrument of war, is also used for the proclamation of peace, when God, the maker and guardian of peace, eliminates factions both in cities and throughout the universe and restores the fertility and the abundance of all things. To us, it seems better to see in this symbolism of the trumpets a reference to the Covenant granted by God both to His people and to all men rather than merely the echo of a Cynical source, as Heinemann asserts.[76] The thanksgiving, then, is a response to the peace which God proclaims to men, and not at all the mere preaching of a pacifist doctrine based on the pattern of the Cynics (Spec. Leg. II, 192).

The sojourn in tents to commemorate the tents in the desert also has a eucharistic meaning--gratitude for the successful conclusion of the migration of the ancestors in the desert and for the settlement of the nation in the land of Canaan. Their descendants re-enact the sojourn in the desert in tents to show their gratitude to God for His abundant blessings in the present, and to conciliate God through their supplications, so that they might never have to repeat the experience of such evils (Spec. Leg. II, 208-209).

Philo does not forget the agrarian character of the feast of Tabernacles. In fact, farmers live in huts in the fall to protect their crop until it is completely harvested. The lesson Philo derives is, once again, eucharistic:

thanks should be rendered to God because He brought the crop
to maturity (Spec. Leg. II, 204-207). He does not mention
the offering of the first-fruits in this context, probably
because they have already been offered, and the basket ceremony occurs not on a fixed date, but depends on the time
when the first-fruits are ripe (Spec. Leg. II, 220-221).

The Fast itself has a eucharistic aspect, for it is
good, Philo says, to abstain for a while from food and drink
in order to realize that we receive our food from God in the
harvest, and to devote some time to giving thanks to God who
provides us with these good things instead of seizing them
immediately as though they were booties which might slip
through our fingers. In this context, Philo mentions the
thanks rendered through hymns and macarisms (Spec. Leg. II,
195-200).

Let us come to the sacrifices offered during this series of autumnal feasts. We find two sections dealing with
them: Spec. Leg. I, 180 and II, 186-189. We learn (Spec.
Leg. I, 180) that on the opening of the Sacred Month (the
feast of Trumpets), the number of burnt-offerings (dora) is
doubled, just as for the Newmoon, with the exception that
only one calf is sacrificed (Spec. Leg. I, 177). We have
already explained the eucharistic meaning of such burnt-
offerings.[77]

The tenth day is the Fast (Spec. Leg. 186-189). Philo
notes that this fast is observed by the majority of the
Jews, even by those who do not show their zeal for piety at
any other time in their life. It is both a feast (hos
heortes and a time of purification from sin (hos katharseos
kai phuges hamartematon), the latter being considered a
grace of God equal to that of the preservation from sin. On
this day, as many sacrifices (thusiais, to be interpreted as
burnt-offerings) are offered as for the Newmoon (Spec. Leg.
I, 177), though with one less calf, as for the feast of
Trumpets (Spec. Leg. I, 187). Three sacrifices are added
for purification (Spec. Leg. I, 188): two kids and a ram.
The ram is offered as a burnt-offering, as well as one kid
designated for this by lot. The other kid, also selected by
lot, is driven out into the desert bearing the curses
incurred by sinners. These holocausts manifest both a
eucharistic and an expiatory character, because of their
relation to the grace of the remission of sins.

On the fifteenth day of the same month, at the full
moon, the feast of Tabernacles is held (Spec. Leg. I, 189).
The sacrifices offered on this occasion are more numerous,

for the feast lasts for seven days: during this period,
seventy calves, fourteen rams, and ninety-eight lambs are
offered, all as burnt-offerings, together with vegetable
offerings and suitable libations; and the number of burnt-
offerings decreases in number each day, according to Numb.
29:12-36. An eighth day is added (Numb. 29:35-38, cf. Spec.
Leg. I, 189; II, 211-213), when only one calf, one ram, and
seven lambs are offered.   On each of the eight days, a kid
is sacrificed for sin.   Such are the sacrifices prescribed
for these feasts, but they do not eliminate the possiblity
also of sacrifices offered by individuals (Numb. 29:39). It
was necessary to outline this particular aspect of Philo's
account of the three feasts of the Sacred Month in order to
faithfully explain the role of eucharistia in the sacrificial order, and to restore a balance in Philo's teaching, a
balance unfairly altered when stress is laid on the ascetical aspect alone, and particularly, with Heinemann, on the
influence of a Cynic source.

    We have already mentioned Heinemann's criticism of
Philo's interpretation of the feast of Trumpets.[78] Later on
using the same method, Heinemann points out other items.
For instance he considers the motive for the fast, with good
reason, as borrowed from the Cynics, although he admits the
presence of the notion of humiliation in parallel sections
(Post. 48; Congr. 106-108). But he fails to notice the commemorative and eucharistic aspect which we mentioned.   The
way in which he understands the Philonic interpretation of
the feast of Tabernacles, namely, as an ascetic performance,
is not wrong, but it is incomplete.   He also notes Philo's
considerations on the number eight in the context of his
discussion of the addition of an eighth day to the feast of
Tabernacles (Spec. Leg. II, 212), and he wonders why Philo
is unfaithful to his "Cynic source" when he mentions "scenes
of folly and joy" (aprhrosunai kai euphrosunai) in his conclusion (Spec. Leg. II, 214).   The context of Philo's last
statement, however, is made obscure by a lacuna.[79]   But
Philo likes to combine the notion of joy with that of
festivity (Spec. Leg. II, 53), and we know that, when he
allegorizes about feasts in terms of a higher form of joy,
he can do so only because these feasts are already
characterized by merriment and many forms of legitimate
rejoicing.

    Is it possible to say that Philo is in agreement with
what modern scholars tell us about the eucharistic aspect of
these feasts?   J. McKenzie writes concerning the feast of
Tabernacles:

Scholars are doubtful that the booths
originally symbolized the desert
sojourn, which was a dwelling in tents,
not in booths. They direct attention to
the common practice of living in booths
in fields during the harvest, and
suggest that this is a feature of the
harvest festival which has been
'historicized' into a commemoration of
the desert sojourn. (At the time of
Philo, joy predominated in the feast of
Tabernacles.)
According to the Talmud people lived in
booths for the seven days of the feast.
On the first night of the feast the
temple area was brightly illuminated by
lamps and torches; ceremonial dancing
was done by this illumination. There
was a daily procession around the altar:
the worshipers carried a branch in one
hand (lulab) and a fruit ('etrog) in the
other, and Ps. 118 was sung. The
priests marched around the altar seven
times. On the last day a vessel of
water was brought to the temple from the
pool of Siloam and poured out before the
altar of burnt-offerings. Horns and
trumpets were blown at all the great
moments of the feast.[80]

6. The Feast of the Basket

     In addition to the feasts mentioned in Spec. Leg. II,
41, and then described, Philo (Spec. Leg. II, 215-222)
speaks of a ceremony with a festal character, but without a
fixed date--the Basket ceremony (Deut. 26:1-11). Heinemann
gives a good description of this ceremony in his book.[81] It
consists of the offering of first-fruits, which is a thanksgiving, accompanied by the recitation, or more precisely the
singing, of an asma taken from Deuteronomy 26:6-10, which is
a type of Credo or confession of the Israelite. Philo
stresses the eucharistic aspect in the literal sense, since
it concerns first-fruits; but he gives an allegorical interpretation as well, inviting us to offer up to God the first-
fruits of the faculties of our soul (Som. II, 272).

VIII. SERVICE OF GOD AND EUCHARISTIA

The notion of serving God is very rich and very complex
in Philo. First, it is opposed to any cult addressed to
others,[82] or to any distortion in the cult of the true
God.[83] It includes all the legitimate forms of worship, and
every man is, under one form or another, expected to worship
God. The most specific term for the service of God is
therapeuein, and the servant of God is called therapeutes.
To become a servant of God, the man who expects God's grace
must take on the attitude of a "supplicant" (iketes).   A
proselyte is a supplicant and a servant of God, because he
trusts in God and tries to honour Him. Tamar exemplifies
this attitude when she enrolls herself for the service of
God, a very bold decision, because she leaves the religion
of her forefathers at the risk of her life (Virt. 221). The
whole Jewish nation shares the condition of being a supplicant and servant of God. To pursue the study of this notion
of the supplicant in Philo, the reader can refer to the
study of V. Nikiprowetzky.[84] Our purpose here is only to
study this notion in relation to eucharistia, and only in
its liturgical aspect.

The service of God involves the entire Jewish nation,
priests and Levites, angels, the world and the Heavens, and
the Divine powers, the Logos and Wisdom at least. Its
object shifts quickly in Philonic spirituality from sacrifices to the offering of prayer, of actions, and of the self
to God, to what is termed "spiritual sacrifice." We take
for granted what we have said above about the role of the
priests in the sacrifices of the Temple. We postpone the
question of the Logos as Universal High-priest, and of
Wisdom as the Paradigm or Absolute of virtue in its eucharistic aspect, to the following chapters. The world, the
Heavens, and the angels all have a part to play in the
Cosmic eucharistia. We retain, in the present section, only
the mediatory function of the priesthood within the nation,
and of the nation within mankind, in relation to
eucharistia. Since this mediation is eucharistic, it
essentially consists of adoration, hymnic prayer, and sacrifice. The author of this prayer is not simply the priest,
but, more generally and on a higher plane, the Levitical
mind. We shall explain just what is meant by this Levitic
ideal, and just how Philo understands spriritual sacrifice.
Finally, we shall try to determine the position of Judaism
concerning aspects of the service of God and of the priesthood, so as to determine once more whether Philo is faithful
to Judaic tradition, while interpreting it in a more philosophical and universalist manner.

1. Levitic Priesthood and Eucharistic Mediation

According to Philo, the entire Jewish nation is endowed
with priestly dignity. The sacrifice of the Passover shows
this very clearly, when every Israelite sacrifices the
Paschal lamb and each dwelling house is turned into a temple
(Q.E. I, 10;12). The right to sacrifice is granted the Jew
on only one day of the year, but this is enough to prove
that the priesthood basically belongs to him as a member of
the people of God, even though the priests are assigned the
office of sacrificing for him during the rest of the year.[85]
The Paschal sacrifice is essentially a sacrifice of
thanksgiving for the preservation of the first-born of
Israel in Egypt and for the liberation of the people from
servitude (Q.E. I,3;7;13). The priests, therefore offer
sacrifices, and many of these sacrifices have a eucharistic
meaning, as we have seen. In this office, the priests are
in the service of the people for whose needs they offer
sacrifice (Q.E. I, 10; Spec. Leg. II, 145). The high-priest
in the Temple however offers the eucharistic sacrifices with
the most universal meaning,[86] because he offers on behalf of
the whole nation and for the whole human race (Spec. Leg.
I, 11-116). Philo sees a two-stage hierarchy in the eucharistic mediation: the priest offers for the nation, and the
nation for mankind (Spec. Leg. II, 163; 168-169; 190); but
the high-priest, who offers on behalf of the whole nation,
exercises the universal priesthood which the nation assumes
within mankind (Spec. Leg. II, 164). He offers on behalf of
mankind as well as for the nation when he makes thank offerings, especially when he offers incense (Spec. Leg. I, 72;
97), and the nation does so particularly in the offering of
the Sheaf (Spec. Leg. II, 167-174). Mediation for the
entire human race is clearly included in the act of thanksgiving, since Philo is surprised that the pagans reproach
the Jews for sinning against humanity. The customs of the
Jews are indeed different from those of other men, but they
serve the true God in the name of all, and especially in the
name of the pagans, who neglect this duty (Spec. Leg. II,
167; cf. Spec. Leg. II, 210-211).[87]

We can now investigate more thoroughly the priestly and
Levitic ideals. When Philo develops the Levitic ideals on
the basis of the term therapeuein, he may implicitly refer
to Plato, who endows this term with a very noble meaning.
According to Timaeus 90c, man, who alone in the Universe
enjoys the upright position, is a heavenly plant rather than
an earthly one--one whose roots are in heaven. He contem-
plates immortal and divine things and partakes of immortality. He ceaselessly worships the Deity (therapeuonta), and

he finds his happiness in pleasing the daimon who resides in
him.   Moreover, man is a possession of the gods, according
to Phaedo 62b, and so cannot commit   suicide without
offending them.   They watch over man like a shepherd over
the sheep, and they guide him as a pilot mans the helm
(Critias 109 b).   As a consequence, man owes the gods
genuine worship, and not a cult corrupted by superstition
(Laws X, 906 a).

     Philo does not openly refer to Plato concerning the
service of God (therapeuein), although he makes use of the
Platonic images mentioned above. He prefers, as is usual
with him, to build his teaching on the word of God.[88]   This
is why he exalts the Levitical ideals.[89]   Levi and the
Levites become the archetype of the servant of God. Levi,
among the Patriarchs, is alloted the service of God and is
the sign of it (to therapeutikos echein auton, therapeias de
ho Levi esti semeion).   And Moses tells us that the sons of
Levi were chosen by God as a ransom for the first-born of
Israel and as servants of Him who alone deserves to be
served (therapeutas ton monon axion therapeuesthai) (Sacr.
118-120).   They obtained the privilege of the priesthood
because of their faithfulness to God during the religious
crises during the wanderings in the desert, when they
rallied with Moses to exterminate the worshipers of the
golden calf (Mos. II, 171-173, cf. Ex. 32), and when they
followed the indignant Phineas in his holy war against the
Israelites who fell into the snare of Balaam and succumbed
to idolatry (Post. 182-184, cf. Numb. 25).   Driven by their
piety towards God, they did not spare even their brethren
and relatives and became murderers and supplicants, though
beyond any praise in these two instances.   Philo includes
this aspect in the Levitic idea, which he transfers through
allegory to the soul of the wise man, the servant of God.
Priests, he remarks (Ebr. 69), do not slay human beings, but

> they cut away from their own hearts and
> minds all that is near and dear to the
> flesh.   They think it appropriate that
> those who are able to be servants
> (therapeutais) of the only wise Being
> distance themselves from all that
> belongs to the created world and treat
> all such things as bitter and deadly
> foes.   To know that nothing else,
> neither wealth, glory, honour, office,
> beauty, strength, physical advantage,
> earth or heaven, nor the whole world
> deserves our service, that only the true

> cause, the Cause supreme among causes,
> deserves our service (therapeias) and
> highest honour, and thus to attain the
> rank of priesthood--this is a marvellous
> privilege and worthy of all our efforts
> (Ebr. 75).

This murder of the irrational part in ourselves, and of out-
ward speech, next of kin to mind, witnesses to the resolve
of the soul to serve (therapeutikon) Him who is Best of all
Existences through that which is best in ourselves (Fug.
91). The rites for the purification and the consecration of
the priests (Lev. 8:24 and 30), performed upon those who are
going to minister (leitourgein) at the altar and in the
Temple, can also reflect this symbolism (Mos. II, 151-152).
The comparison between Moses, the type of apatheia, and
Aaron, that of metriopatheia, which makes of Moses the pattern for priesthood above even Aaron himself, corresponds to
the same idea (Leg. Al. III, 127-132, cf. Lev. 8:29).
Samuel, a Levite, is ranked, according to the etymology of
his name, among the servants of God. Like those mentioned
above, his example applies to us, since, although an individual, Samuel is also a figure, that of the mind which
rejoices only in the service and worship of God (Ebr. 144,
cf. I Sam. 1:11). Among the contemporary examples of the
servants of God, Philo points to the Therapeutae, whose name
means both the healing of the soul and the service of God,
two things which go together (Cont. 2; 11). Philo uses the
same term and the same idea when he speaks of the Essenes,
who are also servants of God (therapeutai), and whose name,
derived from hosiotes, means "holy" (Prob. 75).

With the heroism of the Levites in the service of God
during the religious crisis of Exodus, with the consecration
of Aaron and of the priests, with that of Samuel who was
made a votive offering, with the example of the Therapeutae
who renounced the world to serve God, and with the Great
vow, we reach the notion of the offering of the self to God,
and we come close to the idea of spiritual sacrifice, which
does not consist in the offering of material victims on the
altar, but in the offering of the self,⁹⁰ and of one's
thoughts and deeds, or again in the offering of one's
prayer. These three forms of spiritual sacrifice are found
in Philo, and all three are eucharistic.

The offering of the self is found in the author of the
great vow, who consecrates himself to God because he has
already offered everything else to Him. This offering is
interpreted in the sense of the first-fruits, and therefore

in a eucharistic sense (Spec. Leg. I, 247-254). The
offering of the self particularly belongs to the Levitical
ideal, as we have seen above. But this ideal also extends
to lofty souls and to all those who, in varying degrees open
their heart to it. The Therapeutae, for instance, renounced
their possessions, family, and the world in order to
dedicate themselves to the service of God according to the
rule of their community. Their ideal is the Levitical
ideal, as is demonstrated by V. Nikiprowetzky.[91]
Thanksgiving occupies a large part of their religious
activities, for instance their celebration commemorating the
Crossing of the Red Sea. The prayers at meals and the hymns
of the Therapeutae confirm their eucharistic spirit.
Generally, Philo extols the offering of the self through the
symbolism of sacrifices, as for instance, when he speaks of
the examination of the victims (Spec. Leg. I, 167), or when
he ascribes to the incense-offering the meaning of a thank-
offering for the good things of the soul (Spec. Leg. I, 274-
276).

The eucharistic offering of thoughts and deeds is one
of the ideas to which Philo returns most often. These are
owed to God as first-fruits, and they are represented by
sacrifices, particularly by the incense offering (Ebr. 87;
cf. Q.E. II, 31). Philo is very concerned with the
necessity of uniting deeds and thoughts, and, for this
reason, he cannot be reproached for extolling the mere
intention at the expense of actions. He requires, more
exactly, the purity of intention which directs the action;
thus, in Spec. Leg. IV, 66, for instance, he invites man to
perform the works of justice "justly," according to Deut.
16:20.

2. The sacrifice of prayer

We must now consider the sacrifice of prayer, by which
we mean the offering of praise to God in its eucharistic
aspects. We may begin our investigation of praise from
several starting points. The first is from the point of
view of the works of God, that of the Universe, and here we
find the story of the Muses (Plant. 126-131). According to
this story, the complement of Creation is the word of
praise, a thanksgiving celebrated with hymns: this can be
compared to the offering of sacrifices and all the classical
ways of honouring God, with the difference that praise is
implicitly contained in the works of God and only needs to
be made explicit by a reasonable being with the least

possible amount of artificiality (Plant. 126).   The praise
of God is exteriorized through hymns.

        Another point of departure could be found in the notion
of sacrifice, from there moving to the notion of spiritual
offering (logike   thusia), or   non-bloody   sacrifice
(anaimaton).   But these two expressions are not found in
Philo.   The second is specifically Christian,[92] while the
first belongs to the Hermetic Corpus (I, 31). The sacrifice
of praise, however, appears in Philo (he   thusia tes
aineseos), where it is the todah which completes a sacrifice
of salvation (Spec. Leg. I, 224).[93] It is also connected to
the incense offering, which represents both the sacrifice of
the soul with its faculties, and that which emanates from
them--thoughts, words and deeds.[94]   In Her. 200, about
Cosmic praise, which must be expressed by human lips, we
find, it seems to me, the notion of a sacrifice of prayer.
Philo, however does not cite Ps. 141:2, the prayer rising up
to God like incense offering.

        The third starting point for an inquiry on the sacri-
fice of prayer and of praise in Philo is in the use of
hymns. We must consider terms such as hymnos, epainos,
egkomion, ainesis, eudaimonismos, ode, asma, but chief among
these is hymnos.   As we know, this term generally refers to
a psalm in the Psalter, or to similar, more or less improvised compositions.   The Therapeutae sing hymns and possess
collections of hymns (Cont. 29).   Let us add that everyman
receives from God a vocation of praise which is in common
with the heavenly beings, stars or angels, a vocation which
finds its expression in hymns (Som. I, 35, cf. Spec. Leg. I,
66).   We want to know whether hymns can be considered as
sacrifices and thank offerings.   But we have noted a close
association between hymn, sacrifice, and eucharistia.[95] Let
us recall, in evidence, Plant. 126 and the history of the
Muses which follows.

        3. The service of God and the spiritual cult: Jewish
           positions compared to Philo's teaching.

        A. Jaubert summarizes the complex data pertaining to
the connection between the Jewish positions and those of
Philo on spiritual sacrifice:

            [Philo acknowledges that] the priesthood
            of Israel is exercised in the Temple and
            in the major rites prescribed by the
            legislation of Moses.   But many other

Philonic texts go beyond the narrowness
of this affirmation and point, in the
priesthood of Aaron, of the Levites, and
of Israel, to a priesthood which is
above all one of the soul. Interior
worship is not an innovation in Jewish
tradition, since it is one of the chief
themes of prophetic preaching and is
attested to many times in late Judaism.
The Letter of Aristeas supported the
same principles. Philo is, therefore,
only one of the witnesses of an understanding of worship common in many
Jewish circles, particularly in Hellenistic ones. It is probable, though,
that Philo would have insisted on spiritual sacrifice much less had he not
found in it a common ground with the
most refined aspirations of ambiant
paganism. He is certainly indebted,
like the whole Alexandrian school, to a
large, religio-philosophic movement
which will soon find a remarkable
expression in the Hermetic writings.
The Jewish Alexandrian elite could only
be well disposed toward an idea which
was traditional in Judaism, which con-
formed to the sapiential ideals and was
considered as fashionable among the
pagans. The originality of Philo is
rather to be found in the strength of
his affirmations and in his particular
attention to all the elements of the
official cult.[96]

A. Jaubert then examines the transposition of the
priestly themes to the individual soul and wonders what is
left of the official priesthood of the Temple in light of
the Philonic notion of spiritual priesthood, which becomes
the possession of each individual. We noted, in connection
with the privilege of every Israelite to sacrifice the
Paschal lamb, that this right is in fact a mere privilege,
as it can be exercised only once a year, and that the official priesthood is actually in charge of the liturgy of the
Temple. The basic priesthood of every Israelite and, by
extension, of every man, is situated on an entirely different level, with no danger of interference between the two
kinds of priesthood.

Wolfson, speaking of prayer in Philo, deals with the question of spiritual sacrifice.[97] Philo requires purity of heart in the man who offers a sacrifice, maintains the superiority of prayer over sacrifices, and accepts prayer as a substitute for sacrifices. In this last case particularly, prayer has the value and the effect of a sacrifice, and it is thus possible to speak of a sacrifice of prayer.[98] Wolfson discusses the origin of this notion:

> When improper sacrifices are condemned, the substitute offered for them is always prayer. All this, as we have seen, reflects traditional Jewish views. It is quite possible that Philo was acquainted with some of the sayings of certain early Greek philosophers preserved by later authors to the effect that the gods are to be honored not by luxurious display but rather by deeds of piety or that it must be considered that the noblest sacrifice and best divine worship is to make the self as good and just as possible.[99] If Philo were acquainted with such Greek sayings, he must have found in them corroboration for some of the teachings which he derived from the prophets, and perhaps, in his own mind, he considerd them as having been inspired by the teachings of the prophets. But there are insufficient indications in such Greek sayings to account for the language and the sentiment expressed by Philo in the cited passages.[100]

Here, Wolfson criticizes Heinemann, who supports this opinion.[101] Wolfson makes clear that, before the destruction of the Temple, the Rabbis did not need to stress the importance of prayer, fasting and love as substitutes for sacrifices, but that this was not so in the Diaspora, as illustrated by the example of Philo.

Is there a close connection between the prayer of hymns and thanksgiving in Psalms and the hymnic literature of Palestinian Judaism? First, are there hymns of thanksgiving in the Psalter? It is possible to hesitate before answering positively, as Hebrew has no specific term for thanksgiving.[102] Therefore, in the strict meaning of the term, the so-called psalms of thanksgiving are properly psalms of

praise. Such is the opinion of Westermann.[103] According to
this author, they should be divided into two types: first,
"confessional psalms," which acknowlege the intervention of
God, with this appellation thus substituting for the traditional one of "psalms of thanksgiving"; and descriptive
psalms. This opinion has met with very limited approbation,
because it addresses only the designation, and not the meaning, of these psalms. R. E. Murphy, in a succinct study of
these psalms, says that this type of prayer was probably
used in connection with a thank offering (todah) after a
benefit received from God.[104]   E. Lipinski presents a
detailed analysis of the psalms of thanksgiving, particularly of Pss. 1, 32, 40, 41, 112, 119, 127, 128, 146.   He
sees in these psalms formulas to remind the priests who
welcome pilgrims to the Temple of Jerusalem, to exhort, or
to assist them in the celebration of their thanksgiving.[105]

We have already noted that it would not be fruitful to
establish a parallel between these psalms and Philo, since
he does not comment on them and does not cite them in his
works, which are all devoted to the Law of Moses.[106]   We
have noted the eucharistic aspects of hymnic prayer in
Philo.   We have also pointed out the eucharistic character
of the Therapeutae's Paschal celebration, especially with
the singing of the canticle of Exodus 15.   We may add that
Philo refers to this canticle as a hymn of thanksgiving not
only in Vita contemplativa, but in many other places in his
writings, where he speaks of the liberation from
passions.[107]

The "sacrifice of the lips," which is so strongly
emphasized by Philo, is also highly prized at Qumran.   A.
Jaubert deals with this in the sections entitled L'Offrande
des lèvres," and "Une fonction de louange" in her book, La
notion de l'Alliance dans le Judaisme.[108]

CHAPTER THREE

EUCHARISTÍA AND COSMIC RELIGION

Next, our study turns to the relations between Philonic
eucharistia and cosmic religion. The Philonic eucharistia
offers a cosmic aspect, as is clear from Philo's speculations on the symbolism of the high-priest's vesture, on the
composition of incense, etc. We must avoid too narrow an
approach and present his teaching on the cosmic eucharistia
in all its dimensions, with its philosophical, liturgical,
typological, and spiritual components; Philo's originality
consists as much in widening the scope of the question, as
in focusing on the details. It is time now to confront the
Philonic synthesis on cosmic religion with the philosophical
systems which serve as its base or which he refutes. It is
not necessary to identify all the possible echoes of these
philosophies in Philo, but simply to explain the main points
of his reasoning as he introduces, approves, or disapproves
them, and as he opposes them to his own position--that of a
believer who has discovered the importance and the
complexity of the gift of God in the world, and who suitably
tries to give thanks to God for it. In this section, we
shall also include the data concerning the microcosm, i.e.,
man considered as a miniature of the world in both his
intellectual and corporeal nature: Philo ascribes a similar
nature and similar characteristics to the human mind as to
the heavens (Som. I, 35), and the human body consists of the
four elements like every other earthly thing. It will be
useful to establish, as a preliminary, whether or not Philo
found in his predecessors, in the Letter of Aristeas, the
Wisdom of Solomon, and in the Jewish exegetes of
Alexanderia, some elements and prefigurations of a cosmic
eucharistia, which he then criticizes or completes. We
shall deal with the notions coming from philosophers,
insofar as he recognizes them as pious teachings--we think
most specifically of Plato and of the Aristotle of De
philosophia - when we come to his criticism of philosophies.

We shall proceed in the following order: Philo's forerunners among the Hellenistic Jews; cosmic thanksgiving in
Philo; the philosophies which he disapproves as deficient in
piety toward God, or which he approves; his own religious
philosophy, or his cosmic religion. Finally, we shall examine whether the latter is a deviation or reflects a genuine
aspect of biblical and Jewish religion.

I. COSMIC ASPECTS IN THE FORERUNNERS OF PHILO[1]

Before considering Philo's own notion of the Cosmic
eucharistia, let us see whether he could find an interest in
cosmological speculations and the beginning of a notion of
the cosmic eucharistia in his religious surrounding and in
the writings of the Alexandrian Jews before him. We shall
retain only information given by Philo himself, because it
is relevant and rich, and Philo refers to it explicitly and
implicitly when he repeats or completes it. We shall then
note whether there is something of this kind in Aristobulus,
who is very close to Philo, or in Josephus, who depends on
him; but we shall focus on the Letter of Aristeas which, in
our opinion, Philo certainly knows, and on Wisdom of
Solomon, which he seems to know, though his dependence on it
is not obvious.

1. The Allegory of the "Physicists"

Wolfson[2] describes the milieu and methods of the
Alexandrian Literalists, and even their irritation with
Philo and all Allegorists. Let us remember one thing:
these interpreters have no interest in the cosmic speculations of the Allegorists, which they reject positively.
Philo, however, does not reject the Literalists' literal
exegesis; indeed, he considers it as legitimate and necessary, except for a few instances where it does not fit the
dignity of God, and as dependent on the anthropomorphism of
Scripture. He considers it, however, as too limited in
scope, and accepts the legitimacy of a symbolical or
allegorical exegesis superimposed on a literal exegesis and
occasionally remedying its deficiencies. On the other hand,
Philo, as a man who sincerely believes in the divine
authority of the Law of Moses and of the Jewish institution
which preserves this tradition, i.e., the Jewish people with
their temple in Jerusalem and their synagogues everywhere
in the world, reproaches those among the Allegorists whom he
opposes (Migr. 89-90) because of their distaste for literal
exegesis and particularly for the prescriptions of the law.
The Allegorists live as though the Law were nothing but a
pretext for intellectual speculation and not a body of
rules for life in a particular society.[3] The Therapeutae
are also Allegorists (Cont. 28), but they cannot be faulted
for their neglect of the practice of the law, which they
observe carefully and complete with a more perfect mode of
life. As for the Apostates--Tiberius Alexander, Philo's

own nephew, seems to be the speaker who supports their views
in De providentia--they have intellectually joined the
surrounding pagan world with its schools of philosophy,
although they have not always broken with Jewish society.[4]
They represent neither Judaism nor Philo's ideas, but only
those philosophical systems which he rejects. They are not
therefore relevant to the present inquiry, and we may simply
consider them among the holders of these philosophical
systems. Moreover, they argue against the Law and criticize
it maliciously, or they invent new objections in order to
cast ridicule on it (Agr. 157; Conf. 2), which is the most
certain sign of apostasy.

    Let us consider the exegetes known by Philo, who
practice allegorical interpretation, and who, on the basis
of Scripture develop cosmological or anthropological speculations. J. Daniélou describes them and their speculations
in his Philon d'Alexandrie.[5] We refer the reader to this
book, limiting ourselves here to pointing out a few things.[6]
Philo mentions their interpretations more than once.[7] In
other instances,[8] he, himself produces an interpretation
which is obviously traditional, and not of his own creation.
Danielou even finds forerunners in mystical exegesis (Som.
I, 118), probably among the Therapeutae, who may also be
witnesses to certain cosmological interpretations. Among
these interpretations, let us mention Q.G. I, 10, where the
tree of life, according to some exegetes, means the sun (a
cosmological interpretation), but, according to others,
means the mind or the heart (anthropological interpretations). Philo himself prefers either metaphysical
interpretations pointing, for instance, to the divine
powers--God's sovereignty and kindness as figured by the two
Cherubim standing at the entrance to Paradise (Cher. 27)--or
interpretations bearing on the faculties of the soul and on
the life of virtue. Can we say that these cosmological
exegeses borrowed from his fellow Allegorists lead to a kind
of cosmic eucharistia? Philo does not provide us with an
answer. We may however suppose that these exegetes did not
use cosmology or anthropology on the basis of Scripture only
for the sheer pleasure of speculation, but, like Philo, in
order to reach a deeper understanding of the works of God in
Creation, to build up a sacred science where Scripture could
benefit from the remnants of profane culture. It is also
perhaps to deepen their prayer of praise and thanksgiving,
since the prayers which we preserve from Hellenistic times
expound on the marvels of the Creation, or, at least,
include the title, Creator of the Universe.[9]

2. Cosmic aspects of Wisdom of Solomon

Wisdom of Solomon, with its notion of the God of the Universe, is open to cosmic perspectives. God created all things (1:13). He performed His creative work and now exercises His providence with power and love (12:22-25). We read, for instance: "Who can withstand the might of thy arm? Because the world before Thee is like a speck that tips the scales," and, "Thou lovest all things that exist, and hast loathing for none of the things which thou hast made." These ideas can relate to Timaeus (29e), but they also reflect the best of biblical theology. Let us also note that God creates and works in the world through His Spirit and His Wisdom, two notions which reappear in Philo and which correspond to Philo's far more developed theology of the divine powers or intermediaries. We read (1:6-7): "For Wisdom is a kindly spirit.... The spirit of the Lord has filled the world, and that which holds all things together knows what is said." We are very close to the Philonic and to the Stoic Logos, which are principles of both distinction and cohesion. Divine Wisdom is an "intelligent spirit," a "spotless mirror of the working of God," a "pure emanation of the glory of the Almighty" (7:22-26). "Though she is but one, she can do all things, and while remaining in herself, she renews all things" (7:27). "She reaches mightily (diateinei) from one end of the earth to the other, and she orders all things well" (8:1). "Thou sparest all things, for they are thine, O Lord who lovest the living. For thy immortal spirit is in all things" (11:26; 12:1, cf. Prov. 3:19-20).

To some degree, the proclamation of the works and qualities of God is eucharistia in the sense in which Philo uses this term, since it involves the acknowledgement of God as Creator and Providence and leads logically to praise of Him. But we find these very terms in Wisdom, since we read (13:1): "For all men who were ignorant of God were foolish by Nature; and they were unable from the good things that are seen to know (eidenai) him who exists, nor did they recognize (epegnosan) the craftsman while paying heed to his works." We find the vocabulary of "confession," and we know that Philo uses "to know" and "to recognize" in this sense. We find also the vocabulary of praise. We note, for instance, the presence of hymnein and adein (10:20; 18:9). These words are used in the context of the Passover, and the theme is the liberation of Israel; but God accomplishes this liberation through miracles, for which the Israelites now praise God (ainountes se, 19:8-9). It is not pointless to note this connection between praise and Passover.[10]

Let us also mention the presence of the symbolism of the high-priest's vesture in Wisdom of Solomon 18:4, "For upon his long robe the whole world was depicted, and the glories of the fathers were engraved on the four rows of stones, and thy majesty on the diadem upon his head." This cosmic symbolism of the vesture of the high-priest reveals a religious character of praise and thanksgiving.[11] Coming now to the term eucharistein, we note its presence only in 16:27-28, in relation to the elements whose properties God changes through His miracles: "For what was not destroyed by fire was melted when simply warmed by a fleeting ray of the sun, to make it known that one must rise before the sun to give thee thanks (ep eucharistian sou), and must pray to thee at the dawning of the light; for the hope of an ungrateful man (acharistou) will melt like wintry frost." Eucharistein is used in this context to refer to morning prayer, whatever the form of this prayer. In Philo, we also read that we must pray to God morning and evening, and the terms referring to this prayer are terms of praise and thanksgiving (Spec. Leg. I, 168-171; 296-298). But we must remember that this praise and thanksgiving in Philo, as in Wisdom, are addressed to the divine Creator and Benefactor to recognize His qualities and His gifts in general, and in this instance for the night or the day which draws to a close laden with the gifts of God (Spec. Leg. I, 296-298).

3. The Letter of Aristeas

Philo may or may not have been acquainted with the Wisdom of Solomon, but he probably did known the Letter of Aristeas, since he describes the annual celebration of the Alexandrian Jews on the Island of Pharos in thanksgiving for the Greek translation of Septuagint (Mos. II, 26-44). The Letter of Aristeas is especially interesting for us because of its theology of grace, which is closely parallel to the Philonic theology of grace, and may be a direct source for it. We shall deal in the present chapter only with the cosmic aspects and their eventual connection with eucharistia and related notions. The word itself appears only once (eucharisto, 177), as an expression of the king's gratitude towards the high-priest, who sent him the scrolls of the Law, towards the messengers of the high-priest who brought them to him, and towards God who delivered the oracles. But we did not expect to find this early an instance of this term in relation to the eucharistic praise of the God of the Universe.[12] We are much more interested in the theological contents of the Letter, which positively refer to the God of the Universe (132), to the universal

Benefactor whose example we should follow (205), who confers
on the king the supreme power (219), who is the master of
all hearts (277), who manages the Universe with clemency and
without anger (254), who lavishly bestows good health and
prosperity on men (259), who lowers the proud and extols the
humble (263), who disposes of all glory and grants it to
whom   He pleases (269), who fixes an order of nature and
imposes its laws even on kings (279). A remark by the king
in praise of the delegates of the high-priest summarizes all
this theology, of which we retained only the cosmic aspect
in this section but which carries on in the secrets of the
inner life: "They have given fittin~ answers to those
questions which I have put to them, and have made God the
starting-point of their words" (200-201).

        The best text about the cosmic eucharistia in the
Letter of Aristeas (153-159) does not include the term
eucharistia itself, but plays on the image of the memory of
God and his gifts (Deut. 7:18; 10:21). It does not deal
with the macrocosm, or the Universe, but with the microcosm,
i.e., with the structure of man and the "wonders He has performed in him." We must "remember" these gifts and offer up
their first-fruits before using them. The notion of "first-
fruits" (aparche) as a return of His own gifts to God brings
us even closer to the notion of thanksgiving. Let us add
that part of this text belongs to the prayer of the Shema
(Deut. 11:18-21).

        Josephus presents a parallel to the cosmic eucharist
(Ant. Jud. III, 179-187; Bel. Jud. V, 213). As in Philo
(Congr. 116-117), the curtain of the Temple, woven from
materials of four different colours, represents the four
elements, and the robe, with the ephod and logeion of the
high-priest, also as in Philo (Spec. Leg. I, 96), represents the Universe. The table, the shew bread, and the
candlestick are similarly given a cosmological interpretation.   The term eucharistein is absent, but we find the
image of memory (eis apomnesin, 180).

II. COSMIC THANKSGIVING IN PHILO

        Cosmic symbolism in Philo is far more developed than in
any of his known forerunners because of the large number of
his works and of the particular attention he pays to this
kind of speculation.   But this interest is not for him the
most important, as he prefers psychological symbolism, the
kind of interpretation which sheds some light on the

problems of the life of the soul and of virtue. This is the
kind of exegesis he introduces most often as his own,
whereas he usually only seems to repeat a traditional cosmic
symbolism. His metaphysical symbolism is also original, as
when he develops his theories of the Divine powers and their
missions of creation, intercession, and even of praise. J.
Danielou makes this clear in his section on cosmological,
anthropological, and mystical exegesis. Speaking of
mystical exegesis, Philo includes two notions which we
always find combined because they correspond to the
ascending and descending path of the same sacred
hierarchy--the spiritual itinerary followed by man, and the
way in which God adjusts to the individual and works in him
by means of His powers. We propose in this section to
inquire whether this cosmological and metaphysical
symbolism--of the macrocosm as well as that of the
microcosm--does not have a eucharistic connotation.

We must concede that often, particularly in Questions
on Genesis and Questions in Exodus, where the interpretations are only juxtaposed and presented in catalogue form,
not in the context of a continuous exposition or of a
treatise, which would confer on them a complementary
meaning, it is difficult to recognize a purpose of praise,
of thanksgiving, or even any religious connotation properly
speaking. We must note this connotation when it is
positively mentioned, and, for the rest, proceed by analogy,
with suitable discretion.

We will follow the following order: the world has a
eucharistic aspect insofar as it is a creature and a gift of
God. It praises, confesses, and gives honour and thanks to
God, either directly, or through the figure of the Muses, by
the lips of men. Biblical figures such as Noah, Shem, and
Moses, who represent the ideals of the wise man, are
witnesses of cosmic praise. We shall come next to the
symbolism of the high-priest as a figure of the Logos, who
is the first worshiper of God. On a lower level in the
hierarchy of praise, the high-priest worships together with
the world, since he wears the cosmic symbols on his vesture.
Through the high-priest, we enter the world of liturgical
symbolism, where everything takes on a cultic character and
is oriented to the service of God. The Ark of the Covenant
is charged with cosmic and metaphysical symbolism. It
represents more than the world, but also the hierarchy of
divine powers, or the activity of God diversified according
to the needs of creatures. The eucharistic connotation is
not dominant in this context, but we find it when we reach
the Logos, or the notion of "place," which brings us back to

the Logos' function of adoration mentioned above. Philo's
considerations on the places of refuge provide a close
parallel with the symbolism of the Ark. We find another
parallel in the vision of Abraham at the oak of Mambre.
However, when Philo discusses the Tabernacle and its
furniture--the curtains and veil, the candlestick, the
table, the altar of incense offerings, and the altar outside
the temple--we are no longer in the realm of metaphysical
symbolism of the divine powers, but completely that of
cosmic symbolism. With the altar, we come to the sacrifices, which have both a direct and a symbolic meaning. The
incense offering and the daily sacrifices have the purpose
of praise and of thanksgiving which reaches beyond the
limits of the nation. But the symbolism of the composition
of the incense represents the world, and the division of the
burnt-offering signifies the method of the cosmological and
anthropological thanksgiving. The tenth of an epha of fine
flour, which is the offering of the priests joined to every
sacrifice, takes on the character of a thanksgiving: the
key which explains this is the passage from the number nine
to the number ten--from the numeral of the created world to
that of the Creator. We find a similar explanation for the
first-fruits offered by laymen and by Levites. Let us
mention also the both cosmic and anthropological meaning
given to a famous sacrifices, that of the Covenant granted
by God to Abraham. This link between the cosmological and
the anthropological reappears several times in the lifetime
of Abraham and forms the particular character of his conversion, i.e., the passage of the world and of its miniature,
man, to the transcendent God, who is the Charioteer of both
the world and man. We find it again in the figure of
Besaleel, who stands on the boundary between the visible and
invisible worlds, whereas Moses reaches much higher, since
God speaks to him face to face. We also find it in the
symbolism of the arrangement of the Tabernacle, which is the
work of Besaleel and which represents the division of the
world and of man--the true temple of God - into a visible
and earthly part, and another invisible and heavenly.

1. The world has a destiny of praise

"Surely it is the fitting life-work for the world, that
it should give thanks to its Maker continuously and without
ceasing, wellnigh evaporating itself into a single elemental
form, to show that it hoards nothing as treasure, but dedicates its whole being at the shrine to God its Begetter"
(Her. 200). This principle, pronounced with regard to the

daily incense offering and to the symbolism of its composition, determines the world's <u>vocation</u> of praise or thanksgiving. Such is the essential <u>vocation</u> of a creature:

> The work most appropriate to God is con-
> ferring gifts, that most suitable to
> creation giving thanks, because it has no
> power to return anything beyond this; for
> whatever else it may have thought of giving
> in requital, this it will find to be the pro-
> perty of the Maker of all things, and not of
> the being that brings it (<u>Plant</u>. 130).

The terms are <u>eucharistia</u> and <u>time</u>: thanksgiving and
honour. Of course, this mission is assumed by reasonable
beings, endowed with the gift of expression in the universe,
i.e., the heavens and man (<u>Som</u>. I, 35). For the heavens, we
may mention the Logos, who is in some regards the soul of
the world, but in a particular sense, as we shall see later.
The heavens as such possess a higher nature, a thinking
substance parallel to, or of the same essence as, the human
mind. This substance is the quintessence, or the ether. It
is also diversified into incorporeal <u>logoi</u> and "angels."
The latter seem to be individuals possessing a higher
nature, air or ether, who never come down into earthly
bodies (<u>Q.G</u>. III, 11). They are the heavenly priests, the
servants of the divine powers (<u>Spec. Leg</u>. I, 66). The
heavens can, in some sense, be understood through the image
of Eden, which points to wisdom and happiness. We find in
it the praise of the Creator, which is the fruit of wisdom,
since the Muses, representing praise, are created after
Wisdom, just as Wisdom was created after the world (<u>Q.G</u>. I,
6, 7). This image of Eden, or Paradise, seems to refer to
the whole rational race, far exceeding the garden of the
soul entrusted to the care of a man fashioned from clay and
subjected to a test. Speaking of Divine philanthropy
towards the daughters of Salpaad, Philo refers to the
heavenly praise: "If the stars become a single choir, will
their song be worthy of Thee? If all heaven be resolved
into sound, will it be able to recount any part of Thy
excellences?" (<u>Mos</u>. II, 239). Philo identifies these
higher intelligences with the souls of the heavenly bodies,
as was commonly done from the time of Plato (<u>Laws</u> X, 886d).
The Muses represent the word of praise, i.e., the expression
of praise by all beings, stars, angels, and men, who are
capable of it, and whom Philo calls the race of poets.
Their praise is cosmic, i.e., purely descriptive of the
beautiful things of the world, without adding to them. The
mother of the Muses, "Mnemosyne," which means "Memory," is

the simple reminder of the works of God, which constitutes
perfect and satisfactory praise. The Muses are thus not new
creatures or mythological entities added by Philo to the
number of reasonable creatures.[13]

From among men, let us mention Moses, whose last hymn
of thanksgiving was so perfectly attuned to the music of the
Universe that the heavenly choristers were amazed to find a
man still entangled in a corruptible body capable of singing
a melody comparable to that of the sun, moon, and stars, and
in perfect harmony with God's instrument (Virt. 72-75).[14]
To Moses Philo compares Shem, the man equal in worth to the
world and thus a son of God like the world, in whom God con-
sents to dwell as in His cosmic shrine, because the microcosm is perfectly analogous to the macrocosm.   Philo con-
cludes: "What should he do but requite his Benefactor with
the words, with song, and with hymns (Sobr. 58).   To these
men we can also add Noah, for he represents a new beginning
for mankind, thereby repeating the ideal of man created in
the image of God, living upon earth and in a human body
according to the ideals of the Wise man, Son of God, and
citizen of the world. This man discovers that everything is
grace, that the world is a gift of God, and he thereby manifests his eucharistic disposition (Deus 104-108; Q.G. I,
96).   The whole work of Philo seems to have been written in
order to stir the eucharistic disposition of man with
respect to all things and to warn him against philautia,
selfishness. This anthropocentric disposition refuses, like
Cain, to refer all things to God, or, like Seth, refers them
to God defectively.   Or it sins by some forms of injustice
toward God, which, though superficial, are severe in their
consequences, as in the case of the vainglorious like
Alexander (Cher. 63) and the arrogant who manifest anti-
social behaviour (Virt. 165).

2. Logos and high-priest

The high-priest of the Temple of Jerusalem makes thank-
offerings on behalf of the people, and intercedes for them
in cases of need or sin (Praem. 56; Spec. Leg. I, 229; Ebr.
128-129) He also exercises this function on behalf of the
whole human race, as it is clear from the universal
character of the daily burnt-offerings (Spec. Leg. I, 168-
169) and from the priestly mission of the Jewish nation in
the world (Spec. Leg. II, 166-167).   But we are
particularly interested here in the symbolism of the high-
priest as the figure of the Logos and also in some regards
as the figure of the world. These two symbolisms are in any

case one and the same, but seen under two different angles:
the Logos pouring Himself out as a libation before God, and
putting on the visible ' world like a dress in an act of
cosmic praise and thanksgiving. We find these two aspects
again in man, because the high-priest of the Temple of
Jerusalem is also the type of man, and because we are, as
men, high-priests rather than priests (Spec. Leg. II, 164).

Commenting on Gen. 9:6, "In the image of God He made
man," Philo (Q.G. II, 62) asks only why God does not say,
"in His own image," and distinguishes between the Logos made
as the direct image of the Father of the Universe, as it
were a "second God", and the man made in the image of the
divine Logos, and not in the direct image of God.[15] This
Logos, transcendent to the world and to man as well, is just
like the high-priest, a mediator, particularly on the
highest level, that of creation and thanksgiving. Concerning his creative mediation, let us mention only Q.E. II,
90, 94, and Op. 20. But the eucharistic character of the
Logos is of greater interest for us here. Like every
priest, the Logos is Himself first a worshiper, since he
first offers his own worship before doing so for others. He
is the Cup-bearer of God, "He who pours the libation of
peace, the true high-priest who first receives the loving
cups of God's perennial bounties, then in return he pours
that potent, undiluted draught, the libation of himself"
(Som. II, 183). His human counterpart is reason, the human
logos, which adores by pouring itself out before God just
like the divine Logos. The divine Logos, moreover, has
first filled the cup of the human logos with true ambrosia,
i.e., with a little part of Himself, since the Cup-bearer of
God, the Master of the feast, the Logos, is also none other
than the very draught he pours (Som. II, 249, cf. Som. I,
215). The remarks made above do not assume that the problem
of the personality of the divine Logos in Philo has been
solved. That solution, whatever it may be, has no effect on
the object of our present interest, for the divine powers
seem to be forms of energy rather than persons properly
speaking, forms which appear or vanish when man himself
changes inwardly. The mere fact that we find several
different hierarchies of such powers in Philo (Plant. 86-
89; Deus 108; Q.E. II, 68) invites us to conclude either
that Philo is inconsistent, which is not probable, or that
he is not dealing with a system of personalized eons, which
is our opinion.[16]

Let us come now to the second aspect of the Logos, His
cosmic aspect by which He is involved in the world as a
divine power of division and of cohesion (Her. 205ff; Q.E.

II, 68),[17] and especially by which He has put on the world
in order to celebrate its thanksgiving (Her. 200). His
personal character here has vanished, and we can say that
every reasonable being in heaven and on earth gives thanks,
or the world itself gives thanks. On this level, the high-
priest of the Temple of Jerusalem, in his vesture decorated
with cosmic symbols,[18] is a Figure of the world giving
thanks, and he himself gives thanks together with the world.
The cosmic symbolism of the high-priest's vesture is traditional, for we find it in Wisdom of Solomon (18:24) and in
Josephus.[19]   This symbolism is highly developed by Philo
(Mos. II, 117-135; Spec. Leg. I, 82-97; Q.E. II, 107-124).
The high-priest performs this liturgy together with the
world (sulleitourge pas ho kosmos auto, Spec. Leg.   I, 96).
Philo recognizes two temples of God:

> One of them is this universe, in which
> the high-priest is His First-born, the
> divine Word; and the other is the
> rational soul, whose priest is the Man
> of truth--the outward and visible image
> of whom is he who offers the prayers
> and sacrifices handed down from our
> fathers--who has been commissioned to
> wear the aforesaid tunic, which is a
> replica of the whole heaven, so that the
> universe may join in the holy rites with
> man and man with the universe (Som. I,
> 215).

Philo distinguishes three degrees of priesthood: that
of the Logos, Priest of the universe; that of the reasonable
soul which is its own priest insofar as it is created
according to the image of God; and the high-priest of the
Temple of Jerusalem,[20] who, according to the cosmic
symbolism of his vesture, worships together with the universe. The priestly function, in this context, consists in
praising God for the perfection of His works and in giving
thanks to Him for His gift of the world to us. This is a
lower form of worship, though excellent in itself,[21] since
it corresponds to the way in which Besaleel understands the
construction of the Tabernacle--as a copy of the world -
whereas Moses attains face-to-face contact with God (Leg.
Al. III, 102; Plant. 27; Som. I, 206).[22] The high-
priest--let us understand every man - should be able to
perform this kind of adoration, even if he is unable to
reach higher (Mos. II, 135; cf. Q.E. 40), because this
corresponds to the knowledge of God through His works by
means of reason even when it is not possible to know Him

through revelation or after reaching the summit of the spiritual itinerary.[23]

3. The furniture of the Tabernacle

When we come to the Tabernacle and its furniture, the candlestick and the altar, we are dealing entirely with cosmic and anthropological symbolism, and no longer with metaphysical symbolism. This cosmic symbolism is explained in detail in Mos. II, 72-108 and 136-140 (109-135 dealing with the vesture of the high-priest), and in Q.E. II, 69-103 (see also Her. 215-229). For instance, the fifty-five visible columns of the Tabernacle suggest an anthropological interpretation: the five, added to the fifty, are the senses, which are oriented on the one hand, to things external, while on the other hand they lean toward mind, whose servants they are according to the laws of nature; their bases are of brass, symbol of the senses while gold is the symbol of the mind (Mos. II, 81-82). But the curtains covering the roof and walls, woven with dark red, purple, scarlet, and bright white materials, represent the four elements and, therefore, the universe: this is a cosmological exegesis (Mos. II, 88). The cosmic symbolism returns in the more detailed description of Q.E. II, 83 ff. The veil separating the two internal parts of the Tabernacle (Q.E. II, 93) is placed above four pillars, which represent corporeal things, or three dimensional objects, since three points constitute a surface, and four a volume.

The table and the candlestick are placed outside the veil in order to show that both earthly things (the table) and heavenly bodies (the candlestick) belong to the visible parts of the universe, which are reached by the senses, while intelligible things are not (Q.E. II, 95). The veil also symbolizes the mediating Logos who stands between the incorporeal and corporeal worlds, since this Logos is the tetrad, through which the corporeal solid comes into being (Q.E. II, 94). The outer hanging, called a "covering" and not a "veil," represents sense-perception, which cannot penetrate the secret of intelligible realities closer to God (Q.E. II, 96). The "covering" is placed upon five columns which represent the five senses (Q.E. II, 97). Why this identification of the Tabernacle with the visible and the invisible world? Philo answers:

> Now, as for those who saw the structure
> of the divine tabernacle likened to
> their own dwelling, what would they have

been likely to do other than to bow down
in return for what was done and bless
the Overseer and Guardian and Curator of
His power? (Q.E. II, 83).

The universe, therefore, which is the true Temple of God,
and its miniature, the Tabernacle, are the setting which
reminds man of his duty to pay homage to God and to praise
the divine management of all things.

The candlestick, placed on the south side (Mos. II,
102-103; Q.E. II, 73-82; 103-106; Her. 216-225), represents
the movements of the luminaries above, for the sun, the
moon, and the stars run their courses in the south far from
the north. The refined oil of the lamps symbolizes the
light of wisdom, that is, the pursuit of philosophy, the
queen of sciences belonging to the encyclical studies (Q.E.
II, 103). The lamps must burn from evening until morning in
imitation of the choir of stars (Q.E. II, 104). They are
placed outside the veil of the holy place, because intelligible things possess their own light which illumines the
mind, and they are the measure of all things, whereas
earthly things are characterized by instability (Q.E. II,
106).

The table (Mos. II, 104; Q.E. II, 69-73; Her. 226)
"is set at the north and has bread and salt on it, as it is
the north winds which most provide us with food, and food
comes from heaven and earth, the one sending rain, the other
bringing seeds to their fullness when watered by showers"
(Mos. II, 104). The table also has a moral symbolism, that
of brotherly communion when the food coming from God is
returned to Him in the form of a gift made to men (the
priests) as to brothers (Q.E. II, 69). The cups, censers,
libation-bowls, and ladles suggest the libation of a soul
full of virtue poured out before God (Q.E. II, 71), and the
shew bread placed before the Lord represents the duty of
unceasing thanksgiving in response to God's continuing
liberality (Q.E. II, 72). These exegeses are moral, not
cosmic, but the gold of the table and the gold-wreathed
waves around the table are symbols of the substance of the
world in its greater perfection, as well as of the changing
character of corporeal substance, represented by the
"wreathed waves" (Q.E. II, 69-70). The table and the
candlestick are certainly given a eucharistic, cosmic
symbolism (Her. 226):

In the table, we have thanksgiving
(eucharistian) for the mortal creatures

> composed of the four elements, since the
> loaves and libations which creatures
> needing food must use are placed on it.
> In the candlestick, we have thanksgiving
> for all the celestial world, so that no
> part of the universe may be guilty of
> ingratitude (acharistias), and that we
> may know that all its parts give thanks
> (eucharistei).

An additional eucharistic symbolism is attached to the
candlestick, which "gives light from one part only, the part
where it looks toward God" (Congr. 7-8).[24]

4. The two altars, and sacrifices

The two altars that of incense offering inside the
Tabernacle and that of burnt-offering outside, together with
the sacrifices offered on them, are very rich in meaning.
We retain in the present section only their cosmic symbolism
and its eucharistic aspect. The altar of incense offering,
placed between the table and the candlestick, is "a symbol
of the thankfulness (eucharistias) for earth and water which
should be rendered for the benefits derived from both, since
these elements have been placed in the middle of the universe" (Mos. II, 101). In Her. 226, the symbolism involves
the four elements. With the altar, as shown before (Her.
199), we find the notion of thankfulness (eucharistian) for
the elements, since the altar itself contains each of them.
The wood of the altar belongs to the earth; the incense suggests water, since it melts and turns into small drops; its
perfume refers to the air; and what is consumed, to fire.
In addition, the composition of the incense offering which
includes "sweet spices, oil of cinnamon, cloves, galbanum of
sweetening, and clear gum of frankincense" (Ex. 39:34) is a
symbol of the elements. We know the cosmic symbolism of the
composition of the incense-offering and its eucharistic
meaning (Her. 199):

> The mixture thus harmoniously composed
> proves to be that most venerable and
> perfect work, truly holy work for it is
> the world which, Moses holds, should,
> under the symbol of the incense
> offering, give thanks (eucharistein) to
> its Maker. A product made with the art
> of the performer is burned as incense,
> but in reality, it is the whole world,

wrought by divine wisdom, which is
offered and consumed morning and evening
in the sacrificial fire.

We know that, if the composition of incense represents a
cosmic eucharistia, the offering of incense itself, as well
as the altar, signify the eucharistic offering of the soul
full of virtue, which belongs to a spiritual, and not
cosmic, symbolism of eucharistia (Congr. 114).

The altar of burnt-offerings also has a eucharistic,
cosmic symbolism, the only one we shall mention in this
section, since it also represents the spiritual eucharistia
of the soul (Mos. II, 108; Spec. Leg. I, 287; Q.E. II, 98-
99). We find this cosmic symbolism, together with an
anthropological symbolism, in Q.E. II, 100-102. The four
horns of the altar, facing the four sides of the world, seem
to call for the offering of the first-fruits from every part
of the earth (101). The earth is also suggested by the
bronze of which the altar is made, for bronze belongs to the
things of the earth, where wars are made, since among the
ancients bronze was the material used for weapons of war
(102). The bloody offerings, the offerings of first-fruits,
of fine flour, of wine and oil mixed with the flour, and of
the basket, all refer to earthly and corporeal things, while
gold points to incorporeal and intelligible things, and
silver to the heavenly nature perceived by the senses. Is
this symbolism a eucharistic one? The term is not used, but
the altar itself is called thusiasterion, for it "preserves"
sacrifices (Mos. II, 106; Q.E. II, 98), and the eternal
flame on the altar, which equalizes all sacrifices by combining them in the same consecration by fire, is a symbol of
eucharistia.

Among the sacrifices offered upon the altar, we mention
particularly the daily burnt-offerings in thanks for the
nation and for the whole human race, and the first-fruits,
or the products of the earth, brought to the altar. But
some sacrifices manifest a cosmic, eucharistic symbolism in
the very way they are offered. Burnt-offerings represent
the world consumed in thanksgiving without keeping anything
for itself (Her. 200). The division of the burnt-offering
suggests the division and order necessary in the prayer of
thanksgiving, since we must give thanks, first, for the universe and its parts, second, for the whole human race and
its parts, third, for the individual man and his chief components, fourth, for the works of the mind and of the hands
(Sacr. 74-85; Spec. Leg. I, 205-211). Finally, the offering
of fine flour, added to every sacrifice, made by the priests

in their own name also has an anthropological and cosmic
meaning, as do the tithes delivered by the Levites to the
priests, and by lay people to the Levites (Congr. 94-105).
The offering of the tenth of three measures of fine flour,
which amounts to an omer, symbolizes the offering of the
senses, of speech, and of the mind. The offering of the
tenth of an epha suggests that the priests are elevated
above the number nine, the symbol of the world of sense-
perception, in order to adore Him who stands aloof as the
tenth, and who is the true God.[25] We find the word eucha-
risteteon together with aparchesthai, kathiereuein,
prospherein, timan, anatithenai, which proves that we are
certainly in a eucharistic context.

5. The sacrifice of the Covenant of Abraham

A famous sacrifice, that offered by Abraham when God
granted him a Covenant (Gen. 15:9-10), has an anthropological and cosmic symbolism (Q.G. III, 3-7). Abraham
must offer a heifer, a she-goat, a ram, a turtle-dove, and a
pigeon. The heifer represents the earth; the she-goat,
water; the ram, air; and the birds, the heavens with planets
and stars--such is the cosmic symbolism. An anthropological symbolism is added to it: the heifer represents
the body; the she-goat, the senses; the ram, reason; the
pigeon, the contemplation of the universe (physikes
theorias), and the turtle-dove, the contemplation of the
intelligibles (Q.E. II, 3; cf. Her. 125-127). This is a
sacrifice of Alliance which has on Abraham's part, a character of thanksgiving, since God told him, "Take for Me"
(Gen. 15:9), and not "Bring to Me." Philo comments on these
last words, saying that for a mortal creature there is
nothing properly its own, but that all things are the gift
and grace of God, to whom it is pleasing that one who has
received something should show gratitude with all eagerness
(Q.E. II, 3), thereby escaping the accusation of ascribing
it to itself as the author, and not to God (Q.G. II, 4). We
find anthropological and cosmic symbols again in Abraham's
discovery and confession of God in the divine visitations of
Gen. 17:1 (Q.E. II, 39) and Gen. 18:1-2 (Q.G. IV, 1), and in
God's announcement to him of his death after a happy old
age, Gen. 15:15 (Q.G. III, 11).

III.   THE QUEST FOR A COSMIC AND ANTHROPOLOGICAL PHILOSOPHY
IN AGREEMENT WITH THE PRINCIPLE OF PIETY TOWARD GOD.

     It is not enough for Philo to develop cosmic and
anthropological symbolisms on the basis of Scripture, and to
ascribe to them a eucharistic meaning, together with the
related notions of confession and of praise which accompany
the idea of thanksgiving. Since Philo lives in a milieu
imbued with philosophical culture, and since this culture is
complex--the legacy of several schools of philosophy
mixing their contributions in the melting pot of Alexandrian
Hellenism, and favouring eclecticism--he must make a
choice between what he considers acceptable and what he
thinks should be excluded. Using the criterion of piety
toward God, he distinguishes between impious teachings which
deny his notion of God as Creator and Providence and others
which agree with his principle of piety toward God.   He
approves certain philosophies, for instance those of Plato
and of Aristotle, as "pious," though not without reserva-
tions about some aspects. His fight in the realm of culture
is a fight for piety, similar to that of the great defenders
of God's cause in Scripture. He defends the philosophy of
Moses in the Alexandrian and in the cultural circles of his
time. Does he intend to develop a complete and coherent
system of religious philosophy?   Scholars have successively
affiliated him with almost every school of philosophy, even
reproaching him for inconsistency when, now and then, he
shows some infidelity to the school to which he is supposed
to belong. He is certainly an ecclectic, who borrows from
many different sources, imposing upon his borrowings an
additional meaning to fit the new context.   Wolfson
definitively proved that Philo is a philosopher worthy of
the title, at least in the sense that he founded a
philosophy which became the basis for the philosophy of
Christianity, of Medieval Judaism, and even of Islam.   Let
us, therefore, say that, in his reworking, the elements he
borrowed from the schools of philosophy and integrated to
his own teaching cease to be as disparate as they seems to
those who only pay attention to their origin, but that they
do not become a philosophical system elaborated for its own
sake. Here again, Philo is a man of his time, an essayist
like the authors of "stromata" or "tapestries."

     We do not intend to give a complete description of this
philosophy, or even of all the reasonings by which he justifies his approval or his disapproval of the doctrines with
which he deals, and even less of their sources. This work
has been accomplished by a series of great scholars. But we

can at least give an account of their results, summarizing
the data under a few main headings, in order to prove that
Philo, the preacher of ethics and piety, of the confession
of faith, of the praise of God and of thanksgiving,
sincerely tried to maintain these religious notions and
practices by means of serious and adequate philosophical
research.

We shall proceed in the following order. First, we
shall present his philosophical tenets, or the few
doctrinal points which he considers essential to his
religious faith in the realm of philosophy. We shall then
succinctly examine the philosophical doctrines which he
approves or disapproves. He does this in two different
ways, either directly by explaining them in their own philosophical language, even mentioning the names of their
authors, or in a veiled way, through figures such as those
of the race of Cain, the Chaldeans, Egyptian atheism, and
those removed from the Assembly of God. This second method
is closer to Philo's usual manner of thought and expression,
and enables us to discover more accurately his own position.

After that, we shall take advantage of the light shed
on these problems by recent studies, particularly those of
Festugière and of Pépin, and try to overcome the lack of
clarity about the philosophical traditions which lie behind
the teaching of Philo, especially concerning the kind of
Platonism and of Aristotelianism which he knew and which are
far from their classical representations. It will then be
easy to draw a rough picture of his anthropology and of his
doctrine about the relations between man and God. We shall
also present some Jewish doctrines parallel to those of
Philo. In the present section, we shall limit ourselves to
the cosmological and anthropological problems, i.e., to the
data concerning the constitution of the world and of man in
relation to God, postponing to another chapter the role of
God in the development of virtue, or the Philonic theology
of grace as considered in light of the Alexandrian Jewish
tradition and of Greek philosophy.[26]

1. The philosophial "Tenets" of Philo

If it was unnecessary to demonstrate the principles of
their faith to Jews who practised the religion of Moses in a
close society from their childhood, the same was not true
for those who became more aware of the intellectual implications of their faith in regard to the philosophies of the
Greeks, either learned, or simply popular.[27] For this

reason, at the end of De opificio (170-172), which belongs
to a series of treatises which are more apologetical than
esoteric, and destined for a more diversified audience, even
to pagans, Philo gives a list of tenets to be maintained
vis-a-vis philosophy.[28]

> By his account of the creation of
> the world, of which we have spoken,
> Moses teaches us, among other things,
> five that are fairest and best of all.
> First, he teaches that the Deity is and
> has been from eternity. This is with a
> view to atheists, some of whom have
> hesitated and have been of two minds
> about His eternal existence, while the
> bolder sort have carried their audacity
> to the point of declaring that the Deity
> does not exist at all, but that it is a
> mere assertion of men obscuring the
> truth with myth and fiction. Secondly,
> [he teaches] that God is one. This is
> with a view to the proponents of
> polytheism, who do not blush to transfer
> mob-rule, that worst of evil polities,
> from earth to heaven. Thirdly, as I
> have said already, [he teaches] that the
> world came into being. This because of
> those who think that it is without
> beginning and eternal, who thus assign
> no superiority at all to God. Fourthly,
> [Moses teaches] that the world is one as
> well as its Maker, who made His work
> like Himself in its uniqueness, who used
> all the material that exists for the
> creation of the whole for there are
> those who suppose that there are more
> worlds than one, while some think that
> they are infinite in number. Such men
> are themselves infinitely lacking in
> knowledge of things which it is good to
> know. Fifthly, [he teaches] that God
> also exercises forethought on the
> world's behalf. For it is required by
> the laws and ordinances of Nature that
> the Maker should care for what He
> created, and it is in accordance with
> these that parents watch over their
> children (Op. 170-171).

This list includes five tenets, but it does not represent a "Creed" properly speaking, since they do not refer to
a positive religion. Goodenough sees it as a Platonic and
Pythagorean Creed, since both these schools agree on all
these tenets.[29] Wolfson takes a slightly different
approach when he includes, in what he calls "the scriptural
presuppositions of Philo," three complementary items: one
of these, the existence of Forms, is philosophical; and the
two others, the revelation and the eternity of the Law, stem
from the Jewish religion.[30]

2. Criticism of the Greek philosophies in the language of biblical symbols

In these "tenets," or philosophical principles introduced as basic to religious faith and, consequently, a
criteria for the criticism of philosophical teachings, Philo
speaks clearly, or uses the language of philosophy. We
shall return to this criticism after explaining how he deals
with the "philosophy of Moses" using his favourite language,
the language of Moses himself, that of Scripture. We mean
by this the scriptural images of allegory, through which he
explains his thought on these questions. The chief biblical
images are: the impiety of the race of Cain; that of the
builders of the tower of Babel; that of the Egyptian
atheism; then, the philosophy of the Chaldeans; and the
defects which disqualify one from membership in the Assembly
of Israel.

a. Cain, the Tower of Babel, Egypt

The symbolism of Cain and his descendants is complex,
more important for the chapter on grace than for the present
chapter on cosmology and anthropology, since it points
toward the problems of the soul and of spiritual life. Let
us note only what is pertinent to the present inquiry. Cain
is a sinner, and a sinner is a man who not only offends God,
but is mistaken about the true nature of God. He flees God
as if he were able to escape His presence, whereas he should
know that God is not confined to a particular place, or even
to the universe, since He circumscribes the universe (Leg.
Al. III, 6-7, for Adam). He denies that God is the cause of
everything, or he makes God responsible for both good and
evil without further distinction (Agr. 127-129). He considers God as an instrument, because of an erroneous use of
the prepositions which indicate the different kinds of
causality (Cher. 125-130). He is positively an atheist,

for he pretends to be the measure of all things. Philo thus
identifies Cain and Protagoras, whom he considers as the two
examples of the doctrine that everything, even God, ultimately depends on human opinion--an ancient precursor of
the modern theory of religious alienation (Post. 35). The
descendents of Cain profess materialism, which is the consequence and complement of atheism (Post. 21-123). Moreover, Cain is a sophist who, using the weaponry of
reasoning and persuasion, and showing no regard for truth,
defeats Abel, the man who is sincere and honest, but
inexperienced in the art of discussion (Deter. 1).[31] The
builders of the Tower of Babel, who emulate their forefather
Cain, are, like him, sophists who raise an impregnable
castle against the heavens by producing arguments of impiety
and atheism (Conf. 113). The list of the vices, illustrating the "name" which they create for themselves over
against God, contains all the consequences of atheism as
they can be derived logically, although they are not always
actually seen in atheists; and he reminds us of a similar
development in Paul (Rom. 1:18-32, cf. Conf. 117; Sacr. 32).
We find these atheists and sophists again among the
Egyptians who compel the sons of Israel to build the three
cities of Peitho, Rameses, and On (Post. 54). This image
suggests to Philo the threatening power, the temptation, of
atheism with its sophistic reasonings which ultimately lead
us to become worshipers and servants of man himself, or of
the human mind. Pharaoh's statement in this regard is without ambiguity: he does not know god (Leg. Al. III, 12;
Post. 115). He is an atheist who considers himself as
supreme ruler of the land of the body (Jos. 151; Fug. 148).
Egypt itself seems predestined to be the land of atheism,
since the crops depend on the flooding of the Nile, whose
waters come from the earth and not from the heavens, since
there is almost no rain in this country (Mos. II, 194).[32]
The consequence of the importance granted to the body and to
material things on the one hand, and to the senses and the
passions represented by a nation destined to perish in the
waves of the Red Sea on the other hand, is a form of philosophy which makes pleasure the goal of life, and acknowledges the existence of only the visible world. We easily
recognize in this description the philosophy of Epicurus, as
it was understood in the time of Philo, and all spiritualistic philosophies rejected it with indignation.[33]

b. Those who are removed from the Assembly of God

Two scriptural texts form the basis of the Philonic
discussion about those who are barred from the Assembly and

who represent, in Philo, those whose faith is unsatisfactory with respect to the notion of God.[34]   They are mentioned in Deuteronomy 23:1-3 and 5:2-4:

> He whose testicles are crushed   or whose
> male   member is cut off shall   not enter
> the   assembly   of the Lord.   No bastard
> shall enter   the assembly   of   the Lord;
> even to the tenth generation none of his
> descendants shall enter the   assembly of
> the Lord.   No Ammonite or Moabite shall
> enter the assembly of the Lord;   even to
> the   tenth generation none   belonging to
> them shall   enter the   assembly   of   the
> Lord   for   ever....(7)   You   shall   not
> abhor   an   Edomite,   for   he   is   your
> brother;   you   shall   not   abhor   an
> Egyptian,   because you were   a sojourner
> in his land.   The children of the third
> generation that   are born   to   them   may
> enter the assembly of the Lord.   (The
> second text is Numbers 5:2-4:)   Command
> the   people of Israel that they   put out
> of   the camp every leper, and   every one
> having a   discharge, and every   one that
> is   unclean   through   contact   with   the
> dead;   you shall   put out both   male and
> female,   putting them outside   the camp,
> that they may not defile their   camp, in
> the midst of which I dwell.

    Philo comments at length on Deut. 23:1-3, in Spec. Leg. I,   324-345.   The   man   whose sexual   organs are   mutilated represents those   who deny the existence of   the archetypes, thereby bringing God   into direct   contact with matter.   We should   not   imagine here   a radical   dualism   which deifies matter, or denies its creation by God, since these two ideas are   probably absent from his thought.[35]   Rather, Philo is concerned with anthropomorphism, whose wrong implications he is   always   careful to   correct.   To reduce   creation to   a material   level is to oblige God to work with his   hands like a   craftsman,   whereas   He   only   creates   the   archetypes directly.   The latter   have an energy of their   own and are able to confer a form upon matter.   In other words, a notion of Creation which is too down-to-earth is destructive of the dignity of the Creator   and of   the correct notion   which we should have of Him (ibid. 330; cf. Mut. 204).

The man whose sexual organs are mutilated is an atheist who has lost faith in the Father of all created things.   If he allows others to express belief in God, or even if he himself says that God exists, he does it only because belief in God is useful to men, whom it keeps from wrongdoing, but not because he himself actually believes in God.   He simply supports the notion of God as a policeman, a notion well known in modern times, but already deemed by Plato and the Greeks to be a form of atheism.[36]

The son of the harlot (ibid. 331-332; cf. Conf. 144; Dec. 8) does not know who his father is, and therefore suspects several of his mother's lovers of being the author of his life. He represents the polytheist who worships several gods but does not know the true God.[37]

The Moabites and the Ammonites (ibid. 333ff; Post. 177; Leg. Al. III, 81), descendants of Lot, symbolize the protagonists of the mind and of the senses. They hold the mind to be the father and the senses to be the mother of everything which happens in man: this amounts to the rejection of divine causality and to the deification of man. This symbolism stems from the episode of the daughters of Lot who took advantage of the drunkenness of their father to beget offspring from him (Gen. 19:30-38), and on the eytmology of their names, which Philo interprets as "Deliberation" and "Assent"--the behaviour of a mind which discusses and assents readily to every pleasurable suggestion (Ebr. 162-166).

The Edomite and the Egyptian, who are accepted in the Assembly in the third generation, are not interpreted allegorically in this context (cf. Virt. 105).

The leper and the man with an issue are also excluded from the Assembly (Number. 5:2-3). According to Leg. Al. III, 7, both of them represent the obscuring of the true notion of God, since:

> The former combines God and creation, as
> joint causes which are mutually hostile
> natures, for he shows two different
> colours, whereas there is one single
> Cause, even He who doeth all. The man
> with an issue, on the other hand,
> deriving everything from the world, and
> making it return into the world,
> imagines that nothing has been created
> by God, sharing the opinion of

> Heraclitus in his advocacy of such
> tenets as "fullness and want," "the
> unity of everything", and "the inter-
> changeability of all things".

Here at least is a clearly identified opponent, even if his
work and the transmission of his writings are obscure.

c. The Chaldeans

The identification of the Philonic Chaldeans has been a
challenging problem for scholars.[38]   Are they simple astrologers, supporters of the doctrine of fate like the
Stoics,[39] worshipers of the heavens like some Jews, or more
generally the partisans of cosmic religion in whatever form
it may take? These hypotheses are both too specific and too
vague.   Before choosing between them, we must consider the
biblical images through which, once more, Philo explains his
thought.   The chief texts are: Gig. 62; Her. 96-99; 289;
Congr. 40-51; Mut. 16; Migr. 52-60; Virt. 212-216; Praem.
58, and especially Migr. 176-199 and Abr. 68-88.   Let us
briefly describe their contents. Abraham, who migrated from
Chaldea to the land of Harran, and from there to Canaan,
first represents the man who, like his father Terah, the
biblical counterpart of Socrates, turns away from cosmology
to anthropology.   But, abandoning the pair Terah-Socrates,
he reaches a point where he realizes the impossibility of
self-knowledge and falls into a kind of intellectual despair
at the very end of his philosopical inquiry.[40]   Scepticism,
then, brings him back to God, because the criticism of
knowledge elaborated by the Sceptics of the Academy invites
him to suspend his judgment. In his distrust of his ability
to reach the truth, which is a form of humility of the mind,
he has the proper disposition to listen to God, and he
enjoys a double revelation, the discovery of God as the
charioteer of the world, and as Him whose voice he heard
after he had said: "I am but earth and ashes." His very
name, Abram, which means "Uplifted father," becomes Abraham,
"Elect father of sound."[41] This change means that the
unsuccessful investigator and worshiper of the heavens has
turned into the hearer and servant of the word of God, the
witness of faith in God.[42],[43],[44] The Chaldeans of Philo are
not simply astrologers, nor do they represent a biblical
label for a particular school of philosophy, such as that of
the allegorizing Stoics, as is evident from the hesitation
of scholars about their identity.   Philo thus invents a new
category under this title, at once very precise and very

broad in its implications, thereby freeing himself from the
labels of any particular school of philosophy. He clearly
explains what he means by the Chaldeans and their doctrine
in the following:

> The Chaldeans have the reputation of
> having, far more than other peoples,
> elaborated astronomy and the casting
> natal horoscopes. They have set up a
> harmony between things on earth and
> things on high, between heavenly things
> and earthly. Following as it were the
> laws of musical proportion, they have
> shown the universe to be a perfect con-
> cord or symphony produced by a sympa-
> thetic affinity between its parts, sepa-
> rated indeed in space, but united in
> kinship. These men imagined that this
> visible universe was the only thing in
> existence, either itself God or con-
> taining God in itself as the soul of the
> whole world. And they made Fate and
> Necessity divine, thus filling human
> life with much impiety, by teaching that
> aside from phenomena there is no origi-
> nating cause of anything whatever, but
> that the rotation of sun and moon and of
> the other heavenly bodies determine for
> every being in existence both good
> things and their opposites (Migr. 178-
> 179).

Philo continues with the statement that Moses accepts the
doctrine of the unity of the world and of the sympathetic
affinity of its parts--if we may use a scholastic formula,
he accepts the interdependent "secondary causes," but he
maintains that "neither the universe nor its soul is the
primal God, and that neither the constellations nor their
revolutions are the primary causes of the things that happen
to men" (Migr. 180-181).

3. Criticism of the particular philosophies in their own language

We are already well informed--perhaps in the most
accurate manner--about the Philonic criticism of the particular philosophies from the cosmological and anthropological point of view, through these three large biblical

frescos. But we can do more by positively identifying these
philosophical doctrines.   We do not have to redo here the
work very well done by E. Bréhier, H. Heinemann, H.A.
Wolfson, A.-J. Festugière, J. Pépin, J. Daniélou, and others
on the philosophical influences discovered in Philo.   We
shall limit ourselves to a few important affirmations found
in Philo himself, and to the fascinating problem, apparently
raised and solved by Festugiere and Pepin, whether the Plato
and the Aristotle of Philo fit our classical picture of
them.   We shall note that this discussion dominates the
whole religious philosophy of Philo, and that it is out of a
motive of piety that he accepts, corrects, or completes the
data of the cosmic religion transmitted to the Alexandrian
intelligentsia of his time.

        We shall successively examine his rejection of the
materialism of Epicurus and of Heraclitus, then his criticism of the principles of Protagoras on man as the measure
of all things.   Finally, beyond Stoicism, which does not
alter the nature of the problem, we shall return, together
with Philo, to Plato and Aristotle, who are the two great
authorities in philosophy, especially to Timaeus and the
Laws of the old Plato and to De philosophia of the young
Aristotle.

        4. The rejection of materialism

        Philo shares the indignation common to all spiritualist
philosophers of Hellenistic times about the man who dared--
although he lived worthily and his thought is not trivial--
to propose pleasure as the goal of human endeavour (Fug.
148). Philo, in fact, integrates pleasure into the workings
of sense-perception as a positive thing, created by God, but
he rejects it as a goal, and thereby joins, without further
originality, the mass of those who despise Epicurus.   Moreover, he considers Epicurus to be an impious man and compares him to the Egyptian atheists because Epicurus ascribes
a human form to the gods, and the Egyptians worship animals
(Post. 2).   Similarly, he attacks Democritus, Epicurus, and
the Stoics for their doctrine about the destructibility of
the world:

                Democritus, with Epicurus and the great
                mass of Stoic philosophers, maintain the
                creation and destruction of the world,
                but in different ways. The first two
                postulate many worlds, the origin of

which they ascribe to the mutual impacts
and interlacings of atoms and whose
destruction is due to the counterblows
and collisions sustained by the bodies
so formed. The Stoics admit one world
only: God is the cause of its creation
but not of its destruction. This is due
to the force of the ever-active fire
which exists in things and, in the
course of long periods of time, resolves
everything into itself; and out of it a
new world is constructed according to
the design of its architect. According
to these, the world may be called either
eternal, or perishable--thought of as
a world reconstructed it is perishable,
thought of as subject to the conflagra-
tion it is everlasting through the
ceaseless rebirths and cycles which
render it immortal (<u>Aet</u>. 8-9).

Philo therefore rejects Atomic materialism as equally
atheistic and impious as well as the materialism which sees
fire as a creative power. If Philo ever seems to ascribe
creative power to one of the elements, it is not to fire,
but to the ether, the quintessence, which is the substance
of both the heavens and the mind according to the
Peripatetics, but not according to the Stoics, as shown by
Pepin in his discussion of Cicero's <u>Dream of Scipio</u>, and of
<u>Q.E</u>. IV, 8 on Gen. 18:6-7.[45]

5. The theology of the old Plato and of the young
   Aristotle[46]

The above leads us now to a discussion of the sequel of
the text quoted above, where we find an unexpected judgement
of Aristotle by Philo:

But Aristotle surely showed a pious and
religious spirit when, in opposition to
this view, he said that the world was
uncreated and indestructible and
denounced the shocking atheism of those
who stated the contrary and held that
there was no difference between man-made
idols and that great, visible God who
embraces the sun, the moon, and the
pantheon, if one may truly call it so,

of the fixed and wandering stars. He is
reported to have said in bitter mockery
that in the past he had feared for his
house lest it should be overthrown by
violent winds, terrible storms, passage
of time, or neglect. But now he lived
in the fear of a far greater menace from
the theorists who would destroy the
whole world. Some say that the author
of this doctrine was not Aristotle but
certain Pythagoreans, and I have read a
book of Ocellus, a Lucanian, entitled On
the Nature of the Universe, in which the
author not only affirms, but seeks to
prove by demonstrations, that the world
is uncreated and indestructible (Aet.
10-12).

Let us consider for the moment the label of piety and
of holiness given by Philo to the thought of Aristotle,
which seems to contradict what Philo says elsewhere, in Op.
7:

There are some people who, admiring the
world rather than its Maker, pronounce
it to be without beginning and everlasting, falsely and impiously accusing
God of vast inactivity (tou de theou
pollen apraxian); whereas we ought, on
the contrary, venerate His powers as
Maker and Father, without exalting the
world beyond all measure.

How can Aristotle be praised so warmly in De Aeternitate,
and at the same time be accused of ascribing inaction to
God, which probably refers to the First Mover of the
classical Aristotle? (cf. De Caelo 279a).[47]

Some have considered this to be an inconsistency in
Philo, or considered him in Aeternitate as a mere doxo-
grapher recounting the opinions of others, or have
questioned the authenticity of the treatise itself. But
there is a better explanation: the Aristotle praised by
Philo is not the classical Aristotle, but the Aristotle of
the lost treatise De philosophia, which exercised a large
influence in Antiquity.   Philo knew this treatise, and presents one of the most valuable contributions to its difficult reconstitution.

Festugière explains how the religion of the world
developed in the Hellenistic times, beginning with Plato.
We summarize his exposition. If, for the moment, we put
aside the Demiurge of Timaeus, we note that the Socratic
demonstration of the existence of God leads to the notion of
the Soul of the world rather than to the idea of the
Demiurge. The Soul of the world governs the world and exercises providence over it. Such is the religion of
Xenophon's Memorables and of Plato's Laws. This religion,
which survived together with the prestige of Socrates among
the Cynics and the Stoics, is not concerned with the affirmation of an immanent or transcendent God nor does it get
involved with the mysticism of the ecstatic contemplation of
God. Its God is a cosmocrator, a "master of the world," or
a "political God" on the scale of the Megalopolis, i.e., of
the universe.⁴⁸ What is therefore the place of the Demiurge
of Timaeus in this religion? In the beginning, He is
nothing but a "mythical counterpart" to the Soul of the
world,⁴⁹ who confers a mechanistic connotation upon the
Platonic system of the world, then disappears completely.
He only appears for the purpose of giving the initial push
to set the world in motion, or, rather, to provide a
parallel to such mythical cosmogonies as we find in Hesiod
or in Eastern literature, for instance that of Mesopotamia.
In fact, the Soul of the world, with its power as a final
cause, suffices to govern the world. The creation of
matter, which is a problem in Plato, should not be conceived
with respect to the Demiurge. It must be confined to the
antagonism between soul an body, or, more exactly, to the
conflict between a principle of disorder which is opposed
and ruled by the ordering power of the perfect motion, a
circular motion which is that of the fixed stars, whose
substance is the quintessence, i.e., a higher, thinking
nature, parallel to that of the intellect in man.

How can we, then, explain the importance of the
Demiurge of Timaeus? The answer is that the subsequent
generations took very seriously what Plato had only presented as an essay and turned his myths into religious
dogmas, thus creating a Platonic system far removed from the
true thought of the master. The insertion of a Demiurge as
a second explanation of the world is an addition which is,
actually, foreign to Plato, especially when it is made the
cause of the continuous motion of the world, which is sufficiently well explained by the operation of the Soul of the
world.⁵⁰

Festugière then describes the development of cosmic
religion after Plato. The De philosophia of the young

Aristotle is marked by deep religious feeling and invites
the reader to discover God in the cosmos as in a kind of
sanctuary.[51]   The astral deities are offered for our
adoration, and we are related to them. The existence of God
is proved by the order of the world. The first moving body
is the heavens, and the Prime Mover is the Soul of the
heavens.[52] Since our mind consists of the same substance as
the stars, the ether or quintessence, we are attracted
towards on high. Originally located in a star, our fallen
soul, by the contemplation of the order of the heavens
through the higher senses, is ruled by the heavens, and even
our body must be ruled by music.[53]

Stoicism takes advantage of the notion of our kinship
with the order of the world and with the heavens: we must
obey the same law as the world, the law of nature. The
divine Logos, which permeates every being, reveals itself in
man as intelligence. Man is therefore able to know divine
Reason, which can be defined as the Law of the Megalopolis.
This Reason, or divine Law, expresses an Order which imposes
itself: this is Fate, not in the sense of a blind power,
but of the Intelligible par excellence. Knowing the order
of things, therefore, the wise man adheres to it with love
and "lives according to nature."[54]

We then notice the development of an eclectic dogmatism, which is well represented in the theology of the De
mundo used by Philo.[55] Let us note in this theology the
unity and transcendence of God, from Whom everything comes,
and by Whom everything is maintained, Who governs the universe without effort, the heavens directly, and earthly
things indirectly, as the great Persian king governs through
his Satraps. This God is one, invisible, contemplated by
the soul only, creator of all things. He dwells in the
ether and is called by many names which reflect His majesty
and His mighty deeds.[56]

Pépin, in his reconstruction of Aristotle's De philosophia,[57] uses and interprets the De aeternitate of Philo.
In his opinion, Aet. 10-43 is actually an amplification of
the ideas of the young Aristotle on the eternity of the
world.[58] He writes:

> The De aeternitate mundi provides an
> indication concerning Plato in a section
> (13 ff) which belongs to the same con-
> text as the former ones. After quoting
> the famous text of Timaeus 41ab, and
> describing several exegeses which he

considers to be biased, Philo refers to
Aristotle's   clearly   creationist
interpretation of the Platonic thesis.
Philo states that the opinion of
Aristotle on this point is the best
authority, because he had too much
respect for philosophy to falsify anything, and a teacher can have no more
trustworthy   witness   than   a
disciple.[59]

The essential point of the thesis of De aeternitate is the
affirmation of the creation of the world, and Philo's goal
is to establish the consequence of this, the doctrine of the
indestructibility of the world. With regard to the creation
of the world, Philo knows of an interpretation by Plato
according to which the world is created but does not have
its absolute beginning in creation. But Philo prefers to
refer to the Father and Maker of Timaeus and Hesiod and to
affirm a beginning of the world, although God is not subject
to time. According to Moses, he adds (Aet. 19), the world
is created and indestructible. For the creation of the
world is described in the Law, the Law does not tell us
about the destruction of the world, and we even read in it
that the world will last for ever (Gen. 8:22). Philo, as we
know, confines himself to the Pentateuch and does not
acknowledge the eschatology of later Judaism.

The continuation of this passage rejects the inactivity
of God (Op. 8-12) and presents Moses, after having reached
the summit of philosophy, as being taught by God about the
secrets of nature. Moses is now aware of the necessity that
beings contain, on the one hand, an active cause--the
Mind of the universe, pure and undiluted--and, on the
other hand, a passive principle--itself incapable of life
and motion but, once set in motion, shaped and quickened by
the Mind, transformed into that most perfect materpiece,
this world. Pépin[60] draws our attention to the fact that
this section does not refer to Stoicism, as previously
supposed, but that it might refer to the young Aristotle,
who, in De philosophia, taught about the life and autonomy
of the Soul of the world. The apparent contradiction
between Op. 7 and Aet. 10-12, therefore, seems to be
resolved. The real inconsistency would thus be between the
young Aristotle, the author of De philosophia, and Aristotle
in his maturity, with his theory of the Prime Mover
transcendant to the world. The young Aristotle ascribed the
creative function not to a Deity outside the world but to an
immanent principle, the fifth element, which intervened both

as the Mind of the universe (whose creative power was
already recognized in Laws) and as the substance of the
heavens, invested with a mission which was not confined to
unification among the elements but also included generation
of the universe.[61] He welcomes the Platonic teaching about
creation, and particularly the creative function ascribed in
Laws to the Soul of the world, provided they are understood
ab aeterno and purified from the artificialist metaphors of
Timaeus.[62],[63]

Philo discards this notion of the creative Soul of the
universe when he rejects the idea of a God immanent in the
world or of a Soul of the world; and he considers the
Demiurge as a second God or as the transcendent Logos who
created the world by means of the archetypes. Moreover,
according to Wolfson,[64] Philo restores to the Aristotelian
Forms immanent in visible things a proper existence which
they enjoyed in Plato, but which Aristotle denied. Philo
wants to oppose the deification of the world and to extol
the creator and transcendant God, while granting as much
power as possible to the world of the archetypes and the
visible heavens, though not absolute power (Migr. 179-181).
He sees as pious a system which allows for a Creator, but
this Creator must be transcendant to the world.[65] The
Aristotle of De philosophia, therefore, reasons piously when
he proves the existence of a Creator; but Philo corrects his
system by affirming the transcendance of this Creator, and
he criticizes the mature Aristotle's notion of the
inactivity of the Prime Mover, incapable of exercising providence.[66]

6. The maxim of Protagoras

Although Protagoras' maxim, "Man is the measure of all
things," is refuted by Philo in the context of his theology
of grace, where we shall find it again, we must mention it
in the present chapter because of its importance for the
relations between God and the world, and, more basically,
for the demonstration of the existence of God. Philo
mentions Protagoras by name (Post. 35) even outside his philosophical treatises, which he does very rarely, and he thus
makes of Protagoras one of the great figures of his
Allegorical Commentary, since he identifies him with Cain,
to whom he ascribes the famous maxim. He also mentions this
maxim more than once without naming its author, particularly
in Som. I, 190-194.

We know Protagoras through Plato, Aristotle, and
Diogenes Laertius.[67]   Diogenes Laertius, in his section on
Protagoras says:

> Protagoras was the first to maintain
> that there are two sides to every ques-
> tion, opposed to each other, and he even
> argued in this fashion, being the first
> to do so.   Furthermore he began a work
> thus: "Man is the measure of all
> things, of things that are that they
> are, and of things that are not that
> they are not." He used to say that soul
> was nothing apart from the senses, as we
> learn from Plato in the Theaeteus (152 a
> ff), and that everything is true. In
> another work he began thus: "As to the
> gods, I have no means of knowing either
> that they exist or that they do not
> exist.   For many are the obstacles that
> impede knowledge, both the obscurity of
> the question and the shortness of human
> life."   For this introduction to his
> book the Athenians expelled him; and
> they burnt his works in the market-
> place, after sending round a herald to
> collect them from all who had copies in
> their possession.[68]

When Protagoras writes, "Since, then, man had a share
in the portion of the gods, in the first place because of
his divine kinship he alone among living creatures believed
in gods, and set to work to erect altars and images of
them,"[69] he proposes to justify popular religion and the
cult of the gods through a mythical explanation of the
origins of man.   His radical scepticism about the very
existence of the gods, however, which caused his explusion
from Athens, and his maxim which makes of human opinion the
ultimate warrant of every reality, make him more than a mere
subjectivist, but a dogmatist whose tenets ultimately rely
on man, and who rejects the objective certitude of the
belief in God.[70]   Plato depicts him as a subjectivist and
relativist (Tehetetus, 151 a ff). Philo, in his development
on scepticism (Ebr. 155-205; Jos. 125-148), used his very
relativism against the man who makes himself the measure of
all things, and he looks for a warrant of truth superior to
man, i.e., the word of the living God as perceived by a man
who has confessed his incapacity and his nothingness.   In
Post. 35, Philo labels Protagoras as impious and reproaches

him with denying divine causality and substituting man for
God by attributing the fatherhood and ultimate guarantee of
every kind of thought to the mind and to the senses.[71] For
these reasons, the Cain-Protagoras pair represents the chief
enemy to a disposition of mind which refers everything to
God (Abel), i.e., to eucharistia.

IV. PHILONIC TEACHINGS ON THE RELATIONS BETWEEN GOD AND THE
     WORLD

     Philo did not construct a "world system," and what he
says about the role of God in the cosmos and in man is only
occasional. He is first of all an exegete, and the text of
Scripture provides him with rich materials for his favourite
literary exercise - the investigation of the deeper meaning
of the word of God, in other words, the essay genre.   If
there is any unity in a treatise or in a series of treatises
by Philo, it is provided by his obstinate interest in the
science of spiritual life, which he investigates in all its
aspects, and it is not based on a world system developed for
its own sake and used as a basis for other research. This
does not mean that Philo does not have a world system.   It
is even rewarding to gather its scattered components and to
make a bouquet of them, without binding them too strongly.
Of course, this will only be a summary, completed by a few
remarks confined to theological aspects. For more information, the reader may simply turn to the excellent exposition of the philosophy of Philo by Wolfson.

     Philo does not create out of nothing, any more than
other philosophers. Like them, he repeats the doctrines
accepted in the schools of philosophy, and states his
preference for those which are favoured by the intelligentsia of his milieu. The originality of Philo in the
choice of his ideas is, therefore, often not a genuine one:
he simply reflects the thought of his teachers and the
authorities which he recognizes. J. Daniélou gives a good
description of the Alexandrian cultural circles which formed
Philo's environment.[72] However, scholars have noticed that
Philo rarely accepts a doctrine into his system without significantly altering it. For example, his notion of the
Logos is largely Stoic, but he places over this Logos a
transcendant Deity, and he emphasizes the transcendance of
the Logos with respect to the world and to man (Legat. 5-6).
The heavens and the mind consist of ether, a quasi-divine
substance, the most sublime one according to philosophers,
but Philo grants absolute power neither to the mind nor to

the heavens (Migr. 179-181): he proclaims a transcendent
God and confers a mission of praise on the heavenly bodies
and on men (Som. I, 35). Moreover, the supreme dignity of
the heavens and of man, of the universe, and of the Logos
himself, is that of a Son of God or of an image of God
(Sobr. 56; Mut. 131; Conf. 53; 146; Deus 32).[73] He accepts
the Forms of Plato, but he sees in them the archetypes of
particular things. These archetypes are created in the
thought of the Logos before giving form to matter (Op. 20).
Philo therefore distorts the Forms of Plato by bringing them
closer to particular things, and, on the other hand, he
alters the forms of Aristotle by conferring on them an
existence of their own independent of their visible
copies.[74] He makes these changes so as to extend the
creative activity of God to everything in the world, and, at
the same time, to extol the dignity of the divine creative
activity by adding the preliminary creation of the archetypes, the only objects worthy of being directly created by
God (Spec. Leg. I, 328). He welcomes the Demiurge of
Timaeus, but, following Hellenistic tradition, he sees Him
as the Father and Maker of everything, ascribing to Him
Providence over the universe, an activity which extends even
to the secret part of the human soul, where God assumes the
function of a spiritual Guide (Deus, 27-32). We are far
from the Demiurge of Timaeus, which only gives the initial
push for the work of creation, or of that of De caelo, whose
direct intervention does not extend to the regions under the
moon (Book III), and that of De mundo, who governs the universe through the intermediary of His "Satraps" (397b -
400a). The God of Philo, indeed, operates through the
intermediary of His powers, but these are not mere creatures
like the angels of the Jews or personal beings like the
star-gods of the Greeks. The personal character of the
divine powers vanishes to the degree that they are close to
God, and the highest of them, the divine Logos, withdraws in
his turn when the soul becomes capable of dealing directly
with God (Q.E. II, 40).[75] The powers are, therefore, but
the several faces of the great Pedagogue of men.[76] They are
not however, mere abstractions, but real things, influences
consciously experienced by men, as sorts of divine
"effluence." In this sense, they resemble the abstract
dieties of the Greeks, such as Justice, Peace, but they are
firmly interrelated and subject to the transcendant God who
emits them like a reflection of Himself. The interior
system of the world, or the hierarchy and combination of its
components, including the coordinating operation of the
Logos and the life-giving influx of the ether, reappear in
Philo. Moses, he says (Migr. 180-183), accepts the Stoic
doctrine of sympathy, i.e., the interdependence of the

"secondary causes" of the Scholastics. We can also say
that, with this theory, he acknowledges the existence of the
future field of modern science, which deals with the phe-
nomenon.[77] But there is a place in this structure for the
eventual insertion of miracle.[78] For Philo, a miracle is
basically nothing but a change in the property of elements
by divine decision, with nothing being ontologically added
to the world (Mos. I, 96 ff). Divine causality preserves
all its importance in the transcendent order, so that, without it, nothing could exist or be accomplished in the world
(Op. 20). In this, Philo is attentive to the proper use of
the causal prepositions borrowed by the Stoics from
Aristotle: God, he says, cannot be a cause of inferior
nature, such as an instrument (Cher. 125-130). This role is
assumed by visible creatures, or by incorporeal Forms (Op.
4;19), but we must ascribe supreme causality to God, affirm
that God is the source and the end of everything. The law
of nature, which is the supreme rule of Stoic Physics and
Ethics, is the Right Logos, but it is also the Law imposed
by God on the world, which is found in Scripture (Op. 3').
All created things rank as passive with respect to God, who
alone is the Active Cause (Op. 8; Cher. 77-78). He is the
kairos (Mut. 265) and the aion (Deus. 32), two titles
usually ascribed to the power of Fate, but He assumes them
the way a king possesses absolute power and freedom, and not
as a dependant being, like the link in a chain, or even the
whole chain with repect to the links. He is apoios (Leg.
Al. III, 36), without qualities permitting Him to be classified in the category of particular things.[79] He is the only
Sage, the only Citizen of the world (Ebr. 69; Plant. 38-39;
Cher. 121), and the only perfect and happy one (Abr. 200-
205; Sacr. 40), since all others, including wise men,
possess these attributes only in a limited way, by participation and by grace (Som. II, 70; Spec. Leg. III, 180). He
is the transcendent One (Legat. 5), above the unity which is
the principle of numbers, and above the dyad which is the
beginning of multiplicity and of lower realities (Som. II,
55). Here, Philo shows that he knows the discussions of the
Platonic and Pythagorean schools on the One and the many
very well,[80] but the Divine One is incomparable like the God
of Israel. He is also incomprehensible in His essence
(Spec. Leg. I, 41-44), an idea suggested by Timaeus 28 c
about the Demiurge, and deepened by philosophical tradition.
In Philo, however, the incomprehensibility of God is not
only our inability to understand Him, but a characteristic
of His very unity as transcending every category (Legat. 5).
What can we add to these remarks? The very scepticism of
Philo, a heritage from the Academy, codified by Enesidemus,

is ebbing in Philo, but without leading him towards metaphysical negativism or the confined security of the philosophies of the Absurd. He masters scepticism and uses it
as a weapon to fight subjectivism itself, not in the manner
of a second-rate preacher who may offer faith in exchange
for reason, but as a man who, having reached the end of the
criticism of knowledge with the Sceptics, understands that
man cannot be considered as the measure of all things or as
the ultimate warrant of objective truth. Rather, truth,
i.e., God, can still impose Himself on man with His own
voice if man accepts to suspend his judgment to become
humble and to listen (Her. 30; Fug. 135-136). The Philonic
faith, therefore, has nothing in common with the Platonic
faith which is mere human opinion (Rep. VII, 533 e; VI, 511
e).[81] It is the fruit of an encounter between man and God,
and, in a deeper sense, participation, though very limited
and imperfect yet certain because of the divine influx that
it contains, in the stability of God, who is the only
"Believer," or the absolute Truth (Mut. 54; 181; 186). As
to the problem of evil, we can only say here that it is not
properly speaking a cosmological or anthropological problem,
but only a moral problem, for God is not the cause of evil
(Leg. Al. I, 48-52; Q.E. I, 78).

Is it possible to say that Philonic theology is in con-
tinuity with the theology of the Bible and of Judaism?[82]
Judaism does not have an equivalent to Philo before the
Jewish philosophers of the Middle-Ages, such as Saada Gaon,
Crescas, Maimonides, the Cabbalists, to say nothing of
Spinoza. It cannot however be denied that Philo constructed
a religious philosophy on the basis of the chief tenets of
Judaism, namely, the belief in only one God, who is perfect,
creator and providence, and on the notion of piety toward
God, used as a criterion for every judgment in theological
matters. In addition, Philo, like Judaism, is ultimately
concerned with only one thing - how to obey and praise God,
give thanks to Him, and ask Him for help and mercy. His
religious orientation is so obvious, so conscious, that all
the materials, however unusual, which he integrates in his
teaching, not without giving them a new meaning, cannot lead
to the conclusion that Philo stands just on the edge of
faithfulness to the religion of Moses.[83] Wolfson mentions
many common features. Let us only point out the same horror
of idolatry, the importance granted to the heavens, which
Judaism uses almost as a synonym for God, or which lean it
towards a theology of Fate. We can also mention the presence in Philo and in Judaism of heavenly worshipers,
although Philo, perhaps because he follows the Sadducees, is
almost completely silent about the angelology of which the

Pharisees were very fond, and about the several forms of
eschatological Adventism of Apocalyptic literature.[84]

CHAPTER FOUR

EUCHARISTIA AND THE INTERIOR LIFE OF THE SOUL

The purpose of the preceding chapter was to show how Philo, following the inspiration of Alexandrian Judaism, developed and brought to quasi-perfection his teaching on cosmic and anthropological eucharistia, and how he extended and strengthened it in relation to the particular philosophies of his time. In the present chapter, our task is to show how Philo, as a consequence of his deep analysis of interior life, developed a far-reaching teaching on grace and insisted on the basic necessity of thanksgiving for its defense and confirmation.

We shall adopt the following order. First, we shall inquire, as in the last chapter, whether Philo found among his predecessors the beginnings of a teaching on grace, and the idea that thanksgiving plays an important part in it. We shall find the rudiments of such a doctrine in the Letter of Aristeas, which can be considered, in our opinion, as one of Philo's sources, and in Wisdom of Solomon, which represents at least a parallel, if not a source. Very little, on the contrary, can be found in the Allegorists of Philo's Alexandria, whose cosmological interpretations are better known to us. But we can find a great deal in Philo's meditation on the Bible, not only because the peculiarities of his text of Septuagint sometimes serve as a pretext for exegetical developments in this sense, but, more basically, because the action of God himself takes on a complementary meaning when it is transferred from the context of the external world and the life of the Jewish nation--for instance, the notion of the Covenant--to the context of the internal life of the soul. On the other hand the same can be said of the positive or negative reactions of men to the divine action in Scripture. We have already seen that a symbolic interpretation of events, things, and laws, as well as an allegorical interpretation of the great characters of Scripture in some of their more notable actions, can offer wonderful opportunities.

Passing from scripture to philosophy, or from biblical symbolism, his favourite "language," to philosophical doctrines with their technical vocabulary, we shall seek to determine what Philo has been able to gather in this field. There is no question, of course, of going through the heritage of the Greek schools of philosophy in this regard,

or of gathering every echo of the theory of knowledge and of
virtue in Philo. Our purpose is to determine the chief elements of these philosophies which he selects either to
oppose or to integrate them, though not without significantly altering them.   In other terms, Philo is looking for
a Mantic and an Ethics which fit his ideals of piety towards
God.

After this inquiry, it will be useful to reflect on the
general meaning of Philo's struggle in this area, in order
to determine as clearly as possible what cause he supports.
This is the problem of Philo's originality in his spiritual
teaching; or, if we may use this image, we need to know what
nail he relentlessly hammers whatever the importance for him
of the other points of his teaching.   Several scholars have
made their own suggestions about this, for instance, Brehier
and Goodenough following Pascher and Reizenstein, then
Völker, Daniélou, and, more recently, Arnaldez in an
interesting study of the dialectic of feelings in Philo.[1]
All of them, particularly Arnaldez shed much light on the
question, but, in our opinion, it is still possible to hit
the target more accurately.   Philo fights wherever he spots
a danger to combat or an advantage to win on behalf of his
religious faith. We must consider him as an ascetic already
far advanced on the way to perfection. He knows that everything in the external world, and even in the internal world
of the soul, is grace, but he himself faces the trials of
more advanced souls, or, rather, he has marvelously con-
quered them.   The way to overcome these trials is to preserve piety through a disposition of thanksgiving, when the
soul has, with God's help, almost completed the edifice of
virtue.   There is the danger of stumbling over the final
obstacle, which corresponds to the test of the perfect man,
to award the crown to oneself rather than crowning God for
the acquisition of virtue.   The most typical image to illustrate this stage of spiritual life is that of the
unfinished house from which, because there is no parapet
around the roof, there is the danger of falling off.   The
biblical characters who illustrate this are, among others
who represent more particular aspects of the same thing,
Isaac, the very type of perfection, and the pair Judah-
Issachar, when the progress of the soul has reached its cri-
tical point.   Finally, the problem itself is that of
merit: no   one is as odious, and actually as impious, as a
virtuous man who is satisfied with himself, believes he is
superior to others, no longer feels the need for God, or no
longer experiences the radical poverty of man.

Should we speak of a controversy over merit in the time of Philo? Let us say that certain souls felt very deeply, and others more superficially but perhaps more brutally, the danger in the notion of merit threatening religious faithfulness. We find sufficiently clear echoes of this in the controversy over "Pharisaism" presented in the Gospel. The Targumim also attest to the existence of discussions on merit in Judaism, independent of Christianity. Paul bases his fundamental criticism of the justification by works of the Law upon this controversy. And Origen, among the best representatives of Christian theology in the first centuries, to say nothing of Augustine later, faces the same obstacle in the itinerary of the soul. The problem is nothing less than a true crisis of religious faith, a crisis which takes place on the very threshold of perfection.

I. THE BEGINNINGS OF A THEOLOGY OF GRACE BEFORE PHILO

1. Philo's contemporaries

Philo provides little information on the science of inner life among his forerunners or in his own milieu, although they did deal with some aspects of it. Ethics and contemplative life were the objects of the philosophy taught in synagogues (Mos. II, 216); and a more perfect style of life was represented by the Essenes and the Therapeutae, where we note the ideals of virginity (Cont. 65-68), frugality, the moral virtues of community life, the practice of prayer, instructions given by the elders (Cont. 76-79), and even a particular emphasis on a spirituality where Passover and Pentecost are combined (Cont. 83 ff). The spirituality of the Therapeutae certainly includes the theme of liberation from bondage to the body and to the passions, represented by Egypt and the Red Sea, and thanksgiving for salvation. Should we also mention a pentecostal spirituality properly speaking? In this hypothesis, thanks would also be given for the fulfilment of the divine promises symbolized by the rejoicing at the feast of Pentecost and by the prosperity of the land of Canaan, but this would mean going beyond the text. Among the exegeses received by Philo from his surroundings, let us mention Jos. 51, where the king of Egypt represents the soul claiming ownership of the body, an exegesis which has a moral aspect, since Passover symbolizes the liberation from the bondage to the body and to the passions. The tree of life was also given a number of superimposed interpretations, which Philo records in Q.G. I, 108 (cf. Leg. Al. I, 49), one of which is psychological and

refers to the intellect at the summit of the soul. J.
Daniélou, who quotes these examples,[2] mentions several
others of the same type. He also mentions the existence of
a mystical exegesis in Aristobulus, for whom the seventh
day, identified to the first, is a symbol of wisdom from
which all light originates.[3]-[4] Finally, he refers to Wisdom
of Solomon and to the Letter of Aristeas,[5] which, in our
opinion, are very important for the theology of grace, as we
shall soon see. Let us also mention among the mystagogues,
or spiritual guides from whom Philo learns the secrets of
interior life, Jeremiah (Cher. 49-52), who says, "Didst thou
not call upon Me as thy house, thy father and the husband of
thy virginity?" (Jer. 3:4), and Hosea (14:9-10, cf. Plant.
137; Mut. 138-140). We are here, with the idea of the
divine fatherhood of the virtues in the soul, at the very
center of the problem of grace. We must not forget, finally, to include those in Philo's circles who were
interested in spiritual exegeses, his own listeners and
readers, for whom these exegeses were destined, and who made
them possible at least by their attention.

2. Wisdom of Solomon

Let us turn now to Wisdom of Solomon, which offers, if
not a source, at least a parallel to the teachings of Philo
on grace, as we also noticed in regard to its teachings on
the God of the universe and on cosmic eucharistia. C.
Larcher shows parallels between this book and Philo.[6] He
mentions the notion of God as the principle of every
activity of the soul, of the sciences, the arts and tech-
nics, as for instance in Wis. 8:21: "I perceived that I
would not possess wisdom unless God gave her to me—and it
was a mark of insight to know whose gift she was—so I
appealed to the Lord and besought him." Larcher shows other
parallels between Philo and Wisdom of Solomon on the notions
of the necessity of divine grace (Wis. 3:9; 4:15: grace
and mercy come from God), on antecedent grace (Wis.
6:13: "She hastens to make herself known to those who
desire her"), on grace as supporting the efforts of man
(Wis. 8:21; 9:6; 9:16-17: "Who has learned thy counsel,
unless thou hast given wisdom and sent thy holy Spirit from
on high?"). Let us simply affirm that the doctrinal
parallelism is certain. As for the question of whether the
teaching of Wisdom of Solomon on the Holy Spirit is truly
Jewish, and not Hellenistic, the reader may refer to the
interesting remarks by Hans Lewy which connect the pneuma
sophias of Wisdom of Solomon with Sirach 24:33.[7]-[8]

3. The Letter of Aristeas

The Letter of Aris'teas, on the other hand, probably
offers more than a parallel - indeed it appears to be a
source used by Philo. For the theology of grace in the
Letter of Aristeas is very noteworthy and close to Philo.
Let us mention several of its aspects: God is a universal
Benefactor whose example we must follow (205); He indul-
gently guides all men without exception (207); He loves
truth (206); He is merciful (208) and loves justice (209);
He needs nothing and is not hard to please (211); He brings
to fruition every thought which is oriented toward perfection (216); He offers man mastery over his impulses (223);
people pray to Him in order to win the approval of others
(225), to become liberal (226), to conquer their own enemies
through liberality, because He is the master of all hearts
(227). Piety is a kind of sovereign beauty, whose energy is
love, itself a gift of God (229); everything is accomplished
by God and is organized according to His will (234); to welcome all that is beautiful and to reject its opposite is a
disposition of the soul which we owe to the divine power
(236); we can achieve temperance only if God disposes our
soul to it (237); the accomplishment of our own deeds
depends on God, and we ought to follow His direction in our
choice (239); we must ask God not to fail in our duty, so as
not to surrender to idleness or pleasure (245); to desire
virtue for one's children is an effect of divine power
(248); God's help governs human life, even in resisting
anger against one's wife (251); to be concerned with
avoiding error and doing one's duty is the effect of divine
power (252); a man must be pious in order to have the gift
of counsel (255); he must pray to God in order to obtain the
talent of philosophy (256); eloquence effects persuasion by
the power of God (266); God bestows good judgment (262) and
goodness to men (274); He directs the work of virtue,
although virtue is hated by many (277); God enables us not
to exalt ourselves over others (282); God gives nobility of
nature, meekness and humanity (290).

This enumeration, which covers the totality of virtue,
needs no further comment. Every good thing in the soul
comes from God, and we must ask God for it in prayer. We
must also submit to His guidance. Is there in this context
a notion of thanksgiving for the things of the soul? The
word is absent but, since eucharistia means the recognition
of God as the source of all good things, we can say that the
idea is present. The seventy Jewish sages made God the
foundation of their answers and acknowledged that every

power and every worthy thought has its principle in God
(200-201).[9]

II.   ASPECTS OF GRACE, AND OUR ATTITUDE TOWARD GRACE, IN
SYMBOLS, ALLEGORIES, AND BIBLICAL LAWS, IN PHILO

We can summarize the essentials of Philo's teaching on
grace under three headings: 1)   the symbolism it takes on
when God sends it to us; 2) the allegories which explain the
general mechanism of the life of virtue; 3) the laws which
determine the proper attitude toward Divine grace.   It goes
without saying that this symbolism, these allegories, and
these laws are Scriptural, and therefore, that Philo is
speaking in his favourite language and directly interpreting
the teaching of Moses or, if one prefers, his own understanding of this teaching. In this context, borrowings from
Greek philosophers, and even parallels with the Judaism of
his time, represent a second stage of reasoning and are of
secondary importance.

1. The symbolism of grace

The word "grace" is abundantly attested to in Philo,
but let us consider here the object of grace, under its
different aspects.   These are all governed by the idea of a
God who pours Himself out, or, if we alter the Scholastic
formula bonum diffusivum sui into Deus diffusivus sui, of
a shining God, whose ray is an almost substantial energy,
the efficacy of which is a reality with which we must con-
tend.   This efficacy is first creative, endowing the incorporeal archetypes with a reality of efficacy and of creative
and penetrating power.   it is also providential, since
divine providence is a complement to creation. This gift of
God has several aspects, determined by our needs: light
of the mind, seed of spiritual life and of virtue; covenants
and other help offered by a loving God to His subjects;
powers with multiple names and faces organized into several
hierarchies in order to make the condescension of God more
available to men.   A few words will suffice to explain and
illustrate these ideas.

God is light.   He is perceptible to men--in His existence if not in His essence--by Himself, like the sun by its
rays. We read, for instance, in Praem. 45:

> How this access has been obtained can be
> made clear with an illustration. Do we
> behold the sun' which sense perceives by
> any other thing than the sun, or the
> stars by any others than the stars, and
> in general is not light seen by light?
> In the same way God too is His own
> brightness and is discerned through Him-
> self alone, with nothing else co-
> operating or able to co-operate in
> giving an exact apprehension of His
> existence.

The same can be said of the Logos (Som. I, 85) and of the
Wisdom of God (Som. II, 242). The divine Pneuma itself is
the divine light or, rather, divine life (Leg. Al. I, 31).
The creatures made of quintessence are luminous (Op. 70;
Jos. 145-147). The intelligibles and the archetypes are
endowed with light and are immediately perceptible by the
mind upon which God pours them like rain (Op. 25-27; Conf.
124-127), in the same way that data coming from external
things are perceptible by our senses, and, through them, by
the mind, after God has showered them upon the sense organs
(Op. 25-27).[10]-[11]

Not only does the mind enjoy the help of divine light,
but the soul receives the seed and the increase of virtue
from God. Properly speaking, virtue is our participation in
the life of God. Through it, man participates in "generic"
virtue, which is divine and immortal, and in the stability
of God, who is the only Wise Being, the only Citizen of the
world, the only One absolutely happy, perfect, and sure
(Som. II, 237). We shall return to the role of God in the
development of virtue when we deal with the allegories on
the holy women of Scripture.

The notion of the Covenant bestowed by God upon
believers is also fertile ground for a theology of grace.
The Covenant is the most characteristic example of the
application to an individual believer of a divine disposition concerning the people of Israel collectively. Even
more, it shows the interiorization of Scriptural promises
concerning the bestowal of gifts which are rather external
than internal to the soul. Annie Jaubert dealing with the
doctrine of the Covenant in Philo, summarizes the
characteristics of this notion in Philo as follows:

> When Philo comes across the notion of
> diateke--so central in Scripture that

he was obliged to use it as the theological locus of the relations between God
and His people--he tends to integrate it
partially into his flexible system of
intermediaries between God and man.
Sometimes, he identifies it with the
divine Logos--oath and stability--but
mostly he makes it a symbol of the
highest graces of God, virtue, wisdom,
holiness, these divine fruits of the
Promised Land which, lavishly poured
forth in the soul, enable it to welcome
the presence of God as much as is
humanly possible.[12]

Let us only quote one text (Mut. 57-60):

The frame of mind (Abraham's) which
shrank from Him and fell spontaneously
won God's high approval by thus acknowledging of the Existent that it is He
alone who stands and that all below Him
are subject to change and mutation of
every kind. He addresses him with an
insistence which is also a call to
partnership. "And I," He says, "see, My
covenant is with thee" (Gen. 17:4). The
meaning suggested is as follows: there
are numerous kinds of covenant which
assure bounties and gifts to the worthy,
but the highest form of covenant is I
myself." He shows and points to Himself, insofar as He can be shown Who is
above all showing, by the words. "And
I," and adds: "Behold my covenant,"
the beginning and the fountain of all
bounties is "I myself." For to some men
God is wont to extend His benefits by
other means, by earth, water, air, sun,
moon, heaven, and other immaterial
agencies, but to others by Himself
alone, making Himself the portion of
those who receive Him.

Thus all the gifts of God are contained in the Covenant
granted to man, including God Himself, Who is the source of
all gifts. And the Covenant, once attaining this level of
intimacy and friendship with God, becomes the symbol of the
loftiest, the most direct, and the most loving influence of

God on the soul, as Philo says in the same context: "Now covenants are drawn up for the benefit of those who are worthy of the gift, and thus a covenant is a symbol of the grace which God has set between Himself, who bestows it, and man, who receives it. And this is the crowning benefaction, that there is nothing between God and the soul save virgin grace" (Mut. 52-53). All other powers have vanished away, even the Creator and the Lord, even the Logos and Wisdom, and nothing remains with the soul but virginal grace, or the Charities, symbols of the Covenant, i.e., of the direct gift of divine love.

We have just seen one of the forms of God's operation in the soul, the most direct of all. As for the other forms, they find their way to us through the divine powers combined in various hierarchies, with which we have dealt before.[13]

2. The allegories of virtue

Philo finds allegories of virtue particularly in the holy women of the Pentateuch. Not all women in it are virtuous, indeed, but even those who are not virtuous can, even by their blameworthy disposition teach us something about the attitude we should avoid if we desire virtue. This is not simply a moral teaching about actions we should accomplish or avoid as well as about the corresponding habits, for Philo does not deal with particular virtues, but with the general problem of virtue. Women are the types of virtue, because woman is the symbol of receptivity and of fecundity. Let us put it in this way, coining a formula of Philonic colour: woman is in man the theological locus of virtue, with all the ambiguity such a notion can imply. We shall deal now with the women who represent virtue, or its opposite, in the order in which they appear in Scripture.[14]

First is Eve, then, the woman known by Cain, and then the women of his lineage. We must concede that they are not paradigms of virtue, but they help us to understand how we can fail and even sink into sin. The wives of the Patriarchs and of Moses reveal an opposite process, which is the dialectics of virtue and no longer of sin.[15] In the Adamic allegory, Eve is a figure of the irrational part of the soul, and thus of man's receptivity to the external world through the senses, and, in contradistinction, the reduction of man's attention to the intelligible world and to God. The highest level of impiety is reached when Adam calls Eve "mine" (Gen. 2:22-23, cf. Leg. Al. II, 40), in other words when man sees himself as his own god, creator, and master. This stain on the origin of Cain is reflected in the sentence of Gen. 4:1-2, "And Adam knew his wife and she conceived and bare Cain, and he said, 'I have gotten a man through God'" (Cher. 40), because God is wrongly introduced as merely an instrumental cause (Cher. 124-126). The clause, "Cain knew his wife" (Gen. 4:17) implies the same attitude in Cain with regards to God and the world, as in Adam; but, whereas this attitude was only an error in Adam, who was inexperienced, it becomes a deliberate sin implying a greater guilt in Cain, who comes later. For this reason Cain, and not Adam, is the Protagoras of Scripture, i.e., the man who made man the measure of all things (Post. 33-35). We have studied the meaning of the Cain-Protagoras type in the chapter on cosmic eucharistia. We must now consider the second diptych of the figure of Cain - the father of Enoch, a name which means "thy grace." We are here in the internal domain of the soul, and we see Cain ascribing the absolute authorship of all the operations of the soul to himself. Philo comments on the etymology of the name Enoch "Enoch," as I have said, means "thy gift.". . . "Thy gift" is, on some people's lips, an address to the mind within us; on the lips of better men, it is addressed to the universal Mind. Those who assert that everything which is involved in thought or perception or speech is a free gift of their own soul, seeing that they introduce an impious and atheistic opinion, must be counted within the race of Cain, who, while incapable of ruling himself, made bold to say that he had full possession of all other things as well" (Post. 41). We must remember that, together with Protagoras, Cain is basically an Atheist, and that the understanding of man as the measure of all things should be given its fullest implication. This is more than subjectivism here, which can be interpreted in the good sense of a distrust of the self, but the affirmation that every kind of knowledge is a gift of the mind and of the senses and does not necessarily presuppose the objective existence of the external, sensible, and intelligible world, nor of the Creator, source of all things.

Cain's counterpart in the tenth generation is Lamech, who marries two wives, Ada and Sella (Gen. 4:19). Of course, the wives of him who is "ten times worse than Cain" can only be evils of the soul (Post. 79). Ada represents the success of the impious in the world, a success worse for the soul than failure (Post. 79-83). Her offspring are Jobel and Jubal (Gen. 4:21), respectively the symbols of the instability of the wicked (Post. 100) and of the discordant music of falsity (Post. 111). Sella means "shadow" and is a

symbol of bodily and external goods, which are nothing but
inconsistent shadows of the real goods, those of the soul
(Post. 112-113). Her offspring are Thobel (Gen. 4:22) and
Noeman. Thobel, or "all together," represents the man who
believes that he has acquired absolutely all things when he
has obtained health and wealth, but he does not know God
(Post. 115). Noeman, or "fatness," which is in this context
a symbol of weakness and not of strength, represents those
who deify Fortune and substitute it for God, considering it
as the source of bodily and external goods, while attributing to themselves the goods of the soul. The goods of
the soul are also represented by fatness, in its positive
sense, and destined for the altar, according to Lev. 3:16:
"All fat is the Lord's" (Post. 120-123).

After this series of women who represent the sinking of
the soul into atheistic materialism, let us turn now to the
wives of the Patriarchs and see how they illustrate the conflicts of the soul in the quest for virtue, or the quiet and
joyful possession of perfection. Abraham had two wives,
Sarah and Hagar, whose names respectively mean "sovereign"
and "sojourning" (Leg. Al. III, 244). Since Hagar represents one of the ways to perfection, paideia, i.e., the
school disciplines taught in the Hellenistic times, it was
proper that Sarah, who represents Wisdom or Virtue, should
entrust her handmaid Hagar to the care of Abraham, who was
to beget Ismael, the figure of the Sophist, from her. However, because of the inclination among Sophists to excel in
the art of persuasion without first seeking truth and good,
a correction in the use of paideia was necessary. When
Hagar, rebuked by Sarah, flees from her the first time, she
meets the angel of God, or the Logos, at the well and,
obeying His word, she accepts discipline from Sarah. Later,
Sarah will dismiss Hagar definitively, but for another
reason, because it is not becoming for a cultured man to
stay for ever in the field of sciences and letters, which is
of a secondary interest, considered as only a step toward
wisdom. After acquiring virtue through learning, or, at
best, through the effort of learning, he is invited to
humility by Scepticism, which is the summit of science, and
led to faith; he must, as a man now sufficiently mature in
thought, join the lawful wife, wisdom, represented by Sarah
(Cher. 9-10). Before this moment, Sarah could not beget
children by Abraham,[16] but now she becomes pregnant. In
fact, her pregnancy is the result of the grace of God, who
is the true father of Isaac, the perfect disposition and
happiness (Leg. Al. III, 219). At the same time, God
changes the names of Abraham and of Sarah. We have
explained above the meaning of the addition to the name of

Abraham (Mut. 70), which refers more specifically to the
problem of faith in the context of Cosmic religion. The
change of Sarah's name is more important for us here.
"Sarai," or "my Sovereign," becomes "Sarah," or simply
"Sovereign." In other words, specific virtues, considered
as possessions of man and perishable with him, disappear
with the coming of generic virtue, which is not a human
achievement but a divine power. The man who welcomes
generic virtue and cleaves to it as to a source of energy, a
perfection which comes to him from on high, recognizes it as
higher reality and properly calls it "sovereign" in the
absolute sense of the term. To this woman man must yield.
She becomes pregnant for him, if not by him (Leg. Al. III,
180-181). The plantation of virtue, or the seed of virtue,
which grows in the soul, is of divine origin. Virtue is
properly the life of the soul, a divine plantation and tends
to turn into eternal life. In this sense, we can say that,
for Philo as well as for Origen and the Fathers of the
Church, the soul is both mortal and immortal - mortal when
it is deprived of the life of divine grace, but immortal if
it manages to persevere in this grace. Of course, like
Origen and the platonizing Fathers of the Church, Philo
accepts the teaching of Phaedo on the indestructibility of
the soul and on bodily death. The central point we want to
underline in the teaching of Philo on Sarah is what he
understands as her "mystery" in Scripture (Cher. 43-52).
Sarah, who represents Wisdom, or rather Generic Virtue, is a
woman. As such, she receives seed from God, becomes pregnant, and brings forth Isaac, the symbol of Joy and of the
perfection through nature. But she begets for man and
becomes the possession of man, without ceasing to be a
divine possession for which thanks should be given to God.
In man, she now assumes a quasi-masculine function, just as
she earlier assumed a feminine function with regard to God.
She confers life and immortality on the soul, brings about
good deeds, and invites us to give thanks to God. Blessed
is the man who is willing to be made more manly by the power
of divine Virtue: everything becomes easy for him, and his
offspring will be perfection and joy. He represents the
ideal type of Man, realized through nature, that is to say,
as if through magic. The type of Isaac represents this
divine fruit in man, a type which we may add, is strongly
eucharistic (Cher. 106). Miserable, on the contrary, is the
man who affirms his masculinity over virtue as over every
other thing he finds in himself. This man belongs to the
type of Cain, or of the philautoi (lovers of the self). He
believes that he is the father of virtue (we remember the
interpretation of the name Enoch: "thy grace," i.e., the
things of the soul are the products of the mind and senses),

but he is the father only of perishable things, which are thus marked by impiety. They perish together with him or are themselves a source of death. Denying divine paternity of virtue amounts to failing in our duty of thanksgiving, offending God who is the real author of virtue, and severing ourselves from the source of life either by a conscious or a blind pride. One could even say that Sarah, in becoming pregnant, recovered, rather than lost, her virginity: she has passed from the condition of a defiled woman to that of a virgin, which is natural for her and is not defiled through intercourse with God. In fact, divine penetration makes her as pure and blooming as possible, radiant with divine glory. Philo exploits in this regard the strange statement that Sarah's menstrual periods had stopped long before, so that she could not beget life in a womb which was already dead. The point, of course, is the generation of virtue in man: virtue, defiled by human pride or by self-satisfaction, can, when regenerated by God, regain purity from every impiety and strength from divine power.

This enables us to better understand the mystery of Rebecca, Isaac's only wife, whose name means "constancy." Isaac needs only constancy in virtue, because he already has virtue (Congr. 37-38; Q.G. IV, 146). Philo writes beautiful pages on Isaac and Rebecca (for instance, Q.G. IV, 92-110), although his treatise on Isaac has been lost. The pedagogy of Rebecca is particularly interesting, reminding us of some aspects of the "true Gnostic" of Clement of Alexandria (Strom. VI and VII, particularly VI, 17). Let us note that Rebecca lowers her water-jar at the well of Bethuel to quench the thirst of Abraham's servant, and that she hastens back to the spring to fill the troughs for his camels, who symbolize memory (Q.G. IV, 124). Philo shows through this symbolism the liberality with which a master should bestow his knowledge on his students and the necessity of adjusting his teaching to them. In addition, filling their memory with knowledge, he enables them to exploit the potentialities of his teaching through further reflection in the secret of their souls. The servant rightly pays homage to Rebecca when he presents her with jewelry. The earrings and bracelets represent thanks for the teachings treasured in memory, and for the good deeds which are derived from them (Q.G. IV, 109).

But the point which we want to emphasize more particularly is the youth of Rebecca. Philo asks why Isaac, after he married Rebecca and loved her, was consoled about the death of his mother (Q.G. IV, 146, on Gen. 24:67). The answer is that Rebecca is none other than Sarah, but a

rejuvenated Sarah, blooming in her extra-temporal reality.
She was an old woman when the soul was in need of protection
and of discipline, but now she assumes the appearance of a
glamorous bride in the bloom of her youth, a sign of joy and
unending fecundity. How can we not think of the passage in
Shepherd of Hermas where the church first appears as an old
and crippled lady who progressively recovers the vigor and
the charm of her youth.[17] We find another parallel in Eph.
5:5-33, the mystery of the Church as the Bride and the Body
of Christ,whose union with Christ confers on her a purifying
and rejuvenating power.

Let us come now to the two wives of Jacob - Leah, who
represents hated virtue, and Rachel, who represents the profane judgement passed on the visible world. Leah corresponds to the rational part, and Rachel, to the irrational
part of the soul (Congr. 24-29). The two wives of Jacob,
therefore, symbolize the conflicts which tear the soul of a
ascetic and the choice which he is required to make, probably more than once, between the two antagonists, virtue
and pleasure. Of course, this antagonism reflects a controversy about the notion of happiness, into which, as we
shall see Philo enters. He refers particularly to the trial
of Hercules who, at the cross-roads, was invited to choose
between pleasure and virtue, and elected the latter. Jacob
is, in some respects, the Hercules of Scripture. He is the
type of the ascetic who progresses toward perfection through
practice. The respective situation and behaviour of his
two wives illustrates the problems which the quest for virtue raises for him. Leah is a fecund woman, and Rachel is
barren, because, though hated, virtue is fruitful, but the
predominance of the irrational part of the soul is barren
with regards to the production of the true good. God,
accordingly, "opened the womb of Leah, but Rachel was
barren" (Gen. 29:31, cf. Leg. Al. II, 47). We are once more
confronted with the already familiar theory of the divine
insemination of virtue. But Rachel's demand to Jacob,
"Give me children" (Gen. 30:1-3), introduces a complementary
meaning. The irrational part of the soul, on the one hand,
is easily attracted by the charm of external things and is
even enflamed by pleasure; on the other hand, it tends to
consider the mind as its god and to ascribe the divine
attributes to it. Adam yielded to this temptation, and Cain
made it his own dogma, putting the mind in the place of God.
But Jacob wisely answers Rachel, "Am I in the place of God?"
(Gen. 30:2), implying that the ascetic knows who is his
Master and his God, and that his struggle is not that of a
profane asceticism, but that of religion. Asceticism, for
Philo, consists in obedience to God, in the service of God:

it is theocentric and not anthropocentric. Moreover, it is
also theocentric in its principle, since the ascetic expects
the seed of virtue and the help of divine grace for growing
it from God himself.

Finally, Leah is the mother of Judah, the symbol of
confession, praise and thanksgiving, a fact which confirms
her eucharistic character. Judah, in some respects, is a
second Isaac, a man possessed by God, an enthusiast. The
comparison between him and Issachar, the figure of the ascetic claiming his reward as due to him, will lead us later to
raise the problem of merit, which, in our opinion, is very
important in Philo's thought because it involves the success
or the failure of the ascetic advanced in the way of virtue
in regard to the principle of piety toward God. But our
present concern is the contrast between Leah and Rachel,
which we continue by comparing their offspring. Joseph is
the eldest son of Rachel: as we can expect from such an
origin, he presents a composite character. In allegorical
commentaries, he is judged pejoratively as the symbol of
those compromises with the world which in practice ruin the
ideals of contemplative life and perfection. We shall find
him again in the next section, which deals with Philo's cri-
ticsm of specific philsophies. In De Josepho, as we said in
another study,[18] following E.E. Goodenough, Joseph represents another aspect of the quest for perfection, namely,
the political man. This man is divided, threatened, and
sometimes enslaved by his own passions in his soul and by
currents of popular favour from outside. His vocation, however, is a lofty one, and his intervention is beneficial if
he manages to remain free and able to govern. He will be,
within himself and in the government of the city, the inter-
preter of the dreams of life, the judge of genuine values,
and the prudent and incorruptible leader who prefers to be
victimized rather than to give up his own ideals of political life. This image of Joseph is found in the servant of
divine providence who saves his own people, at least on the
level of earthly things, who introduces himself as a "man of
God" in spite of his internal division (Jos. 266; Migr.
22), and whose bones are honored by being carried to the
sepulchre of his forefathers as a sign of personal salvation. We are all, in the city of our own individual life,
types of Joseph, and we are all called to be Joseph in the
larger circle of domestic society, of our ethnic community,
and of the city. Philo himself, to some extent, represented
this type. His ideal of perfection is not without diversity, since besides contemplative life, there is a place for
active life and nobody, in his opinion, is well-prepared for

contemplative life unless he has first proved himself in the
duties of active life (Fug. 34-38).[19]

We could discuss with Philo the complementary light
shed upon the problem of virtue by the allegories of the
concubines of Abraham, Jacob, and others. Jacob's concubines are Zilpah and Billah - reasoning and adequate expression respectively (Congr. 30-33). There are also those of
the wicked like Amalek (Congr. 54-60), and the Canaanite
wives of Esau (perhaps Congr. 61). But we would not learn
much more from this discussion about the problems with which
we are concerned. Tamar is a far more original figure, with
a complex meaning, two aspects of which deserve to be
pointed out in this context. She is the symbol of the
insemination of virtue by God when Judah acknowledges that
he did not give her to any man. She is also the symbol of
asceticism when she gains possession of Judah's staff and
belt, which represent discipline and firmness against the
passions (Mut. 135-136).[20] Moses' wife, Zipporah (Ex.
2:21), whose name "bird" represents the winged, inspired and
prophetic nature, is not taken as a wife by Moses, but is
given him by God (Post. 77), and she is inseminated by God,
not by Moses (Cher. 41-47), in keeping with the theory of
the divine origin of virtue. Moses also receives the
Ethiopian woman as a wife from God (Numb. 12:1), and it is
unjustly that his sister Miriam finds fault with him, "for
this Moses deserves much praise that he took to him the
Ethiopian woman, even nature which has been tried by fire
and cannot be changed. For even as in the eye the part that
sees is black, so the soul's power of vision has been called
a woman of Ethiopia" (Leg. Al. II, 67; cf. Leg. Al. I, 76).
Here, the Ethiopian woman represents perfect nature, completed with virtue, which Moses was worthy to receive. One
final woman deserves to be mentioned among the symbols of
virtue, although she does not belong to the Pentateuch--
Hannah, the mother of Samuel, whose name appears repeatedly
in Philo. This is not surprising, for Hannah means "grace"
(Mut. 143-144). She is also the symbol of the soul made
pregnant by God: "But the word 'barren' she applies to the
mind which refuses to accept any mortal insemination as
fruitful, and which, rejecting and suppressing all the inti-
macies and the matings of the wicked, holds fast to the
'seventh' and the supreme peace which it gives. This peace
she wishes to bear in her womb and be called its mother" (Mut.
144; cf. Deus. 10; Praem. 159-160). As a consequence, there
is in Hannah a joy which overflows into her canticle (I Sam.
2:1-11), the sober drunkenness of ecstasy or of the divine
possession of the soul, which is a prophetic charism.
Hannah is also called to the highest form of sacrifice, the

offering of the self to God (Ebr. 143-153). Accordingly, her son is properly called Samuel, or "appointed to God" (Deus 5-6; 10-13), since she returns him to God who had first given him to her in a gesture of eucharistic character (Deus 5-7).

3. The laws on the attitude to be taken toward grace

We have already observed the eucharistic character which completes the various allegories about the life of virtue as the fruit of grace. We take this for granted, and we shall add here only those precisions which stem from the laws about thanksgiving. These laws determine the attitude we must adopt or avoid toward grace. We have already presented them for the first-fruits and the first-born in their literal meaning (the material offering required for obedience to the Law of Moses) and in their symbolic meaning (the offering of the goods of the soul and that of the soul itself).[21] For what concerns us here, the relations between divine grace and the life of virtue, we can hardly depend on literal exegesis, which usually refers to external things, but we must expect to see these laws interpreted symbolically.

Among the laws on the first-fruits, let us consider Deut. 8:12-20: "Beware lest you say in your heart, 'My power and the might of my hand have gotten me this wealth.' You shall remember the Lord your God, for it is he who gives you power to get wealth; that he may confirm his covenant which he swore to your fathers, as at this day" (17-18). Philo does not challenge the literal implication of this law, but directs his exegesis toward the goods of the soul for which thanks should be given. It would be vain and disastrous, indeed, to progress in the way of virtue and to crown oneself for this progress, as if God were not its principal cause. What would the pursuit of virtue mean, if it should end in the impiety of philautia (self-love)? (Agr. 169-173). The interpretation of Deut. 6:10-13 is quite similar: we must acknowledge that the goods of the soul as represented by the cities, houses, cisterns, vineyards and olive-trees--generic and specific virtues, as well as good deeds--are the gift of God (Fug. 176-201, cf. Deut. 6:10-13). The same can be said for the law on loans (Spec. Leg. IV, 30-38, concerning Ex. 22:6-14), which is also interpreted in the sense of the goods of the soul in Her. 110 (cf. Spec. Leg. II, 7), and for the law on the Nazir (Numb. 6:21), because the offering made by the author of the great vow according to the power of his hands represents the

virtues or talents which everyone has received from God and
for which he must pay homage to God (Mut. 218-225). On the
contrary, the man who inscribes himself as a slave forever
(Cher. 72-74, cf. Ex. 21:5) represents the one who has
accepted the mind and the senses as his master instead of
God, whose service is the equivalent of freedom (Ebr. 144).

The laws on the first-fruits and on the first-born are
similarly interpreted. In addition to their literal
meaning, they refer to the homage due to God for the goods
of the soul, and especially for virtue and its resulting
fruits, thoughts and deeds. Such is the meaning given to
the law of Lev. 19:23-25, concerning the fruits of a four
year old tree (Virt. 159), of Numb. 28:2, on sacrifices,
which reappears so often in Philo (Deus 6-9; Leg. Al. III,
196; Cher. 84), of Lev. 2:1-2, and Ex. 29:38-39 concerning
daily burnt-offerings accompanied by an offering of fine
flour from the priests (Her. 174; Som. II, 71-74), of Ex.
23:19; 25:1-2; 13:1-2, on the first-fruits and the first-
born (Sacr. 74; Her. 113; 117-118), of Lev. 23:10, on the
first sheaf (Som. II, 76), of Lev. 27:30-32, on tithes
(Congr. 96), etc.

A third series of laws may be mentioned which, in addition to their literal implication, also have a symbolic
meaning concerning the manner in which thanks should be
given without delay, just as a vow should be fulfilled without delay, according to Deut. 23:21 (cf. Sacr. 52-53), and
first for the highest goods, i.e., for the good movements of
the soul, then for the body and the rest, according to Ex.
23:19 (cf. Sacr. 72-73). In fact, such a law is unnecessary for a righteous man, who shows his gratitude spontaneously, without waiting for an injunction, because gratitude is not something which can be commanded (Q.E. II, 50
about Gen. 8:20, Noah building an altar without being
ordered). And we are familiar with the laws concerning the
division of burnt-offerings (Lev.1:3-17, and Lev. 2:14),
which represent the order to be observed in giving thanks,
mentioning first the universe and its parts, then the entire
human race, individual man, the things of the soul, in order
to escape confusion and to omit nothing important (Spec.
Leg. I, 198-219; Sacr. 82-85; Q.G. I, 64). We also know
that nothing doubtful or evil must be offered to God,
because God is the cause of every good, but not of evil.
For this reason, Seth is blamed (Q.G. I, 78, about Gen.
4:25), and the offering of the harlot is rejected (Deut.
23:18, cf. Spec. Leg. I, 280-284). All those who try to
secure the favour of God by bribe, often with dishonestly
acquired money are identified with the harlot, since God

cannot accept becoming their accomplice.   Nor are the heart
or brain of the victims offered upon the altar (Lev. 3:3),
for these organs are associated with the sovereign part of
the soul, which is capable of both good and evil and is
therefore not essentially good (Sacr. 136-139).

III.   PARALLELS TO THESE TEACHINGS IN GREEK PHILOSOPHY AND
       IN JUDAISM

    1. God as source of light

    The teachings of Philo on these questions are not
entirely of his own invention.   He probably found them more
or less complete in Alexandrian Judaism and in Greek philosophy, and they are not without parallel in Rabbinic
Judaism.   We have made such an investigation above for
Alexandrian Judaism, and we have discovered, particularly in
the Letter of Aristeas, a highly developed notion of grace.
We now turn to the philosophers and to Judaism.   We are
looking for teachings concerning God as enlightening minds,
as sowing the seeds of virtue, and as giving them growth;
concerning the nature of ideas or energies which come to man
from on-high; concerning the various aspects of virtue and
the method of its acquisition; and finally concerning prophecy and ecstasy, or the way in which inspiration appears
in man. We know that Philo is precise and original, on all
these points because he examines them by means of his
favourite allegories, those of the wives of the Patriarchs,
who illustrate the relation of the life of virtue to God.
Philo, indeed, depends on others for these teachings, but he
confers such a personal stamp through allegory on his
borrowings that they are restructured.   In addition, the
context into which they are inserted is proper to Philo.   In
our identification of these materials, we must therefore
remember that they are only sources or parallels.

    The first of these teachings is the notion of God as
source of light, radiant with grace, counsel, and force.
The biblical sources of this teaching are so well known that
it would be useless to enumerate them, and it is better to
take them for granted. We shall simply mention a few biblical images of grace and illustrate each of them with an
example from Philo.   There is, for instance, the image of
rain, very frequent in Philo (Deus 155; Spec. Leg.   II, 53),
that of the manna (Leg. Al. III, 166-171),[22] of the source
(Deus. 155), of the radiance of God (Praem. 45), of
purifying and repairing warmth (Q.E. II, 28-29), of the
pedagogue using chastisement out of love for the advantage

of his disciple (Sacr. 101), of help (Post. 31), of the
benefactor (Congr. 171), of the pattern offered for our imitation (Dec. 73), of the judge (Ap. A. on Gen. Book I, no.
89), of the sower (Migr. 139-142), and of the father. The
last image may either have the same meaning as the one which
immediately precedes it, or it may simply refer to the providence of a father toward his children or of a worker
toward his work (Op. 23:25).

        In the philosophers, these ideas appear insofar as they
have a theology, although this theology is sometimes
vitiated by pantheism, for instance in the Stoics, or, on
the contrary, it teaches a God so completely transcendent
that He cannot exercise direct providence in the world and
in the human soul. Philo certainly depends on Plato and on
the young Aristotle of De philosophia for his belief in the
reality of the Forms or of the Heavens, and in their
influence on the intelligence and will of man, as well as
upon the whole of the universe.²³ He also certainly depends
on the Stoics and probably on the Cynics when he applies the
maxims concerning the wise man to God: God alone is wise,
free, happy, immutable, and the only citizen of the world.²⁴
Consequently, every wise man on earth is wise by participation in God, the only wise One. On the other hand, the Hymn
of Cleanthes presents such a clear parallel to Philo that we
would be tempted to consider it as a direct source if the
teachings contained in it were not commonplace in the time
of Philo. We read in the Hymn, for instance, that everything except for the crimes of the wicked, depends on God,
that God is Saviour and Benefactor, that He provides the
goods of the soul, and that the soul will praise God if it
has previously received the illumination of God. It is not
irrelevant for our inquiry to note in Cleanthes the idea
that, in return for the divine gift--let us understand by
this the contemplation of the order of the world by the
mind--the soul sings to God (time, verse 35-39). This is
close, if not identical, to the Philonic idea of eucharistia
for the goods of the soul.²⁵

        Is there in the philosophers, or in Judaism, a teaching
on the operation of God in the world, and especially in the
soul, comparable to Philo's theory of the divine powers? On
the Jewish side, there are certainly semi-hypostasized
entities, considered as created before the world, whose
influence is destined to intervene in the world and in the
hearts of men at the proper time. Wolfson notes, in relation to Philo's famous distinction between God and Lord, the
former (theos) corresponding to the Hebrew Elohim, the
latter (kyrios), to Yahweh, that an ancient Palestinian

tradition identified the goodness of God with Elohim, and His severity with Yahweh.[26] On this point, therefore, Philo may not be alone in Judaism. Can the same be said concerning the other Philonic powers? To speak about angels in Judaism would not help very much, although angels occupy a far more important place in Judaism than in Philo. However, whether they are messengers of God as found in Judaism, or souls of the heavenly bodies and non-incarnate souls, as we find in Philo, they are creatures and not powers of God. In order to find a parallel to the Philonic powers, we must turn to the Jewish speculations concerning Wisdom, the Law, the Shekinah (the Presence of God), the Word, which are creatures of God, but anterior to and superior to the world, and which exercise a quasi-divine power over the world, particularly among men. These entities which reappear deeply altered in Philo's hierarchies of divine powers, may be considered as of Jewish heritage.[27-28]

We find parallels in Hellenism to the Philonic powers which are as interesting as those within Judaism.[29] There are many deified abstractions, such as Justice, Peace, Victory, Grace, Fate, etc., not to mention the multiple names ascribed to the classical gods, names which confer upon them a certain plurality of meaning. It would be wrong to assume that the Greek contemporaries of Philo considered these deities as persons properly speaking, even when they worshiped them. Nor is it exact either to consider them as mere abstractions, for they appear as energies, whose reality we perceive by experience. This notion becomes current in Hellenism through the Stoics, whose pantheism consisted of abstract deities of this kind and of popular gods who became mere names for elements or forces of nature. Bréhier makes this observation in his section on the mythology of the powers.[30] Philo, he says, inherits this notion, but, if he knows forces like these--either accepting them as in the case of Justice (Jos. 170-171), envy (Jos. 5), or the Charites (Migr. 180-183), or rejecting them partially as in the case of Fate (Migr. 180-183), or conferring on God divine titles or attributes current in Hellenism, such as Soter, nikephoros, euergetes, tropheus, ploutophoros, megalodoros, etc.--he nevertheless turns to formulas borrowed from Scripture and uses them to build his diverse hierarchies of powers: for instance, the Word of God, the Ark of the Covenant, the cities of refuge, the distinction God-Lord, etc. The powers are the many instruments used by God to work in the world, and particularly in souls.[31]

We may consider in this section about the God who
radiates with light and energy the notion of prophecy. This
notion undoubtedly belongs to the biblical heritage, and
such is the affirmation of Philo. He knows three forms of
inspiration: prediction through the divine spirit when the
prophet is in ecstasy; prediction or legislation through
divine voice, as on Sinai; and prophecy through the intermediary of angels. He also accepts the inspiration of the
translator in the case of LXX (Mos. II, 37-40). On the
other hand, he recognizes four functions or charisms in
Moses: king, priest, lawgiver, and prophet (Mos. II, 1-7).
This analysis is the fruit of Greek thought, and Philo
transposes it into the domain of Holy Writ, just as he does
for many other philosophical teachings. The three types of
inspiration have parallels in Plato, for instance in Timaeus
71 e -72 b,[32] and in the Stoics, for instance in Posidonius
concerning the interpretation of dreams, according to
Cicero.[33] And the four powers of Moses as king, priest,
lawgiver, and prophet in relation to the four forms of prophecy (mania) also appear in Plato.[34] For the question of
prophecy in all its aspects, we refer the reader to Wolfson
and to Hans Lewy.[35]

2. God as Sower

The allegories of the divine generation of virtue,
using Sarah, Rebecca, Leah, Hannah, etc., form the center of
Philo's esoteric teaching. They are not, however,
unparalleled in Hellenistic culture and in Judaism. It is
important to know what sources Philo could have used in this
regard. Bréhier tries to identify the elements of Philo's
theory of the divine generation:

> We are confronted with one of these
> hierogamies which are found throughout
> Greek religion, and especially in the
> mysteries of the Hellenistic times. But
> we can be more precise: the essential
> feature of this mythology is the virgin-
> bride of God (or of the Logos), called
> sophia, episteme, or arete, who brings
> forth the world. The idea of a bride-
> mother preserving her virginity is
> familiar to the Orphists: in the latter
> writings known through the testimony of
> Proclus, Korah is the undefiled virgin
> who preserves her integrity in genera-
> tion. Moreover, although married to

Zeus, the same virgin (nymphe achrantos)
is the life-giving cause of the world;
in the cycle of her three lives, this
goddess, like Sarah, is virgin and
mother. On the other hand, Wisdom, in
Philo, is the daughter of God: Sarah
(the sophia or arete of Cherubim) is
without a mother (ametor): in other
words, she does not originate from
matter, which is called the mother of
existences, but from the Cause and
Father of the universe. One immediately
thinks of the Athena of Greek mythology,
who is called ever-virgin and without a
mother. The combination of bride and
daughter of God has a striking parallel
in the combination of Artemis and Athena
in the Orphists. However, the triad
cause-virtue-product of both also
requires an explanation. There are many
triads in Hellenic and Hellenistic
mythology: their symbolic interpretation explains how they may have found
access into Philo's thought; John Lydus
cites from Terpander the triad
Zeus-Persephone-Dionysios. But the
allegories of De Iside et Osiride provide the chief contribution: Osiris is
principle; Isis, receptacle; Horos, the
product.[36]

Bréhier then points out Philo's originality with regard to
these presumed sources in an observation of the greatest
importance: "However, there is still a difference; Philo
almost entirely substitutes the moral generation, happiness
and virtue, for the explanation of the world."

Goodenough goes further. Generally agreeing with
Pascher's conclusion (Konigsweg, pp. 60-68) about the
"Persian source," he introduces the three sources of
Plutarch as found in some way in Philo:

I do not think that Pascher has said the
last word on the matter. I feel that he
has not recognized the problem of the
two types of Mystery, that of Sophia and
that of the Powers, and that he has
similarly confused the Persian source
with the Isiac. Plutarch has actually

three sources, not two, for the
mythology of his De Iside, one Egyptian,
one Persian, and one Greek, the three
fused and interpreted in mystic philosophy of Greek origin. How much the combination of the three mythologies, or
their interpretation, is his own work it
is now impossible to say, but the
writings of Philo seem to me to indicate
that they were all in process of combination at least by his time.'⁷ . . .
What is clear is that a pleroma conception of the Light-Stream, apparently of
Persian origin, and a Female Principle
conception, of whatever origin, have
both forced themselves upon the Judaism
Philo represents,and that he is content
with treating them, like Plutarch, as
parallels, without adequately fusing
them.³⁸

Festugière opposes the historians of religions in their
tendency to look to the East for the source of Hellenistic
teachings:

The idea of the First Principle as
"male-female" may be commonplace in the
East. However, before inquiring in this
direction, and absolutely affirming that
this notion must come from the East,
when, I repeat, no ancient text witnesses to a direct transmission, why not
look to Greece, where explicit texts
show how this idea appeared?³⁹
(Commenting on Leg. Al. III, 180-181,
concerning the Philonic theory of the
seeds of virtue Festugiere adds:) I
quoted this pious amphigori in its
entirety because it witnesses to an
important step in the long history of
the wedding of God and the soul. In
Philo, there are probably many origins
for this idea. There should be an echo
of the hieros-gamos, peculiar to certain
initiation rites: otherwise, we do
not see any reason for such a broad use
of the language of mysteries in this

text.   Philo also   probably has in mind
the biblical image of   the marriage
between God and Israel (Os. ch. 1 and
3: Ez.   ch. 16 and 23).   But another
influence seems essential to me, that of
the Symposion of Plato.   The ascent   to
the Beautiful is also   presented as an
initiation with several steps (209 e 6-
210 a 2).   Similarly there   is a
mystagogue   or hierophant (211 c 1-4),
and the goal of the initiation is a
generation (212 a).   The soul, marrying
not an appearance of the Beautiful but
the Beautiful itself,   therefore, begets
not appearances of virtue   but true
virtue, thus becoming herself immortal.
Moreover, this idea of the generation of
virtue at the conclusion of the intia-
tion only   repeats one of the chief
themes of   Diotime's   discourse,   the
fecundity of the soul (208 e -209 e).
And this theme itself is brought in by
the general idea of the book, the love
for beauty.   For the idea of love, in
the Ancients,   easily leads to that of
procreative   union: "By   begetting
children,   one   seeks   to   acquire
immortality, lasting fame, and happiness
for the future" (208 e).   It therefore
seems to me that we should see in this
discourse of Diotime the   direct source
of the Philonic elucubrations.[40]

The same is not true for the symbolism used by Philo to
express this idea, and Festugière does not know of any
source for it anterior to Philo:

There is still a difference, as noted by
Bréhier.[41]   Philo's symbolism, like that
of all our texts, does not refer to the
genesis of the cosmos, but to spiritual
generation, either of the virtues in the
soul (Philo, Corpus Hermeticum IX 3; I
Petri; Passio Caeciliae), or of the new
man (Corpus Hermeticum XIII, Pap. Mag.
Paris).   This is an original aspect
whose source I cannot identify.   The
Greek mysteries have nothing of this

> kind, and, even supposing that all our
> texts depend on it, we should still
> accept that someone, for the first time,
> has transposed rites and formulas to the
> moral domain, which referred very con-
> cretely to the divine uiothesia (son-
> ship) of the initiated man. Who is this
> innovator? That, we do not know.[42]

Monique Alexandre, who agrees with Festugière concerning the philosophical sources of this theory, underlines
the importance of biblical sources:

> The pre-existing Wisdom who lives with
> God (Prov. 8:22, quoted in Ebr. 31) can
> easily be represented as the bride of
> God. The books of Wisdom tell us about
> the wise man that he desired to be
> united to Wisdom as to a wife (Wis.
> 8:2.9.16). The idea of the love of God
> for Israel may also have contributed to
> the formation of the symbolism of the
> wedding of God and the soul, as shown by
> Philo in Cher. 49-51, referring to Jer.
> 3:4.[43]

Mrs. Alexandre, at the same time, points to the eucharistic
aspect of the virginal fecundity of wisdom in Philo:
"Wisdom, 'bearing ceaselessly' (Congr. 3-4) and 'for God
only,' 'thankfully rendering the first fruits of the
blessings, bestowed upon her, to Him who, as Moses says,
opens the womb which remains virgin" (tas aparchas on
etuchen agaton eucharistos apodidousa to ten aeipartheon
metran... anoixanti, Congr. 7, cf. Gen. 29:31).[44]-[45]

Let us add one observation: the theory of the divine
seeds of virtue certainly precedes Philo, and he could
easily be acquainted with it, for there are many signs of
its existence in his time. Certain connections, however,
such as those with the "Persian and Egyptian" sources presented by Brehier, Pascher and Goodenough, can be
challenged, because the best texts which are brought for-
ward, Chaldaic Oracles, Corpus Hermeticum, and Plutarch's De
Iside et Osiride, although echoing earlier teachings, are
generally posterior to Philo. Great discretion is therefore
necessary in the use of non-Greek sources. On the other
hand, as we have shown, Philo's synthesis is consistent,
developed, and biblical, even when he discovers in biblical

figures ideas which have nothing in common with the literal meaning.   We must, therefore, grant the biblical sources a great importance with regard to form, and also some importance with regard to ideas.[46-47]

3. The three ways to acquire virtue

Having discussed the mystery of the divine generation of virtue, we may now come to less esoteric teachings and discuss the three ways leading to perfection, or the three ways to acquire virtue.   This discussion is classical from the time of Plato.   Philo recognizes in Abraham the way of learning, in Isaac inborn virtue, and in Jacob the way of asceticism.   For each of these three ways, it is the matrimonial situations of the Patriarchs, as we observed before, which provide materials for the discussion.   Hagar represents the way of learning, since Encyclopedic studies pave the way to the acquisition of wisdom.   Rebecca symbolizes that constancy which the perfect one should preserve in the love for virtue.   Leah and Rachel represent the internal conflict of the ascetic who must choose between pleasure and virtue, and the choice which he must make in favour of the hard way.   Of course, these three ways are not independent, but concurrent and complementary (Abr. 52-54). Actually, the type of each of the Patriarchs is found in each of us, although in different proportions.

What can be the background for this discussion? Bréhier, who studies this question in his chapter on moral progress summarizes the sense and development of the debate:

> Cynicism was one of the most exclusive
> moral doctrines of antiquity; in it,
> asceticism is the only way to virtue.
> The Cynics did not think that nature
> could predispose to virtue, and they
> virulently rejected the doctrine of the
> Sophists that culture can lead us to
> fulfil the ideals of life. Socrates was
> less exclusive when, although putting
> the science of concepts at the basis of
> virtue, subjected the development of
> this science to a condition in the
> will: self-mastery (egkrateia).   Plato,
> after doubting for a long time whether
> virtue can be learned, finally accepted
> the necessity of, in the one hand,

science and, on the other, of some
natural or innate dispositions, which he
ascribed to the operation of God.
Aristotle gives a definitive formula of
the same idea, admitting that virtue is
acquired through nature, asceticism, and
instruction (physei, askesei, mathesei),
thus combining the teachings of his
forerunners in a striking formula
(Aristotle, ap. Diogenes Laertius, V,
18). The Stoics, who first laid the
emphasis upon the development of the
will, admitted that virtue is as theore-
tical as it is practical. This problem,
indeed, was one of the most debated in
the time of Philo.[48]

a) The way of learning

Philo accepts the three ways. The problem, for him, is
to see that they lead us to our goal and bring us to a
eucharistic disposition. We remember the type of Cain who,
because of self-confidence (philautia), killed the opposite
disposition represented by Abel, which consisted in
referring every good thing to God (Sacr. 88). Cain is the
anti-type of eucharistia. We also remember the Sophists,
the great builders of towers and strongholds against God
(Conf. 113; 129). The pursuit of learning and of dialectics, in the service of pride and in a quite anthropocentric
way, leads them to despise truth, God, and even their
brethren. We know how much Philo insists upon the idea that
all knowledge comes from God, and that the disorder inherent
to man, or original sin if one prefers, consists in the
failure, by forgetfulness, malice or error, to recognize God
as the author of all good things (Sacr. 52-58). Philo is
here condemning an intellectually oriented culture which is
self-satisfied to the point that it keeps man prisoner
within its limits rather than leading him to wisdom, i.e.,
to the generic virtue which is fruitful through and for God.
The conflict between Sarah and Hagar illustrates this idea
very well (Congr. 68-80; Leg. Al. III, 244-245; Q.G. III,
23-26), and there is no reason for further development in
this regard. We shall, therefore, only shed some more light
on it with a remark by Festugière concerning the specific
approach to, and evaluation of, science in antiquity:

> Man is created in order to contemplate
> the order of the universe, and, through
> this contemplation, to return to God
> (Timaeus 90 a-e). This conception, so
> detrimental to science, will become the
> rule later on. Learning physics will
> most often consist--after mentioning a
> few "harmonies of nature" which are
> almost always the same (the order of the
> heavens, the functional organization of
> the body)--in praising and blessing
> divine Providence which instituted so
> beautiful an order and arranged the
> human body so well for the functions
> which man must fulfil. Even more, every
> science which does not lead to this
> praise will be considered as unworthy of
> study. The author of Asclepius states
> this explicitly.[49]

Philo does not come to science as a lazy man who is
only looking for motives to bless God, without taking the
trouble of learning. His own formation is wide and up-to-
date,[50] and his scepticism is not the result of a vulgar
ignorance but a knowledge aware of its own limitations.[51]
The arts and sciences, however, are for him servants of
Wisdom, just as Hagar is the handmaid of Sarah. Moreover,
all the trouble which we take in learning, - often, he says,
the only fruit we derive from learning is the effort which
we have made, which has its own value in the eye of God, and
which is itself a gift of God (Sacr. 112-114) - is justified
only if done for a higher end, such as service to our
brethren (Jos. 54-57), the service of God through the prayer
of praise or of thanksgiving (Spec. Leg. I, 84-97), and the
posession of wisdom whose eucharistic character is known to
us (Congr. 6-8).

b) The way of nature

The second way is that of nature, and is represented by
Isaac. We have already noted the eucharistic character of
the divine Wisdom which permeates and guides Isaac, whereas
Rebecca represents its preservation and care. Isaac calls
our attention to the higher goods, since he is in possession
of the highest of all, Virtue, or Wisdom.[52]

Philo participates in the debate of philosophers concerning the nature of the good.   There are three kinds of
goods: external things, bodily things, and the things of
the soul.   Philo's position is well-balanced in this regard
and reflects that of Aristotle (Nic. Ethics, I, 1098 b).
Here he parts from the Stoic and Cynic ideals of perfection,
which do not acknowledge the value of earthly things.
Bréhier explains Philo's position concerning the three kinds
of goods in relation to philosophy:

> We know, from the 4th book of
> Cicero, De finibus, that Antiochus
> borrowed arguments from the Peripatetics
> for the attack on Stoic Ethics.   The
> Stoic ideals, which seems to be the
> chief reason for his attack, would be
> good for creatures reduced only to mind
> (De fin. IV, 12, 28), but for man bodily
> goods are truly goods.   We have seen
> that, also for Philo, Stoic perfection
> went beyond the limits of human nature
> and was only fit for pure intelligences.
> This is also the reason for which he
> sees value in Peripatetism, a meek and
> sociable philosophy which is fitting for
> us who are imperfect, for it affirms the
> goodness of external and bodily goods
> and of practical and political life.
> But in Philo, Peripatetism is not free
> of Stoic elements.   In his long exposi-
> tion of the theory of virtue as a middle
> between two extremes, the virtues chosen
> as examples: courage and piety, are
> defined in a Stoic manner.   Similarly,
> when he adopts the threefold division of
> the goods of the soul, the body, and
> external goods, ascribing the authorship
> of bodily goods to the tension of the
> mind, which, on its own endows the body
> with all the goods proper to it, he is
> interpreting Peripatetism in a Stoic
> sense.   These developments on a deeply
> altered Peripatetism, on the contrary,
> manifest close links to the conceptions
> of Antiochus. Like him Philo accepts
> the existence of inborn virtues such as
> domestic feelings and the happy disposi-
> tion.   In Philo, moreover, we find an

explanation of the idea that the doctrine of the threefold division of good
belongs to the political man. But we
know that Antiochus criticized the
Stoics precisely for completely elimin-
ating the political aspect by subordi-
nating all ethics to the portrait of the
Sage, and he shows how important this
aspect was for the Peripatetics.[53]

We must now determine the position of Philo on the
three kinds of goods in the context of his spiritual
teaching. Without insisting on the value granted by Philo
to material and bodily goods, let us only say that he
invites us to give thanks for them. He also urges us to
give thanks for spiritual goods: faculties of the soul,
virtues, and good deeds (Q.G. II, 52; Spec. Leg. I, 168-171;
270-284; Sacr. 73-76). We may add that Philo is not simpli-
stic on this question of the respective value of the three
goods. It would be wrong to consider him as a purely contemplative man, for he criticizes those who enter this way
of life without having first fulfilled their social duties
and found the best preparation in the acquisition of practical virtues for moving to a higher form of perfection, contemplative life.[54] On the other hand, although he complains
about the difficulties of active life--we know that he
accepted the courageous mission of defending the rights of
the Jewish community of Alexandria before the unpredictable
Emperor Caligula, and that, according to Goodenough,[55] he
probably assumed responsibilities and functions for
an unspecified number of years in his community of
Alexandria--his eagerness for the contemplative life did
not thereby diminish (Spec. Leg. III, 6). Moreover, if he
extols contemplative life, he also depicts the virtues of
practical life, and especially of social life, with much
warmth.

Philo, therefore, was a divided man, but the contradiction in his judgments in this regard is the mere reflection
of an inner conflict, or, rather, of a tension, never denied
and, always present, in the direction of higher ideals.
This brings us back to the ideals of contemplative life seen
only in its intellectual aspect. His ideal is wisdom, which
is knowledge and contemplation, as well as the possession of
virtue.[56] The representative of this ideal is Isaac, and we
thus return to the way of nature, which is the topic of the
present section. We now realize how easy it is to misunder-
stand the implications of this way and form of perfection.
We cannot consider it as the easy kind of perfection of a

mediocre or a lazy man, or of the too humanly cheerful and
sociable man. Moreover, if every virtue involves an element
of joy, according to Aristotle (Nic. Eth. 1098 a 16; Eud.
Eth. 1219 a 38), and if it is at the same time a true participation in divine perfection, the consequence is that virtue is divine, and that the accompanying joy is also
divine.[57]   God is wise, and God alone is happy. Isaac
possesses a happy disposition because he fosters the highest
ideal, and because he shares with God. Such is the position
Philo takes in the debate about happiness and the classifi-
cation of the goods. As he does on so many other points, he
resolves the problem ultimately by referring to God, who is
the principle and end of all things. Once more, the key to
his thought is found in the eucharistic disposition, or in
the perspective of faith and piety, or again in wisdom mani-
festing itself as confession and imitation of God. At the
same time we discover the bias which he imposes on all the
teachings which he integrates, and the complementary meaning
which he confers upon them.

c) The way of asceticism[58]

The way of asceticism is that of Jacob. It also leads
to perfection, or, more precisely, as we have seen, to contemplative life, for which it is the preparation. Such is
the meaning of the change of the name Jacob, the ascetic, to
Israel, the contemplative man, or the man who sees God (Ebr.
82-83). He has two wives, Leah and Rachel, who illustrate
the conflicts of his soul. What are the philosophical ante-
cedents of the Philonic teachings connected with these
persons? Briefly, the entire philosophy of the Greeks presents itself as a search for "better living," which, for the
best thinkers such as Plato and Aristotle, means contemplative life (Spec. Leg. I, 339).[59] Moreover, the conflict
between duty (virtue) and vice (yielding to pleasure) is an
old theme already illustrated in the Apologue of Hercules in
the Memorabilia of Xenophon (II, 1), who ascribes it to the
Sophist Prodicus. Hercules must choose between a harlot,
who represents pleasure, and the woman who represents
virtue. Similarly, Philo places man between vice and virtue
and obliges him, after listening to the plea of the two
parties to choose between ease and effort (ponos) (Sacr. 14-
15). The hated woman, who symbolizes virtue acquired by
effort, is Leah, and her counterpart is Rachel; but Leah is
privileged, since the Law acknowledges the right of first-
born of the son of the hated woman by granting him a double
portion (Deut. 21:15-17). Marguerite Harl brings this pair

of opposites to light in her interpretation of the two women
of Her. 47-51:

> The allegorical interpretation of the
> two women of Deut. 21:15-17, introduces
> the antithetic pair ponos-hedone (see
> this pair in the Stoics). The "hated"
> woman represents the kind of virtue
> requiring effort: she is assimilated
> by Philo to Leah, about whom Scripture
> says, "she was hated" (Gen. 29:31,
> emiseito); but God opened her womb (see
> Leg. Al. II, 47; Mut. 254; Cher. 41,
> etc.). The "loved" woman is pleasure:
> the same text is commented upon in Sacr.
> 20 ff, in terms which remind us of the
> fable of Xenophon in Memorabilia II, 1
> (Hercules sees vice and virtue coming
> near).[60]

In the present context, it is not necessary to further
investigate these data, but rather to reflect upon the
problem which ponos, virtue acquired through effort, poses
for Philo.[61] This problem is very important. On the one
hand, Philo praises effort and invites us to practise it:
on the other, he warns us again its danger in spiritual
life. Already, Bréhier observed,

> There is a strange contrast between this
> strong Cynic Ethics, which grants so
> much importance to the person and to the
> human will, and Philonic mysticism.
> Philo introduces a distinction which
> reduces this importance. Being the work
> of man, asceticism, according to Philo,
> is a form of action more apparent than
> real. It is the intermediary between a
> point of departure, a happy disposition
> and a goal, perfection, neither of which
> depends on man (Migr. 33).... We must
> love effort and pain and consider it not
> as suffering, as most men do, but as
> very pleasurable. This is possible only
> through love for the good which is the
> consequence of this pain and which makes
> it true nourishment or the soul. The
> love which makes effort lovable is the
> mystical love which God inspires in us

> when He attracts us to Himself, the
> close association with and the merging
> into the object of our desire.[62]

Bréhier is correct, but, in my opinion, he does not get to
the heart of the question. The Philonic teachings show
several different aspects which are all authentic.
Certainly, Philo is a Platonist who makes virtue a higher
reality which deserves to be loved for its own sake, even
more than for the advantage we derive from it. He is also a
Peripatetic who considers nature as the point of departure
and the ideals of perfection as the goal of virtue, with the
already noted distinction of Philo's notion of nature with
regard to Isaac. He is a Cynic and a Stoic in his exaltation of duty and effort over against vice and pleasure.[63]
He is also a Cynic and a Stoic in his interest in effort, in
which he recognizes a moral value, although he does not seem
to grant any value to suffering.[64] But he is also a Jew,
permeated with biblical thought. Bréhier more than once
insists on the importance in Philo of the religious perspective characteristic of Judaism, which is determined by faith
in God and which grants the first place to the virtue of
piety toward God. As a matter of fact, the great danger for
an ascetic, because of the very effort accomplished by him,
is precisely to fall into the insidious temptation of spiritual pride, that is, to sin by impiety. We shall find this
problem again in our discussion on merit.

IV.   THE PROBLEM OF MERIT

      1. In Philo

      At the beginning of this chapter, we announced our con-
clusion, namely, that the chief and constant concern of
Philo was to dissuade the ascetics--he was one of them--
from spiritual pride, and to attract them to the practice of
thanksgiving as a remedy for the impiety which threatens the
more advanced souls, and as the crown and summit of the
edifice of virtue.

      Let us briefly explain his teaching on this point. The
danger of pride and of ingratitude is not great at the
beginning of ascetic life, when the soul enters and wins the
first battles against the passions, because the help of God
is more manifest at this stage, and because the condition of
man at this point--a sinner under the bondage of his

passions--invites him to humility. In addition, any deliverance from this bondage is so wonderful that the soul spontaneously sings the hymn of thanksgiving like the Hebrews on the banks of the Red Sea. Such is the meaning of the ritual of Passover in the Philonic allegory (Sacr. 63; Agr. 79; Migr. 25).

But the same is not true after the soul has been straightened and strengthened. Now standing through the grace of God, the soul thinks of erecting a pillar to itself and not to God: this is forbidden by the Law as impiety (Som. I, 244-246). This soul, therefore, risks to sin by self-love (philautia), like Cain. We should not consider Cain as a common sinner, but precisely as a man who assumes that he is the father of his thoughts and deeds, or of his virtues, and fails to thank God for them (Post. 33-39). When this defect is rather superficial, its consequence is vanity (typhos) and puffiness (ogkos), which are closely related to real pride (oiesis) and to inhumanity. The remedy is to pursue the opposite virtues: simplicity (atuphia), humility (oudeneia),[65] philanthropy (philanthropia), and the love for, or the piety toward, God. Let us note that there is a close kinship between philanthropy and eucharistia: the offering of the first loaves (Spec. Leg. I, 132) and of the first-fruits, by reminding us that we receive everything from God, keeps us from attributing a superiority over our brethren to ourselves.[66] The remedy to pride, therefore, is a eucharistic disposition (Virt. 165-174).

However, when self-complacency is found in a man already much advanced in virtue, this is an obstacle which is much more dangerous, because it is less apparent. The crisis which faces the soul is illustrated by the figure of Issachar as opposed to that of Judah. The ruby and sapphire on the logeion of the high priest correspond to Judah and Issachar respectively,

> For the one who exercises himself in the practical wisdom of God shows his gratitude to Him who unstintingly bestowed good; while the other is engaged in noble and worthy works. Now Judah is the symbol of the man who makes confession of thankfulness and after his birth Leah bears no more (Gen. 29:35); but Issacnar represents him who is

engaged in noble deeds, for he submitted
his shoulder to labour and became a
tiller of the soil (Gen. 49:15). In his
case, as Moses says, when he has been
sown and planted in the soul there is a
reward (Gen. 30:18), which is to say
that his labour is not in vain, but
crowned by God and awarded a recompense.
That he refers to these patriarchs is
clear elsewhere when he says of the
high-priestly garment: "And thou shalt
weave together in it precious stones in
fourfold order: there shall be a row
of precious stones, sardius, topaz,
smaragdus, making the one row"--Reuben,
Simeon, Levi--"and the second row will
consist of a ruby and a sapphire" (Ex.
28:17f.¹): but the sapphire is a green
stone. Now Judah is engraved in the
ruby, for he is fourth in order, and
Issachar on the sapphire. Why then,
while saying "a green stone," does he
not also say, "a ruby stone?" Because
Judah, the disposition prone to make
confession of praise, is exempt from
body and matter. But for Issachar, who
has advanced through his effort, there
is a need for a material body. For how
can he hear the words of encouragment
without ears? ...That is why he is
likened to a stone. In addition, the
colours differ.⁶⁷ To him who makes
confession of praise belongs the hue of
the ruby, for in giving thanks to God he
is permeated by fire, and he is drunk
with a sober drunkenness. But the hue
of the green stone is proper to him who
is still labouring, for men who exercise
and train are pale, both because of the
tiring labour and because of the fear
that they may perchance not obtain the
result that accords with their prayer
(Leg. Al. I, 80-85).

We may read Plant. 134-138 as a parallel.

We are faced with two types of virtue, the one
following the way of effort, and the other the way of

nature. Issachar resembles Jacob, whereas Judah resembles
Isaac. Like Isaac, Judah is radiant with divine wisdom,
cheerful, motivated and quickened by God.   He easily accomplishes good deeds and is always disposed to give thanks, as
if he were immaterial, i.e., free from the pressure of the
body and of the passions. He reminds us of the true Gnostic
of Clement of Alexandria, who lives in God so intensely that
his thoughts and deeds proceed, as it were, from God Himself
(Strom. VII, 14; VI, 14).   Issachar, on the other hand, is
material, i.e., he heavily feels the weight of the flesh.
His past efforts and victories appear to him as a valuable
achievement, which indeed they are.   Until now, we see him
only as an industrious, though blameless, ascetic.   However,
the comparison of him with Judah implies the existence of an
imperfection very close to sin. His name is Issachar, which
means "wages," or "rewards."   This man, therefore, does not
think of giving thanks, but considers his work as deserving
of reward.   He ascribes the merit of his progress in virtue
and of his good deeds to himself, rather than giving thanks
for them to God. His fault corresponds to the third form of
ingratitude toward God--the error committed by those who
consider themselves, because of their past merits, worthy of
the graces of God (Sacr. 52-58).   Their fault, however, is
smaller than that of those guilty of blatant forgetfulness,
or of those who, like Cain, sin by atheistic pride.   They
are, however, deserving of blame. Their moral situation can
become very dangerous, precisely in the degree to which they
are progressing toward perfection.   Philo compares their
situation to that of the unfinished house and recalls that
Moses ordered the construction of a parapet round the roof
lest someone happen to fall from it inadvertently, thus
making the owner guilty of a violent death in his own house
(Agr. 169-173, cf. Deut. 22:18). He specifies:

> For there is no fall so grievous as to
> slip and fail to render honour to God by
> ascribing the victory to oneself rather
> than to Him, and so to become the per-
> petrator of the murder of one's kin.
> For he who fails to honour Him who is
> slays his own soul, so that the edifice
> of his education ceases to be of any use
> to him (Agr. 171).

And he cites the law of Deut. 8:18, "Remember God who giveth
strength to acquire power" (Agr. 172).   This warning has
many parallels in the references to ogkos, tuphos, oiesis,
etc.   Thus it is not simply a pious thought among many, but
a repeated warning, a lasting concern.[68]   Philo greatly

fears the fall into impiety at the very threshold of perfection, and we easily understand this in a man such as him,
who is far advanced in the steps of spiritual life. Origen,
who is also interested in guiding souls on the itinerary of
spiritual life, mentions this final obstacle in Homilies on
Numbers (27:12). But Origen is even more precise on this
point when he comments on the episode of the crossing of the
lake, where he first sees the struggle of the soul against
the passions represented by the waves tossing the boat, and
then the trial of Peter, who, presuming to be able to walk
upon the water of righteousness, owes his salvation to his
calling Jesus for help as he sinks (Commentary on Matthew,
XI, 5-6).

        Bréhier, in his section on moral conscience, or
elenchos, a notion whose authorship he ascribes to Philo,
recognizes the importance of the theme of pride in Philo:

> From the point of view of interior life,
> sin leads to pride (oiesis, tuphos). To
> be proud is to ascribe to oneself more
> than to God, and to believe oneself to
> be master of the faculties of the soul
> and of external things as well. It is
> also, if we must seek a deficiency of
> judgment, an intellectual defect. But
> this error is the same thing as the vice
> itself. It is an insidious evil from
> which we are dissuaded only through
> self-knowledge. It is the evil of those
> who believe they can prophesy, of
> princes who believe they are the masters
> of the universe. It causes the soul to
> extol itself and to puff itself up, thus
> losing all humility, and becoming
> unaware of its own nothingness.[69]

2. The controversy on merit at the time of Philo

J. Daniélou writes:

> De sacrificiis Abelis and Caini, shows
> the sin in Cain contrary to eucharistia,
> which is philautia. The three faults
> against thanksgiving are forgetfulness,
> pride, and the attitude of the man who,
> while he ascribes grace to God, claims
> it as his own merit. This could well

> have been a controversy against some
> Jews. And the reason for it is
> notable: "It is not because of thee,
> but because of my Covenant" (diateke).
> But the Covenant is symbolically repre-
> sented by God's graces (Sacr. 57).[70]

Commenting on the same text, Annie Jaubert also refers to
the existence of a controversy about merit among the Jews:
"This text represents a very interesting reaction to a
theology of merit; the attack is against Pharisaism in this
sense of the Gospel."[71]

Wolfson observes that

> When the rabbis urge men to serve God
> without the expectation of any reward,
> they merely wish to emphasize the prin-
> ciple that one is to serve God out of
> love, not out of any doubt that a reward
> will be forthcoming but because the ser-
> vice of God out of love is intrinsically
> the highest kind of service.[72]

We know in the Synoptic Gospels the caricature of the
Pharisee who finds pleasure in his own justice, despises his
neighbour, and considers himself as justified before God.
The Targumim offer even better evidence, not tarnished by
the bias of Christian opposition to Pharisaism, since it
comes directly from the Synagogue. R. Le Déaut writes on
this subject:

> The Pauline reaction to confidence in
> one's work (Rom. 10:3; Phil. 3:9) is
> better understood when we see it
> repeatedly emerging in the Commentaries
> of the Synagogue (cf. Targ. Ex. 13:18;
> Numb. 31:50; Deut. 16:16, etc.). Had
> Paul known a Palestinian targum like
> Neophiti, how would he have reacted to
> the systematic substitution of the love
> for the Law for the love of God in all
> of Deuteronomy?[73]

Festugière mentions a parallel in the Hermetic literature:
the reason given in Poimandres for the fall of the soul is

its temerity and, first, its desire to exist independently
from God.[74]

There existed, therefore, a controversy on merit at the
time of Philo, as revealed by the importance granted by them
to the letter of the Law and which threatened to turn religious practices into a means of securing the approval of God
rather than of serving God.   Paul takes advantage of this
controversy to show that justification does not come from
the Law or from the merits acquired through observing it,
but from faith in Christ, through Whom we receive the grace
of God.   Philo also takes advantage of this controversy, but
he does not use it as a means for another purpose. He stays
within its limits so to speak, and makes it an essential
part of his spiritual doctrine.   If one does not avoid that
false theology of merit which consists in relying on one's
deeds and in finding one's own glory in virtues, Philo seems
to say, one will certainly sin by impiety, which is an evil
comparable to the bondage of the passions.   To serve the
self instead of obeying the passions is not to serve God,
and to consider man as the author of what is best in himself, i.e., virtue is to reject faith in the operation of
God in man.   The remedy is thanksgiving, which returns to
God what belongs to Him through confession and praise, in a
movement of gratitude.   It is also the most sensible attitude for man, at whatever stage of spiritual life he might
be to give thanks to God for every good thing, and this is a
sign of sound spiritual realism.[75-76]

CONCLUSION

The study of Philonic eucharistia brought us to extend
our research progressively in several directions. The word
itself, eucharistia-eucharistein, obliged us not only to
make a complete inventory and analysis of the references and
allusions to it, but also of the parallel terms in
concurrence with it. In order to reach a correct understanding of the terms and notion of the Philonic
eucharistia, we had to trace its origins in the Hebrew
Bible, and from there, through the LXX, to return to Philo.
The doctrine of thanksgiving is enriched by the contribution
of biblical images such as the memory of God and of His
blessings, consecration, loan, and much sacrificial data.
Our terminological inquiry invites us to insist upon the
foundation of the Philonic eucharistia in the Law of Moses
rather than in Greek philosophy or in a Synagogue so
emancipated as to focus on the hymnic praise of God and on
philosophy, and to sever itself from the Temple and the Law.
In particular, the fact that the images used by Philo to
express and develop the notion of thanksgiving are already
laws with an impact on the life of the faithful through
practice, and which are simply extended to a new domain,
namely, cosmological speculation and interior life, proves
that Philo proposes to present a eucharistia of biblical and
Jewish character. His originality, besides the allegorical
method, consists, first of all, in extending the implications of his biblical faith and of the terms and images used
for its expression to cosmology, to anthropology, and to the
life of virtue. On the other hand, the use of eucharistia-
eucharistein, which he found in the Jewish community and in
Hellenistic civilization, enables him to recapitulate, so to
speak, his teaching on thanksgiving in one principal term.
He adopts this term without hesitation, as though it is
already assimilated to the Jewish heritage, and gives it an
importance unprecedented in Judaism and in Greek philosophy.
Eucharistia-eucharistein pervades the entire domain of
theology and of liturgy in his writings, to such an extent
that we may wonder whether his usage of it does not lead to
an incorrect interpretation of the faith and rites. In
reward, it is its extention to this domain which enables us
to define it in the least ambiguous manner. Reduced to mere
praise, or to benediction understood in the sense of praise,
this term is not given full justice and seems emptied of its
biblical contents. It appears as a Greek notion, namely,
the idea of praise common to all the families of Hellenistic
religiosity. Its presence on each page of the Commentaries
of Philo, especially in the context of laws and sacrifices,

179

is an invitation to grant it a much richer meaning and to
return it to its place in biblical theology. We may, as a
consequence, inquire whether the laws and rites were
actually granted a eucharistic connotation by the Jews at
the time of Philo, particularly in the temple of Jerusalem
itself.

It is precisely this eucharistic interpretation of the
liturgy of the Temple which most surprised us and which
seemed the most striking to those who knew of our inquiry.
This interpretation was found in the speculations of Philo
about the vesture of the high-priest, the furniture of the
Temple, the cosmic, anthropological and moral interpretation
of which had attracted the attention of scholars much more
than the eucharistic aspect. It was also found in the
eucharistic connotation which Philo ascribes to the first
fruits generally, to some classes of sacrifices, such as the
sacrifices of salvation and burnt-offerings, and
particularly to the feasts of the calendar. The eucharistic
connotation of the feasts is based, on the one hand, on the
"agrarian" nature of the religion and on the events of the
history of Israel, which exegetes easily accept; but, on the
other hand, and perhaps more directly, it is based on the
nature of the sacrifices offered at these feasts, for
instance, the sheaf, the unleavened bread and the Paschal
lamb, the first-fruits of Pentecost, the burnt-offerings
multiplied in all feasts, and especially at the Autumnal
festival. The "feast of every day" finds its justification,
according to Philo, in the daily burnt-offerings rather than
in the cynical developments which this image occasions.
According to Philo, these sacrifices have a eucharistic
aspect, and constitute a basis for the eucharistic interpretation of festivals, or, in some cases, provide almost the
only basis for such an interpretation. The offering of the
first-fruits, for instance, confers its eucharistic
character on Pentecost, and Philo does not refer to the gift
of the Law on Mt. Sinai and to the sojourn in the Desert in
this context.

From the consideration of the Liturgy, it is natural to
pass to that of the ministers of the liturgy, that is, to
the priests and Levites. Philo says nothing of the Levitic
guilds in charge of music and choirs, probably because his
subject is the Law of Moses and not the usages of the Temple
in his own time. On the other hand, he makes an important
contribution to the development of the priestly idea. There
are cosmic aspects to the service of the high-priest, which
are not unimportant. But the Levitic priesthood, crowned by
the service of the high-priest, is not only in charge of the

sacrifices of thanksgiving offered by individuals, but
performs the eucharistia on behalf of the whole nation
because of the Covenant and even worships in the name of
mankind, regardless of racial distinctions, because every
man has the vocation of praise and thanksgiving, a vocation
which, unfortunately, most forget through ignorance of God
or through impiety. This eucharistic mediation of a more
universal character belongs chiefly to the high-priest. The
notion of the priesthood, therefore, expands directly in the
eucharistic line of thought. It also develops in the sense
of the mediation for the forgiveness of sins, which itself
carries a eucharistic connotation, since, if it is fitting
for us to give thanks to the Divine Creator and Benefactor,
we must also give thanks to the merciful and Saviour God.
On this basis, Philo develops his thoughts on the priestly
or Levitical ideal and enlarges on spiritual sacrifice.
This kind of sacrifice is not so much pure praise in the
vague sense of the term as the offering of prayer, of good
deeds, good thoughts, and of the self, understood as a
sacrifice.

The cosmological aspect of the Philonic eucharistia is
the first to attract the attention of the reader, for it
appears everywhere, even in the symbolism of the furniture
of the Temple, and particularly in the interpretation of the
vesture of the high-priest and of the figure of the Muses.
In these two cases, as in many other instances, the cosmological reference is directly eucharistic. We can associate
anthropology to cosmology in the speculations of Philo,
particularly with regard to thanksgiving, because man is in
his structure a microcosm, or a world in miniature.
Speculations of this nature were current at the time of
Philo and were already supported by old traditions. The
Stoics in particular enjoyed such speculations, and Philo
finds ample materials among the allegorizing interpreters of
the Bible. We also find a remarkable example of cosmic and
anthropological thanksgiving in Letter of Aristeas, where
the image of Memory expresses the idea of thanksgiving without making use of eucharistein.

With regard to these speculations on cosmology and
anthropology, Philo takes two approaches. First, he invites
us to give thanks for the universe and for man, both as a
whole and for each of their parts, so that nothing noteworthy might be omitted. This invitation and this well-
ordered division of the parts reappear too frequently in his
writings to be a mere accident or even simply a personal
idea. They must correspond to some liturgical data. But,
admitting this, does Philo follow a Greek pattern, such as

that of the Hymn of Cleanthes, or a Jewish practice? The
presence of cosmic and anthropological symbolism in
Alexandrian Judaism, and the cosmological developments of
the Bible in Genesis, Psalms, the books of Wisdom, and the
Prophets, lead to insistence on Jewish sources and usages.
Ancient Jewish prayers, moreover, to which we may add the
Christian prayers of the first centuries, particularly those
of book VII of Apostolic Constitutions, extend their thanksgiving in this direction, and rely for that purpose on the
cosmic developments in Scripture rather than on those of the
Greek philosophers. In Philo, cosmic eucharistia culminates
in the speculations on the high-priest as the image of the
Logos of God. The high-priest is a mediator who transmits
the pardon and the healing of God through sacrifices for sin
and votive offerings to men, but he is also established in
order to fulfill their duty of adoration through sacrifices
of thanksgiving, burnt-offerings, and the sacrifice of
incense. His mediation seems to reach its greatest scope,
however, in the cosmic eucharistia. Here, according to the
cosmic symbolism of his vesture, which was accepted at the
time of Philo, he represents adoration for the world. Man,
because he is the thinking part of the universe, ought to
give thanks for the universe. Moreover in man, the
universe, even those of its parts deprived of thought, finds
the possibility to give thanks to God. And the same can be
said for the microcosm, where the high-priest in man is his
logos or his reason. Philo does not rely, in suggesting
this form of worship, solely on the symbolism of the vesture
of the high-priest; and his reason for doing so, in any
case, is the priestly character of man and his idea that
this priesthood is essentially a mission of adoration.
Cosmic adoration, however, is only a step toward pure adoration, i.e., that in which the Soul makes abstractions of
everything below and considers nothing but God alone. Here
again, the Logos of God makes his contribution by pouring
the libation of His own adoration into the soul of man,
until man no longer needs any other priest but himself,
because he is priest and worshiper by natural vocation,
just as the created beings who have never descended upon
earth. The figure of the Charites, or the Graces of God
which assist man when there is no longer any intermediary
between him and God in adoration, shows the eucharistic
nature of adoration at the summit. Can we say the same for
wisdom? In Philo, Wisdom seems to be interpreted as generic
or divine Virtue, which is eucharistic when she resides in
man, rather than as a parallel of the Logos in his cosmic or
anthropological function.

The second approach taken by Philo when he turns to
cosmology or anthropology is more apologetical than
philosophical. His concern in this context is to defend and
to affirm the very existence of God, to whom thanks are
offered. It is therefore necessary to know to what God we
ought to give thanks or consider as the source of every good
thing. Here, Philo has to fight against the several forms
of materialism represented by Democritus and Epicurus among
philosophers, by the biblical symbolism of Egypt, or by that
of the second wives and concubines of the Patriarchs, the
women descended from Cain, the Moabite women, etc., to say
nothing of Eve herself. But the cult of the true God has
two challengers which are even more dreadful, namely, man on
the one hand, and the world and the heavens on the other.
The man who considers himself as the center, or the measure
of all things, is represented by the pair Cain-Protagoras.
This pair interests us in this section because it ultimately
subordinates the existence of God Himself to human opinion.
Philo fights against the man who deifies himself and denies
the existence of God. It seems childish, at first glance,
to worship the heavens or the world, but we must remember
that the doctrine attacked here is no longer materialism,
but pantheism. It is the classical doctrine of the Soul of
the world. We hardly realise its power of seduction among
the ancients, for we oversimplify it by emptying it of the
most important of its contents. We are especially mistaken
about the true meaning of the Platonic and Aristotelian
tradition, which we contrast too easily with the Stoic positions. Recent research has shown the importance of the
theory of the Soul of the world in Plato and in the young
Aristotle, hereby establishing the tradition of this
doctrine through the Stoics down to Philo, who knew the lost
treatises of the young Aristotle. The Soul of the world is
the heavens, and the world, or the Whole, is her body. We
also find a heavenly part, of the same nature as the Soul of
the world, in man, namely, the rational part of the Soul,
which governs the Whole of man. Philo starts from these
data, which are highly spiritualistic, since the heavens and
the mind in man consist of ether, which is a rational and
thinking substance. But he is not satisfied with this
theology, in spite of its affirmation of the divinity of the
heavens, because it does not teach the existence of a God
transcendent above the world and the Soul. Philo succeeds
in getting out of this blind alley only through scepticism,
which at his time challenged the very power of human reason,
and through religious experience, when the Soul, removed
from its divine throne under the pressure of scepticism and
acknowledging itself to be but dust, becomes disposed to

listen to the word of God and to become a believer.   God,
then, appears as the Master of the world and of man.   God,
in this process, is returned to the world, and the world is
returned to God.   Thanksgiving rediscovers its raison d'être
and can consequently flourish under its cosmological and
anthropological form.   Philo ascribes cosmic religion and
the adoration of the heavens to the Chaldeans.   The
Chaldeans of Philo are a biblical image connected with
Abraham, who is the type of the believer who rediscovers God
through a crisis of scepticism about the power of man to
know the world and himself.   But we should not forget that
his criticism is aimed at the Greek doctrine of the Soul of
the world.   Socrates, with his scepticism toward cosmology,
appears to him as the first step in the rediscovery of God.
His biblical counterpart is Terah, the father of Abraham.
Socrates turns to the knowledge of himself with the same
scepticism, which has become for him a method of inquiry.
Abraham, according to Philo, draws the consequence of this
scepticism, since the "Know thyself" brings him to affirm
the nothingness of man and the existence of God.   The theory
of the Soul of the world, which imposed itself on minds with
the authority of Aristotle and of the Stoics, called for a
reaction from Philo.   Philo adopts its contents in his
cosmology and his anthropology, but he proves its basic
theological deficiency.

     The final chapter deals with the interior life of the
Soul and with the life of virtue.   Philo, following the
Letter of Aristeas and the Greeks, explains very well how
God is the father of virtue in man.   His theology of grace
is complete.   He had its elements readily at hand in the
Bible, where the living God intervenes in the interior life
of men.   Because of his interest in psychology, he
developed, with the help of allegory, all the aspects of the
divine operation in the Soul.   In particular, he uses the
symbolism of the wives of the patriarchs, and the women of
the Bible more generally, to depict the main stages of this
divine operation, its methods, success or failure.   This is
what we ought to consider as the Philonic "mystery," because
it is concerning this symbolism that he uses the language of
the mysteries and calls on the arcana against those who
could vilify it.   Here again, he places himself within the
biblical tradition, which likes to speculate on the
symbolism of woman, and he does not onesidedly depend on
Greek, Egyptian, or Persian speculations.   Philo, therefore,
teaches that we must give thanks for the goods of the Soul,
because they belong to God, who is their author and their
source in ourselves.   The interior life of the Soul is the
domain par excellence of divine activity.   For this reason,

it would be very unjust on the part of man to substitute
himself for God as the author of the goods of the Soul.
Those who do so sin by the common ingratitude of forgetfulness, or by that of atheism as in the case of Cain, who
substitutes himself for God when he makes himself the
measure of all things. But there is another form of
ingratitude, that of "acquisition," when man believes in God
but attributes the merit to himself, as if God had only
contributed the means to achieve the works of virtue. But
to affirm one's own merit is the same as to make God an
instrument and man the real author of virtue. Virtue
thereby becomes a human work, perishable together with him,
a pillar erected to the glory of man and not a divine work
consecrated to the glory of God. A eucharistic disposition,
kept active by obedience to the laws of the first-fruits
which daily remind the Israelite of his duty of thanksgiving, is the remedy to the pride of ascetics advanced in
virtue. We noticed indications of a controversy on merit in
the Judaism of the time of Philo. By the development of his
thought in the direction of interior life and of its
problems, Philo ranks among the great masters of spiritual
life.

We are aware that we have pointed out some important
aspect of the eucharistic teaching of Philo, sometimes new
or unexploited ones. We wish we could find the opportunity
to do further research on some of his teachings, but our
best reward would be to see others pursue these inquiries
with their own qualifications as scholars of Judaism, of
Hellenism, and of Philo. May this modest essay contribute
to reveal the grandeur of eucharistia.

FOOTNOTES TO THE PREFACE

1. Review published in *Irenikon* 1974, 4, pp. 574-575; *Bul. de Lit. Eccl.*, 1974, 1, p. 68 (H. Crouzel); *JBL* 92, 4, 1973, pp. 630-631 (R.G. Hammerton-Kelly); *Theologische Revue* 70, 1974, 3 pp. 205-206 (Otto Michel); *Theologische Literaturzeitung* 98, 1973, 8, pp. 593-594) (Gerhard Delling); *La Maison-Dieu* 114, 1973, pp. 127-134 (I.H. Dalmais); *Münchener Theologische Zeitschrift* 1975, p. 413-416 (Michael Schmaus) etc. See also the articles of Charles Perrot, "Le repas du Seigneur," *Maison-Dieu* 123, 1975; Henri Cazelles, "Bénédiction et sacrifice dans l'Ancien Testament," *ibid.*; and the book of Lothar Lies, *Wort und Eucharistie bei Origenes*, Innsbruck, 1978.

FOOTNOTES OF THE INTRODUCTION

1. The English version used in this book is that of F.H. Colson, *Philo*, in ten volumes and two supplementary volumes, The Loeb Classical Library. For the sake of stylistic unity and easy reading, the text of this version and of other books in English has been slightly altered. I also chose to translate quotes of studies published in other languages.

2. F.J.A. HORT & J.O.F. MURRAY, "Eucharistia-eucharistein", JTS 3, 1902, pp. 594-598.

3. T. SCHERMANN, "Eucharistia und eucharistein in ihrem Bedeutungswandel bis 200 n. Chr.," *Philologus* 69, 1910, pp. 375-410.

4. P. SCHUBERT, *Form and Function of the Pauline Thanksgiving*, Diss, Univ. of Chicago, Illinois, 1935 (ms.).

5. R.J. LEDOGAR, *Acknolwedgement, Praise-verbs in the early Greek Anaphora*, Rome 1968, especially pp. 94-98, abbrev. *Acknowledgement*.

6. E. BREHIER, *Les Idées philosophiques et religieuses de Philon d'Alexandrie*, Paris 1959 (2d ed.), abbrev. *Idees*.

7. I. HEINEMANN, *Philon Griechische und Judische Bildung*, Darmstadt, 1962, published between 1929 and 1932, abbrev. *Bildung*.

8. E.R. GOODENOUGH, *By Light Light, The Mystic Gospel of Hellenistic Judaism*, New Haven 1935.

9. H. WOLFSON, *Philo*. 2 vol. Cambridge Univ., Mass. 1947.

10. *Ibid.*, pp. 237-252.

11. J. DANIELOU, *Philon d'Alexandrie*, Paris 1957.

12. *Ibid.*, pp. 175-181.

13. E.R. GOODENOUGH, *The Jurisprudence of the Jewish Courts in Egypt*, New Haven 1927.

14. K. HRUBY, "Les heures de prière dans le judaisme à l'époque de Jésus," *La prière des heures*, Paris 1962, pp. 59-84.

15. E. LEPINSKI, "Macarismes et Psaumes de congratulation", *Revue Biblique* 75, 1968, pp. 321-327.

16. R.K. YERKES, *Sacrifice in Greek and Roman Religion and Early Judaism*, London 1953, abbrev. *Sacrifice*.

17. H. CAZELLES, "L'anaphore et l'Ancien Testament", *L'Eucharistie d'Orient et d'Occident*, Paris, 1970, pp. 11-21.

18. A. Jaubert, *La notion d'Alliance dans le Judaisme aux abords de l'ère chrétienne*, Paris 1963, abbrev. *Alliance*.

19. A.-J. FESTUGIERE, *La Révélation d'Hermès Trismégiste*, 4 vols., esp. *Le Dieu Cosmique*, 1949-1954.

20. J. PEPIN, *Théologie cosmique et théologie chrétienne*, Paris 1964.

FOOTNOTES TO CH. I

1. *Cain* and *Abel*. See A. Measson, *De sacrificiis*, Introd. p. 36-37 (*Les oeuvres de Philon d'Alexandrie* 4, published under the patronage of the University of Lyons by Roger Arnaldez, Jean Pouilloux and Claude Mondésert, Le Cerf, Paris, France, from 1961 on, here abbreviated as *Les Oeuvres*).
-*Enoch*, See J.G. KAHN, *De confusione*, complementary note on *Conf.* 123, pp. 173-174, (*Les oeuvres* 13) and A. ARNALDEZ, *De mutatione*, note 2 on *Mut.* 34, p. 49 (*Les oeuvres* 18).
-*Israel*, See A. BECKAERT, *De Praemiis*, note 1 on *Praem.* 44, p. 64 (*Les oeuvres* 27), and J.G. KAHN, *De confusione*, complementary note on *Conf.* 92, pp. 162-163 (*Les oeuvres* 13).
-*Jacob*. See M. ALEXANDRE, *De congressu*, note 1 on *Congr.* 24, p. 122 (*Les oeuvres* 16)

-Leah, ibid., note 2, pp. 122-123.
-Rachel, ibid., note 3, and 4, pp. 123-124.
-Isaac, ibid., note 1, 2 and 3, pp. 130-131.
-Rebecca, ibid., note 5, p. 131.
-Sarah, ibid., complementary note on *Congr.* 1, pp. 233-234.
-Abraham, ibid., complementary note on *Congr.* 1, p. 234.
-Judah (praise, or *hodah*) in the rabbis of the fourth century, cf. R.J. LEDOGAR. *Acknowledgement*, 118.
-Jethro, cf. R. ARNALDEZ, *De opificio*, Introduction generale, p. 39 (*Les oeuvres* 1).
-Senaar (*Gen.* 10:10) is Babel. Do not look into LXX, but the Rabbis offered an etymology reminding of Philo's: "to shake, to shake something down". Cf. J.G. KAHN, *De confusione*, note 1 on *Conf.* 68-69 (*Les oeuvres* 13). See also A. MEASSON, *De sacrificiis*, note 1 on *Sacr.* 13, p. 74 (*Les oeuvres* 4), and M. ALEXANDRE, *De congressu*, complementary note on *Congr.* 58, p. 241 (*Les oeuvres* 16).
-Damascus figures sackclothe and blood. See M. HARL, *Quis rerum divinarum heres sit* (here abbrev., *Heres*), note 2 on *Her.* 54, p. 192 (*Les oeuvres* 15).

2. T. SCHERMANN, "Eucharistia" und "eucharistein" in ihrem Bedeutungwandel bis 200 n. Chr." *Philologus* 69, 1910, pp. 375-410.

3. P. SCHUBERT, *Form and Function of the Pauline Thanksgiving*.

4. R.K. YERKES, *Sacrifice in Greek and Roman Religions and Early Judaism*.

5. L. HALKIN, *La supplication d'action de grâces chez les Romains*, Bibliothèque de la Faculté de Philosophie et Lettres de l'université de Liége, CXXVIII, Belles Lettres, Paris, 1953, 136p.

6. LEDOGAR, *Acknowledgment, Praise-verbs in the early Greek Anaphora*.

7. HERODOTUS, I, 32,9; XENOPHON, *Oec.*, 5, 10; *Cyr.* 2,2,1; *Cyr.* 8,3,49.

8. W. v. CHRIST, *Geschichte der griech Literatur 5*, Aufl., besorgt von W. Schmid, Munchen 1908, I. Teil 595 ff.

9. *Psephima*, DEMOSTHENES XVIII, 91-92, cf. T. SCHERMANN, "Eucharistia und eucharistein," p. 376, n.6.

10. MENANDER, 693.

11. For all this section, see GONZELMANN, "Eucharisteo," etc. TWNT,IX,7, p. 397-398 (English edition).

12. T. SCHERMANN, "Eucharistia and eucharistein," p. 376-377.

13. For instance, in Papyrus London III,879,11 (123 B.C.).

14. W. DITTENBERGER, *Orientalis graeci inscriptiones selectae* (OGIS), vol. II, 1905, inscriptions 730,11, p. 470.

15. T. SCHERMANN, "Eucharistia und eucharistein," p. 378.

16. *Ibid.*, p. 378.

17. DITTENBERGER, OGIS, 1905, inscription 717,3,13, p. 456.

18. POLYBIUS, 16,11; 18,46,13, cf. LEDOGAR, *Acknowledgment*, p. 92.

19. T. SCHERMANN, "Eucharistia und eucharistein," pp. 381-382.

20. POLYBIUS and DIONYSIUS OF HALICARNASSES, cf. H. ETIENNE, *Thesaurus graecae linguae*, tertio ed., C.B. Hase, G. and L. Dindorf, Vol. III, Paris, 1935, 2513, cf. T. SCHERMANN, *ibid.*, p. 383.

21. GIG (*Corpus Inscriptionum Graecorum*, ed. K. Boekl, vol. I, Berlin, 1924, n. 502, where we read on a votive tablet, *Klaudia eucharisto upsisto*, and GIG, n. 54, *Mantheos Dithou eucharistei Dii epi nike perthathlou paidos*, a prayer of intercession and thanksgiving in SB (*Samnelbuch Grieschische Urkunden aus Eegypten*, ed. Preisigke, Berlin, 1915 and 1922), 4117, a report on four cures in SIG (*Sylloge Inscriptionum Graecorum*, ed. W. Dittenberger, vol. I-IV, 3d ed. Leipzig, 1905-1924), n. 1173, the earliest instance of *eucharistia* on papyrus, in 168 B.C., in UPZ (U. WILKEN, *Urkunden der Ptolemaerzeit*, vol. I, II, Leipzig, Berlin, 1922, 1935), n. 59, *eucharisto tois theois*; finally, the examples of construction with *epi* and *para* for the introduction of the motive of thanksgiving, in SB, n. 7172 and *Pap. Giessen* (*Grieschische Papyriim Museum des oberhessischen Geschichtsvereins zu Giessen*, Leipzig, 1910-1912), n. 77.

22. *Iliad*, VI, 93 ff, and 274 ff.

23. *Ibid.*, VIII, 287-291.

24. XENOPHON, *Anabasis*, III,2,12.

25. Cf. W.H. ROUSE, *Greek Votive Offerings*, Cambridge, 1902.

26. ROUSE, *op. cit.*, gives a list of these offerings, pp. 394-408.

27. ROUSE, *op. cit.*, pp. 57,89,92,122,214,230,234,254,262, 265,295,296,328,329,330.

28. YERKES, *Sacrifice*, pp. 61-62.

29. *Od.*, X,518-540; Sophocles, *Antigone*, 998-1023; *Iliad*, XII, 8.

30. PLUTARCH, *Lycurgus*, V,3.

31. APOLLODORUS, *Bib*. II,8:IV.

32. *Iliad*, III,103-106; 264-301.

33. SIG, 289,14; 384,19; 388,9; 466,9.

34. SIG, 384; 391. XENOPHON, *Anabasis*, III,2,9; V,1,1.

35. APOL. RHOD., *Arg*. IV, 1185-1188.

36. POLYBIUS, V,14,8.

37. SIG, 533,545,656,731,800.

38. SIG, 748,798.

39. *Michel* (C. MICHEL, *Recueil d'inscriptions grecques*, Bruxelles, 1900,1912,1927), 516,546,993.

40. *Michel*, 993.

41. SIG, 559.

42. SIG, 336,547,590,834.

43. SIG, 285.

44. SIG, 374,485,587,731,912,1099,1102.

45. SIG, 346,615,721.

46.   YERKES, *Sacrifice*, pp. 102-104.

47.   LEDOGAR, *Acknowledgment*, p. 92.

48.   POLYBIUS, 6,14,7; 39,7,2.

49.   SUICERUS, I,1296.

50.   SOPHOCLES, III,2513.

51.   *Plant.* 129; *Spec. Leg.* II,146,203, *ff.*; *Sacr.* 53.

52.   L. HALKIN, *Supplication*, p.12.

53.   *Ibid.*, p. 17, n.4.

54.   *Ibid.*, p. 53, n.6.

55.   LEDOGAR, *Acknowledgment*, pp. 101-106.

56.   *Letter of Aristeas*, 177, SCH.

57.   J.P. AUDET, "Esquisse historique du genre littéraire de
la bénédiction juive et de l'eucharistie chrétienne,"
Revue Biblique 65, 1958, pp. 371-399.

58.   J. GUILLET, "Le langage spontané de la bénédiction dans
l'Ancien Testament," *RSR*, 57, 1969, pp. 163-204.

59.   K. HRUBY, "La notion de la *Berakhah* dans la tradition
et son caractère anamnétique," *Questions Liturgiques*,
Louvain, 2, 1971, pp. 155-170.

60.   BEYER, *TWNT*, *Eulogein* vol. II, pp. 754-765 (English
edition).

61.   J.M. ROBINSON, "Die Hodajot-Formel in Gebet und Hymnus
des Fruhchristenstums," *Apophoreta, Festchrift fur Ernst
Haenchen*, Berlin 1954, pp. 194-235.

62.   G. BORNKAMM, "Lobpreis, Bekenntnis und Opfer,"
Apophoreta, id., pp. 46-63.

63.   MICHEL, *Homologein*, TWNT, vol. V, pp. 199-220.

64.   S. DANIEL, *Recherches sur le vocabulaire de culte dans
la Septante*, Paris, 1966, ch. XIII, pp. 273-297.

65.   R.K. YERKES, *Sacrifice*.

66. LEDOGAR, *Acknowledgment*.

67. Examples of *ainein* translating *hillel*:   Ps.   23:24;
35:18;   56:5; 64:6;   69:31.35; 74:21; 84:5;   107:32; 109:30;
115:17;   119:164;   135:3;   146:2;   148:2.3.4.5.7.13;   149:3;
150:1.

68. *Ainesis* translating *tehillah* in   psalms: Ps.   9:15;
22:4; 34:2;   40:4; 48:11;   51:17; 65:2;   71:8;   78:4; 79:13;
102:22; 106:2.12.47; 109:1; 111:10; 149:1.   Besides Psalms:
Is. 38:18; 62:9; Jer. 20:13; I Chr. 16:4.36; 23:5; 29:13; II
Chr. 5:13; 7:8-14; 20:19.21; 31:2.

69. Ps. 35:28; 22:4.

70. Ps. 40:4.

71. Ps. 66:2.

72. Other examples, for *hymnos*:   Ps. 65:2; 100:4; 119:171;
148:14; for *hymnesis*:   Ps. 22:23;   Is. 42:10;   for *epainos*:
Ps. 22:26; for *epainein*:   Ps. 56:5;   115:17.   Other forms:
Ex. 15:11; Is. 43:21; 60:6; 63:7.   Ledogar notices, as
another translation of *tehillah, kaukema* (Jer. 13:11;
17:14), *arete* (Is. 42:8.12.21; 63:7), *doxa* (Is. 61:3),
endoxos (Is. 48:9).

73. S. MOWINKEL, *The Psalms in Israel's Worship*, transl.
D.R. Ap. Thomas, Oxford, 1967, vol. I, pp. 207-210.

74. Collective: Ps.   136; 67; 124; 129; individual: 30;
32; 34; 40:2-12; 66:13-20; 107; 116; 138 (cf. J. McKenzie,
Dictionary of the Bible, p. 705).

75. LEDOGAR, *Acknowledgment*, p. 76-82; v. Rad, TWNT, vol.
II, pp. 238-242.

76. Josuah 7:19; Is. 24:15;   42:12; Jer.   13:16;   I Chr.
16:28; Prov.   25:2; Ps.   3:4; 19:2;   29:1;   62:8; 96:7.8;
145:11.

77. Josuah 7:19; Is. 42:12; Ps. 29:1.

78. Ps. 145:11; 29:9.

79. Examples of *kbd* translated by *doxazein*:   Ps. 22:24;
50:23; 86:12; I Sam. 2:30.

80. Prov. 3:9; 14:31; Is. 29:13.

81.   Is. 43:20; 25:3.

82.   LEDOGAR, *Acknowledgment*, p. 80.

83.   I Sam. 15:30.

84.   Examples of *baruk* translated by *eulogetos*:   Gen. 9:26; 14:20; 24:27; 29:31.33; Ex. 24:27; Ruth 2:20; 4:14; I Sam. 15:13; 22:47; 25:32.39; II Sam. 18:28; I Kings 1: 48; 5:2; 8:15.56; I Chr. 16:36; 29:10; II Chr. 2:11; 6:4; Esdras 7:27; Ps. 28:6; 31:22; 41:14; 66:20; 68:20; 72:18.19; 89:53; 119:12; 124:6; 135:21; 144:1.   Examples of *berak* translated by *eulogion*:   Gen. 1:28;   12:2; 17:16;   22:27; 24:1.35.48; 27:27;   28:14; 32:27-30;   48:15-16; Ex.   12:32;   23:25; Lev. 9:23; Deut. 26:15; 28:12;   8:10; Judges   5:2.9;   22:33; Ps. 5:13; 16:7;   26:12; 34:2;   63:5; 66:8;   68:29;   96:2; 100:4; 103:1; 104:1; 132:15; 135:19; 145:2.

85.   Ps. 118:26; Deut. 28:3.6; I Sam. 26:25.

86.   BEYER, *TWNT*, vol. II, p. 754.

87.   K. HRUBY, "La notion de *Berakhah* dans la   tradition et son caractere   anamnetique," *Questions Liturgiques* 2, 1971, pp. 155-170.

88.   According to N. Dembitz in article "Gomel" (*The Jewish Encyclopedia*, V, p. 40), Talmud (*Ber*. 54 *b*) derives from Ps. 107 the duty of giving thanks for having been protected in danger, especially after crossing desert or sea, or been in jail, or grievously sick.   This thanksgiving must be accomplished publicly, i.e., when at least ten men are gathered in a religious assembly.

      Kaufmann Kohler,   article "Benedictions" in *The Jewish Encyclopedia*, III, pp. 10-12, gives the list of the Hundred Benedictions prescribed in the Talmud and adopted in the liturgies.   Each of them begins with the formula, "Blessed art Thou, O Lord, God of the Universe".   They are meant to be the consecration, not only of directly religious actions but also of the whole profane life.

89.   E.J.   BICKERMANN, "Benediction   et   priere," *Revue Biblique* 69, 1962, pp. 524-532.

90.   According to J. GUILLET ("Le langage   spontane de la benediction dans l'Ancien Testament," *RSR*, 57), the language of Benediction is used in the spontaneous expression of praise and thanksgiving, and makes it clear that, when a man

is declared blessed, God is the author of the blessings
conferred on him.   J. Guillet also shows the importance of
benediction in Semitic manners: the benediction, or the
wish of peace, which is expressed in the gesture of welcome
and farewell, has a sincere and profoundly religious
character.   It includes an appeal for divine grace, and is
thus very close to thanksgiving. Since spontaneous benediction reveals the gift of God to man in the relative clause
usually following the word "blessed", often it amounts to a
thanksgiving, if the latter is understood to be an act of
gratitude or acknowledgment of the name of God.   E.-J.
Bickermann, in the article, "Bénédiction et prière" (op.
cit.) shows that the Hebrew has no special term for the
expression of gratitude, and is satisfied with using the
language of the benediction for that purpose.   We should
not, though, see in this a deficiency, since the lesser
(gratitude) is included in the larger (benediction), and
does not require to be made explicit in a particular formula
(cf. A. CONZALEZ, "Prière dans l'Ancien Testament," Suppl.
Dictionaire de la Bible, fasc. 44, pp. 580-581).

91. Examples of *hodah* translated by *exomologeisthai* in
Psalms: Ps. 6:6;   7:18; 9:2; 18:50; 28:7; 30:13; 42:6.12;
44:9; 45:18; 49:19; 52:11; 57:10; 67:4,6; 71:22; 75:2;
76:11; 79:13; 86:12; 88:11; 99:3; 100:4; 105:1; 106:1;
107:1; 108:4; 109:30; 111:1; 118:19.28; 119:7; 138:1.2.4;
139:14; 142:8; 145:10.

92. One exception; Ps. 79:13, where LXX translates *hodah* by
anthomologeisthai.

93. *Ainein*: Gen. 49:8; Is. 38:18; I Par. 16:7.30.41; II.
Par. 6:26; 7:3; *Hymnein*:   Is. 12:4; 25:1; II Esdras (Neh.)
22:24.46; *Eulogein*:   Is. 12:1; 38:19, cf. LEDOGAR,
Acknowledgment, p. 73.

94. Lev. 5:5; 16:21; 26:40; Numb. 5:5; II Esd. 10:1; 11:6;
19:2.3; Ps. 32:5; Prov. 32:5.

95. MICHEL, *TWNT*, vol. V, p. 201.

96. LEDOGAR, *Acknowledgment*, p. 75.

97. *Shema* (Numb. 15:40-41).

98. BORNKAMM, "Lobpreis, Bekenntnis und Opfer," *Apophoreta
Festchrift fur E. Haenchen*, Berlin 1954, p. 49 *ff*, for
instance, Ps. 32:5; Prov. 28:13; Lev. 5:5; 16:21; Numb. 5:7;
Dan. 9:20; Neh. 1:6; 9:2; Ez. 10:1.

99. BORNKAMM, *Ibid.*, pp. 51-52.

100. ROBINSON, "Die Hodajot-Formel," *Apophoreta, op. cit.*

101. Ps. 6:6; 7:18; 9:2; 18:50; 28:7; 30:13; 42:6.12; 44:9;
45:18; 52:11; 57:10; 67:4.6; 71:11; 79:13; 86:12; 88:11;
92:2; 99:3; 100:4; 105:1; 106:1; 107:1; 108:4; 109:30;
111:1; 118:19.21.28; 119:7; 138:1.2.4; 139:14; 142:8;
145:10.

102. II Esdras 10:11, where *ainesis* means the confession of
sins, cf. LEDOGAR, *Acknowledgment*, p. 73.

103. Neh. 12:27.31.38.40.

104. Ps. 42:4; 69:30.31; 95:2; 100:1; 147:7; Is. 51:3, for
the confession of simple praise.

105. One exception: Jonas 2:9.10, *phones aineseos kai
exomologeseos.*

106. Lev. 7:12.13.15; 22:29; II Chr. 29:31; 33:16; Ps.
26:7; 50:14.23; 56:12; 107:22; 116:17; Jer. 17:26; 33:11;
Amos 4:5; Jonas 2:9.10.

107. S. DANIEL, *Le vocabulaire du culte dans la Septante*,
ch. XIII, pp. 273-297.

108. For the notion of peace as plenitude, see the article
by I. DURHAM, *"Shalom* and the Presence," *Old Testament
Essays in Honour of Gwynne Henton Davies*, John Knox Press,
Virginia, 1970, pp. 272-293.

109. *Ibid.*, p. 280.

110. BORNKAMM, "Lobpreis, Bekenntnis und Opfer," *op. cit.*,
pp. 52-63.

111. Examples for vow: Ps. 22:26; 61:6-8; 76:12; 132:2;
Prov. 20:25; 31:2; Eccl. 5:3; Nahum 2:2. Examples of vow
ending with a sacrifice of thanksgiving: Ps. 50:14; 56:13;
116:14; Prov. 7:14.

112. Prov. 20:25; Eccl. 5:3; Ps. 76:12.

113. Prov. 7:14; Ps. 116:14; Ps. 50:14.

114. YERKES, *Sacrifice*, pp. 64-67 (Hebrew vows), and
pp. 189-192 (vow of the Nazir).

115. Concerning musical terms, cf. *Virt*. 72-75; *Cont*. 29; 80;83; *Mos*. II, 256-257; *Plant*. 130-131.

116. Homage paid to virtue: *Spec. Leg*. II, 160;170;204; *Conf*. 108; *Jos*. 167; *Leg. Al*. III, 167; *Sacr*. 16; *Abr*. 218-219.

117. *Ebr*. 17; *Dec*. 120; *Spec. Leg*. II, 253; *Leg. Al*. III, 10; *Deter*. 53-54.   V. NIKIPROWETZKY (note 2, pp. 124-125), and complementary note on *Dec*. 106, pp. 154-156, *De Decalogo, Les oeuvres* 23) explains the philonic use and gives the Greek sources for the relation parents-children, showing that parents appear as a counterpart of God, and God's cooperators in the procreation of children.

118. *Spec. Leg*. I, 56-57; II, 145; III, 124-127; 173; *Mos*. II, 166-175; *Congr*. 98-105; 132-134; *Post*. 182.

119. *Spec. Leg*. I, 52-56; IV, 178; *Virt*. 102; 220-222.

120. A study of *therapeuein* (to serve God through worship) in relation to Levi, the Levites, the priestly ideal of the Therapeutae, and the cultural vocation of everyone of the faithful contributes to the understanding of the Levitical ideals and its various degrees in Philo.   About the Levitical ideals, see V. NIKIPROWETZKY, "Les Suppliants chez Philon d'Alexandrie," *REJ*, 1963.

121. *Sacr*. 53; *Agr*. 79-81; *Plant*. 130-131; *Q.G*. IV, 130, cf. Ap. A. Greek frg. on Gen. Book IV, n.130 (Loeb Suppl. II).

122. P. 90.

123. In *Migr*. 106, Philo distinguishes between *eulogemenos* and *eulogetos*.   The former refers to the benediction received by Abraham from men, who, as such, are fallible and inconsistent.   The latter refers to the true benediction, which has God as author.   Here Philo relies on LXX (*Gen*. 12:2) which offers these two forms.   Elsewhere, he does not stick to this distinction.

124. BEYER, *TWNT*, vol. II, p. 754.

125. *Q.E*. II, 18 on Ex. 23:25 *b*, and frg. 18, App. A. Greek frg. on Ex. Book II, Suppl. II, p. 246.

126. *Spec. Leg*. II, 175.

127. A similar shift can be observed in *Leg. Al.* I,17; *Migr.* 115-118.

128. We can compare Philo on Biblical heroes to *Sirach* 44-46, on Enoch, Noah, Abraham, Isaac, Jacob, Moses, Phineas, Josuah, Caleb, Samuel.

129. F.J.A. HORT and J.O.F. MURRAY, "Eucharistia-eucharistein," *JTS* 3, 1902, pp. 594-598, make some good remarks about *Spec. Leg.* I,224-225, which deals with the sacrifice of salvation including *todah*.

130. Philo, according to E.R. WOLFSON, *Philo* II, p. 240, proved to know the three meanings of the Hebrew term *todah* when he explained the etymology of the Hebrew name Judah as follows: 1) "praised (*ainetos*) by God" (*Plant.* 33; 135); 2) he "who blesses (*eulogon*) God" (*ibid.*, 136); and 3) "confession (*exomologesis*) of the Lord" (*ibid.*, 136 and parallels). We can observe that the various titles of Judah correspond to the various constructions of YDH.

131. *Ho exomologoumenos*: *Leg. Al.* I,79-84; III,26; *ho exomologetikos tropos*: *Leg. Al.* II,95-96; *Leg. Al.* I,79-84; *Mut.* 136; to *homologeisthai*: *Leg. Al.* II,95-96; cf. I,79-84; *he exomologesis*: *Plant.* 134-136; Som. I,37; *Leg. Al.* III, 146.

132. *Leg. Al.* I,79-84; II,95-96; III,26;146; *Plant.* 134; *Som.* II,37; *Mut.* 136; *Congr.* 125; *Ebr.* 94; *Q.G.* IV,123.

133. ROBINSON, "Die Hodajot-Formel," p. 199.

134. *Deus* 71; *Ebr.* 16;192; *Jos.* 191;230; *Conf.* 5;22; *Fug.* 205; *Abr.* 86.

135. For instance, for *nomizein*: *Leg. Al.* III,100;209; *Post.* 121; *Deus* 87; *Agr.* 169; *Congr.* 49; *Som.* II,116; *Mos.* II,168; *Dec.* 65; *Spec. Leg.* I,258;275; *Praem.* 162; *Prob.* 84; *Cont.* 86; *Legat.* 115;164. For *gnorizein*: *Deter.* 142; *Deus* 161; *Plant.* 64. Pour *gignosko*: *Leg. Al.* III,12;99;126; *Deus* 143; *Fug.* 8-10; *Mut.* 205; *Spec. Leg.* I,53;332; *Conf.* 24;27;144; *Op.* 8.23; *Ebr.* 41-43; *Mos.* I,203; *Post.* 37. For *legein* and *phaskein*: *Op.* 4;5;9;170; *Leg. Al.* II,40; III, 12;29;72;99;198; *Cher.* 71;73; *Post.* 41;115; *Plant.* 52; *Her.* 14; *Congr.* 133; *Fug.* 10; *Her.* 98. For "to inscribe": *Conf.* 106;144; *Fug.* 114; *Som.* I,78; *Mos.* I,299; *Spec. Leg.* I,252; *Praem.* 43. For other formulas such as "to think" (*oieo*): *Leg. Al.* I,51; *Op.* 170; *Cher.* 51; "to forget": *Som.* I,246; *Virt.* 163; "to judge" (*krino*): *Leg. Al.* II,50; III,209; "to

let understand" (*eisegein*): *Op.* 171; *Conf.* 144; "to assume"
(*hypolambanein*): *Plant.* 51; *Migr.* 194-195; *Abr.* 69; *Dec.*
58; *Spec. Leg.* I,13.   Other formulas   could be added, such
as, "not doubting":   *Op.* 170;   "to put" (*anatithemi*):   *Op.*
45; *Abr.* 84; *Praem.* 12; "to maintain", "to profess", "to
blaspheme".   The meaning is often confirmed by the addition
of "dare" (*tolman*):   *Op.* 4-5;45;   *Leg. Al.*   III,198; *Post.*
115.

136. For instance, *dokein*:   *Leg. Al.* III,6; *doxazein*: *Op.*
19; *Leg.   Al.* III,35; *dogma*:   *Sacr.* 3-5;50;64;   *Cher.* 6;32;
48;66;132; *Deus* 88; *Plant.* 52;77; *Conf.* 35; *doxa*:   *Leg. Al.*
I,20; III,31;126; *Deter.* 7; *Post.* 34-36; *Agr.* 130;   *Abr.* 70.

137. *Sacr.* 52-88.

138. *Q.G.* I,78.

139. SCHERMANN, "Eucharistia und eucharistein," p. 385.

140. Other references in this sense, *Spec.   Leg.* I,210-211;
275; *Virt.* 72-75; *Cont.* 87.

141. *Legat.* 118; *Virt.* 165; *Her.* 226.

142. LEDOGAR, *Acknowledgment*,   p.   95-97.   Concerning
whispered, loud,   and silent   prayer in Philo,   see WOLFSON,
Philo II, p. 249.

143. Concerning persons: *Legat.* 60; *Jos.* 99; *Leg. Al.*
III,245; *Deus* 4;7-9;48;73; *Ebr.* 94; *Spec. Leg.* I,287; II,
174; *Mut.* 222; *Plant.* 136; *Her.* 302; *Congr.* 6-8; *Q.G.* II,50.

      Concerning dispositions: *Mos.* II,207; *Virt.* 74; *Spec.*
Leg. II,180; 208-209.

      Concerning action (deeds and words):   *Plant.* 135; *Ebr.*
115; *Mos.* I,180; *Cont.* 87; *Mut.* 216-217.

144. Other examples, with *epi*:   *Mos.* I,58; *Migr.* 142; *Agr.*
79; *Spec. Leg.* II,192; with *eis*:   *Spec. Leg.* II,146;156;
Her. 226.

145. An individual man: *Spec. Leg.* I,283; II,185; III,6;
Her. 31; *Virt.* 72; *Congr.* 114; *Mut.* 222; a group of men or a
nation: *Mos.* II,42; *Spec. Leg.* II,203; *Flac.* 121; the world
or parts of the world: *Her.* 226; *Spec. Leg.* III,210-221.

146. The Jewish tradition generally explains the divine attitude towards Cain from the neglect of the latter in the accomplishment of his offering. S. DANIEL, *Vocabulaire du culte*, p. 209-210, notices that his sacrifice is a *thusia*, whereas that of Abel is called a *dora*. Far inferior to *dora*, which could refer to the perfection of the gifts brought by Abel as a sign of his homage and submission to God, *thusia*, which was but the ordinary name of a sacrifice, did not suggest a valuable offering, or one of any importance at all. The terms *thusia* and *dora* translate the same Hebrew term *minhah* with the addition of the aforesaid distinction.

147. Similarly, when Judas Macchabeus shows the head of Nicanor to the crowd, the shouting of benediction coming from them is not motivated as much by the death of a hated enemy, as by the enthusiasm caused in them by the gesture of the God of awe, who has just directly assumed the defense of His temple (II Mac. 15:34). Cf. J. GUILLET, "Le langage spontane de la benediction," *RSR* 57, 1969, P. 197.

148. The terms appearing in this text are: *memnemes, mneme, mneia, lethe, epilanthaneisthai, eucharistia, acharistia, philautia*.

149. We find also *mnemeion* and *hypomnema* used in the sense of a memorial of a divine gift (*Congr*. 100), or of the gratitude of man (*Spec. Leg*. II,146), and *hypomnesis* (*ibid*., 146) as memory of the first Pasch.

150. Concerning the restitution of a loan, which was so common a problem in the Egypt of Philo, see the note of J. POUILLOUX on *Plant*. 101, *De Plantatione*, p. 70, note 1, *Les oeuvres* 10.

151. *Q.G*. III,3.

152. Other examples of "to take": *Spec. Leg*. I,144, of "to keep for God": *Post*. 175, and of "to keep for oneself": *Leg. Al*. III,20-23; *Cher*. 63.

153. LXX reads, *ta dora mou domata mou karpomata mou eis osmen enodias diateresete prospherein en tais heortais mou*. The quotation is not always given completely by Philo, for instance, in *Leg. Al*. III,196, "Thou shalt preserve my gifts, My grants, My fruits". This law expresses the principle of thanksgiving, according to Philo: to acknowledge the gifts of God and to give them back to Him.

154. Concerning the prayer of petition, see Curtis W. LARSON, "Prayer of petition by Philo," *JBL*, 1946, pp. 185-203.

FOOTNOTES TO CH. II

1. In this chapter and the following, we use *eucharistia* and thanksgiving as a translation of the Greek *eucharistia*, without suggesting a distinction between these two words in English. The notion of *eucharistia* in Philo is now clear enough in the mind of the reader as distinguished both from a flat gratitude and from the Christian notion of the Eucharist in its particular developments.

2. E.R. GOODENOUGH, in his entire and in many regards remarkable book, *By Light Light*, supports the thesis that Philo was acquainted with a kind of mystery religion peculiar to his congregation, and following the principles of the mystery religions of the Greek-Roman paganism. He finds the doctrinal roots of this mystery in the Greek Orphism, in the Persian theology, and in the Egyptian mysteries of Osiris. The figures of this mystery, he says, are Jewish, indeed, and Philo did not indulge himself in religious syncretism, or deny his faith, but, in the Alexandrian Diaspora already, the Jewish faith had long ago laid hold, through the theory of the Greek borrowings from Moses, on the best of the Greek theology and mysticism, and used it for quite orthodox purposes. These ideas are especially the theme of the light-stream, which is particularly Persian and Orphic, and the male-female principle, which is particularly Isiac, but there are many other items perhaps less directly connected to mysteries, such as the migration of the soul, the Hellenistic ideals of kingship, the Natural Law and the Orthos Logos, the living Law as opposed to the written Law, etc. Goodenough finds all these themes in Philo. He gives, in this perspective, an excellent description of the figures of the patriarchs and of Moses idealized by Philo, although, in our opinion, he combines his findings too artificially and, as a consequence, offers too heavy a picture of these philonian heroes. What, in Philo, is pure symbolism, with the diversity of the particular meanings and the simplicity resulting from the very fact that these items are left loose, becomes, with Goodenough, a system, the richness of which, thus artificially displayed, seems, indeed, to justify his hypothesis of a Jewish mystery. From this construct, we can understand how easily Goodenough arrives at the idea of a liturgy, which he believes to be found in

the prayers of the seventh Book of *Apostolic Constitutions*.
He also supposes a liturgical apparatus of the type of
mystery religions, with rites, initiations, robes,
processions, thiases, and a sacred banquet (cf. *By Light
Light*, p. 261-264). The existence of the community of the
Therapeutae seems to confirm this view. If his hypothesis
were true, we should, as Goodenough does, consider it as the
basis to spiritual and liturgical life in Philo, which would
mean a complete overthrowing of our representations. However, our study shows that, although Philo likes the
vocabulary of mystery religions, which was so common in his
time that his use of it does not confirm the existence of a
mystery religion properly speaking among the Alexandrian
Jews. The use of these terms, when his tone becomes more
solemn and when he appeals to the arcana, is actually very
narrow, and refers to a Scriptural figure requiring, in
order to be understood as Philo means it, a fitting
spiritual and exegetical preparation. Therefore, the
Philonian use of these terms is simply a problem of
exegesis, especially when the matter concerns sexual
symbols, and does not justify at all the hypothesis of a
liturgy patterned on that of the mystery religions. Philo,
by principle, knows of only one liturgy: that of the Temple
of Jerusalem. The Therapeutae practice a liturgy of the
kind fitting their community life, but we do not find it in
any essential component of mystery religions. The
Therapeutae are exegetes, who practise asceticism and
contemplative life, have their religious assemblies, meals
and celebrations. But their liturgical celebration is a
Paschal celebration, the only one which is possible outside
of the precincts of the Temple, and probably without the
actual sacrifice of a lamb. They do not celebrate the loves
of Sophia and other myths. Philo also knows of the
Synagogal meetings, but he wants to consider them as mere
schools of philosophy, a restriction which leaves us without
any information on the prayers made in the Synagogue. The
grouping of such various elements in order to prove the
existence of a Jewish mystery religion can give the illusion
of a demonstration, but the analysis of each of these items
gives a very negative result.

3. The Rabbis refer to Deut. 8:10 for the benediction
recited over the meal and for the threefold benediction
which follows it (*Ber*. 21 *a*; 48 *b*; *Tos. Ber*. VII,1; compare
to it *Sybillines Oracles* IV,25; Josephus, *B.J.* II,8:5;
Letter of Aristeas 184). Cf. K. KOHLER, *The Jewish
Encyclopedia*, III, p. 9, article "Benedictions."

Concerning the *Graces* recited at meals by the Jews of the time of Philo, see Louis FINKELSTEIN, "The Birkat Ha-Mazon," *JQR*, 19, 1928-1929, pp. 211-262, particularly p. 213. the three first prayers are substantially earlier than Philo. They include a thanksgiving for the food taken in the meal and for the fecondity of the land granted to Israel. A prayer for Jerusalem and the Temple was also attached to it. The mention of the Covenant with Abraham for which graces ought to be given certainly goes back to a time of persecution, when it was forbidden to observe the Law. We also know that the mention of the *Torah* goes back to the second century B.C. Louis Finkelstein gives in parallel the three first benedictions of the "Birkat Ha-Mazon" and the three benedictions of *Didache* 10 (X,3;X,2;X,5), which are very similar (pp. 215-216), and he compares to them those of *Book of Jubilees* (22:6-9) (p. 219).

See also J.M. BAUMGARTEN, "Sacrifice and Worship among the Jewish sectarians of the Dead-Sea scrolls," *H.T.R.*, 46, 1953, pp. 252-253, for the practice of *Graces* at Qumran and the blessing given by the priests. We can suppose that Philo knew a formula of thanksgiving at meals for the gift of the food and for that of the good land of Israel, according to Deut. 8. But nothing backs the supposition of the mention of Jerusalem and of the Temple in this prayer, since Philo develops his thought and his spiritual life on the basis of Pentateuch, i.e., on the Patriarchs, the deliverance from Egypt, the liturgy and the Law given in the Desert.

4. Paul SCHUBERT, *Form and Function of the Pauline Thanksgiving* (Diss. in Phil., The University of Chicago, 1935, ms.), notes that the use of *eucharistia* and cognates is almost exclusively confined in Philo to their speculative function on the basis of the liturgical and ritualistic data. We have insisted enough on the sacrificial nature of the Philonian *eucharistia* to accept this remark. However, we should acknowledge Philo's serious interest in the literal meaning besides the speculations, since, for him, *eucharistia* is both a practice rooted in the rites and letter of Scripture, and speculatively developed on that basis. But we part from Schubert when he qualifies as Neo-Pythagorean speculation the sections where Philo speaks of *eucharistia* as the work of God and not of men, or when he sees in Philo a follower of the Stoic ideology concerning *eucharistia*, because he finds in these sections Stoic terms. His comparison between Philo and Epictetus is also very artificial (*ibid.*, p. 199).

5. J.P. AUDET, "Esquisse historique du genre littéraire de
la 'bénédiction' juive et de l'Eucharistie' chrétienne,"
Revue Biblique 65, 1958, pp. 371-399.

6. J.P. AUDET, *Didachè*. Etudes Bibliques, Gabalda, Paris,
1958, pp. 375-400.

7. *Ibid.*, p. 309.

8. *Ibid.*, p. 372.

9. LEDOGAR, *Acknowledgment*, p. 124.

10. H. CAZELLES, "L'Anaphore et l'Ancien Testament,"
Eucharisties d'Orient et d'Occident, Lex Orandi 46, ed. B.
Botte, Paris, 1970, pp. 11-21.

11. Luke 22:17-19: *eucharistein*; Mark 14:22-23: *eulogein*
and *eucharistein*; Mat. 26:26-27: *id.*, I Cor. 11:24:
eucharistein.

12. COLSON, *Philo*, cf. Ap. A. Greek frg. on Gen. Book IV,
frg. 130, Suppl. II, p. 223.

13. *Ibid.*, Note *a*, Suppl. II, p. 120.

14. *Ibid.*, Ap. A. Greek frg. on Ex. unidentified, Suppl.
II, p. 262.

15. H. CAZELLES, "L'Anaphore et l'Ancien Testament," *op.
cit.*, p. 11-21.

16. *Ibid.*, pp. 16-17; abbreviated.

17. *Hymnois te kai eudaimonismois kai euchais thusiais te
kai tais allais eucharistiais euagos ameibesthai. A de
panta sullebden hen onoma tes aineseos elache.*

18. Concerning merriment with wine drinking, singing and
dancing after a sacrifice among the Greeks, see YERKES,
Sacrifice, pp. 108-109.

19. ATHENEAS, *Epit*. II, 40 *c*.

20. E. LIPINSKI, "Macarismes et Psaumes de congratulation,"
Revue Biblique 75, 1968, pp. 321-367.

21. K. HRUBY, "Les heures de prière dans le judaisme à l'époque de Jésus," *La Prière des heures*, Lex Orandi 35, Le Cerf, Paris 1963, pp. 59-94.

22. Concerning the daily prayers of the Jews and what can be conjectured about them for the time of Philo, see the article just mentioned, p. 76-83. Concerning the prayers extracted from the Talmuds of Babylon and of Jerusalem, see the same author, "L'action de grâces dans la liturgie juive," *Eucharisties d'Orient et d'Occident, op. cit.*, pp. 45-49.

23. K. HRUBY, "L Action de grâces dans la liturgie juive," *Ibid.*, pp. 70-71.

24. *Ibid.*, pp. 23-51.

25. *Ibid.*, p. 36.

26. FINKELSTEIN, The Development of the Amidah, *JQR*, XVI, 1925-1926, pp. 36-40, note 86, quoted by Hruby, *ibid.*, p. 35.

27. K. HRUBY, "L'Action de grâces dans la liturgie juive," *op. cit.*, p. 41.

28. K. HRUBY, "Les heures de prière dans le judaisme à l'époque de Jésus," *La prière des heures*, pp. 69-75.

29. The Greek burnt-offering does not have the same meaning as the biblical burnt-offering. R.K. Yerkes notices (*Sacrifice*, p. 128): "Rendition of *'olah* into Greek was one of the problems of the translators of the LXX. Any Greek rite in which an animal was completely burnt was a rite not of worship and adoration but of aversion and placation. The Greek *karpoun* occurs twice to describe such a rite. The noun *kautos* likewise occurs twice to describe the animal so burned. The verb *holokautein* or *holocautoun* occurs twice. The translators of LXX carefully avoided all these words to render *'olah*, but used other words from the same roots, most of them apparently invented for the purpose, thus leaving no doubt that *'olah* connoted a victim completely burned".

Concerning *minah* and *'azkarah*, see, R.K. YERKES, *Sacrifice*, pp. 161-168. *'Askarah* refers to the incense added to the shew bread and burnt upon the altar, and as well to the portion of the *minhah* burnt upon the altar. Its meaning is "memorial", but in a sense more rich than the simple memory, remembrance, or even commemoration in

English.   A precision is added by the qualification of "a
burnt offering of sweet odor".   See *ibid*., pp. 212-214,
concerning   the   sense   of   'memorial'   in   the   Christian
Eucharist.

       Ishsheh can refer to   all rites in which fire was used
for sublimation of all or part of a victim into smoke which
ascended to Yahveh.   The exception of Lev. 24:7-9 is solved
by the fact that *'ishsheh* in this passage refers to the
frankincense, which was   placed in a pot beside the shew
bread, and was burned on the altar when that bread was eaten
by the priests in the sanctuary (R.K. YERKES, *Sacrifice*,
p. 129).

       Concerning the sacrifice *zebah*, see R.K. YERKES,
Sacrifice, pp. 146-160).   This term is translated by *thusia*
(138 times) or by one of the immediate cognates like *thuma*
or *thusiama* (24 times).   It is the earliest kind of
sacrifice, performed in the context of the family, but only
later on by a priest.   *Zebah* is used as a general term for
sacrifice, and is determined by the addition of *shelem* or of
todah.   Even the Pasch is twice called a *zebah*.   Concerning
the sense of *zebah* *todah*, see *ibid*., pp. 151-154.   R.K.
Yerkes explains the difficulty for the translation of *todah*
(8 Greek words or phrases, and 13 in the Latin) by the
evolution of this form of sacrifice.   The meaning of *todah*
as a kind of *zebah* is not always realized.   This word
appears only 31 times in the O.T., and always refers to an
object which ought to be given to Yahveh and to Yahveh only.
Todah was definitely an act of worship.   In every instance
it expressed an act or attitude addressed solely to Yahveh,
and always characterized by rejoicing and singing.   As a
cultic act, it was obviously a kind of *zebah*.   The chief
difference between *todah* and the other kinds of *zebah* seems
to be that the flesh of the *todah* was to be eaten the same
day that Yahveh's portion was offered.   Nothing was to be
left for the next day.

       Yerkes writes (*ibid*., pp. 151-152), "The word *todah*
means "thanksgiving", which played an increasingly important
role in the worship of Judaism and in the Achean, the
Hellenic and the Hellenistic cults on both the Eastern and
Western coasts of the Aegean Sea.   It is scarcely known in
any other semitic religion or in the native religion of the
Latins.   It is significant that, in the two religions which
gave form to the worship, thinking and living of early
Christianity, the very phrase *sacrifice of thanksgiving*
should have been so prominent.   It is significant also that,
in all three religions, the same phrase describes both a

cultic and a spiritual attitude".   Yerkes adds (*ibid.*, pp.
159), "Thanksgiving to God forms the contribution of the
zebah.   The Greek *thusia* had already begun to stress the
idea.   It remained for the *zebah* to enlarge and extend and
spiritualize it.   When we consider the close etymological
and logical and factual connection between remembering and
thinking and thanking, we can understand that constant
thanksgiving to God represents the highest possible development of religion.   To be thankful to one for a gift is not
merely to speak some formal words.   The words are well and
fitly spoken; they must entail constant "bearing in mind" of
the fact of the gift.   None but a churl would receive a
gift, say, "Thank you" and then abuse or forget the giver.
Genuine thanksgiving has no end.   It might be thought of as
constant cooperation with the giver in the tiniest and in
the greatest acts of life.   To be thankful is never to
forget the donor".

        According to S. DANIEL, *Vocabulaire du culte*, pp. 239-
240, a *'olah* is a burnt-offering.   It refers to a sacrifice
in which the victim is entirely burned on the altar, and the
word can as well refer to the victim directly.   It is the
basic rite of public cult: every day, in the morning and in
the evening, a *'olah* is offered for the entire people on the
altar of the Temple, and an additional one is offered on
every Sabbath, Newmoon, and in the great solemnities.   The
meaning of it is not, for as much, perfectly clear.
Scholars agree on seeing it as the feminine form of the
participle *HLH*, "to rise up", in the Qal.   But if, according
to the general agreement, it means "that which is rising
up", opinions are divided concerning the following.   For
some, the *'olah* is the victim itself, which goes up, or
which is made to go up, on the altar.   For others, who
represent the majority, the *'olah* is the offering which,
once placed upon the fire of the altar, goes up in the form
of smoke to the heavens.   This sacrifice occupies an
essential place in religious life.   An Israelite can offer
it spontaneously, as a confirmation of a personal request,
or as a thanksgiving, or in order to accomplish a vow.   He
is obliged to offer it in certain circumstances of his life,
such as after a birth, or after a disease.   Concerning the
way Philo translates *'olah*, see *ibid.*, pp. 257-258.

        Concerning burnt-offerings, see also the chapter on
Ishsheh in S. DANIEL, *Vocabulaire du culte*, pp. 155-174.
The word *'ishsheh*, exclusively reserved to the language of
worship, is found almost only in Pentateuch, and seems to
refer more particularly to the offerings destined to be
burned upon the altar, and not to those which are delivered

to the priests or the faithful.   LXX translates by *karpoma*.
This term has the advantage of including the relation of
'ishsheh to fire, however without, like Aquila's *pyrron*,
violating the usage of the Greek language, but, on the
contrary, in agreement with the meaning of *karpoun* in its
religious use among the pagans. In addition, because of its
apparent synonymy with *karpos*, understood figuratively,
karpoma suggests that *'ishsheh* is also a gift, the only idea
preserved in the *qorban* of the Aramean *Targums* (p. 174).

According to S. DANIEL, *Vocabulaire du culte*, p. 201-
204, *minhah* refers to an offering which man addresses to the
Deity.   In this sense, *minhah* can be a very general term,
like *qorban*, and referring likewise to all kinds of
offerings destined to the celebration of sacrifice.   But it
can take on a more specific meaning, and refer to a well
definite kind of offerings, that is, the vegetable offering
under its various forms and according to the various
compositions prescribed by the sacrificial code (cf. Lev. 2;
also Lev. 14:10-21; 23:16.17; Numb. 28:26; Lev. 5:11-13;
Numb. 5:15).

In the cultic domain, *minhah* is generally translated by
thusia.   LXX offers at least 94 instances of this usage: 2
in Genesis; 2 in Exodus; 34 in Leviticus and 56 in Numbers.
LXX also uses *thusia* for certain connotations of *'ishsheh*
and of *'olah*, but uses it regularly as the equivalent of
another important term of the religious language, *zebah*,
which refers to the sacrifice of an animal, either in a
quite general sense, or in the more restricted sense of a
sacrifice which is not a burnt-offering.   But *zebah*, being
clearly attested in a context which also includes the verb
z.b.h., "to offer", and the substantive *mizbeah*, "altar",
which are more often translated into Greek by *thusia* and
thusiasterion, appears with more rights over *thusia* than
minhah can claim, since the latter is isolated in the Hebrew
to such an extent that its root is not even discerned with
certitude.   For *soleth* (fine flour), of which the *minhah*
most often consisted, LXX uses the phrase *he thusia tes
semidaleos*, and for *zebah*, in the restricted sense of the
sacrifice of an animal not as burnt-offering--a *zebah
selamim*--LXX uses *he thusia tou soteriou*.

According to S. DANIEL, *Vocabulaire du culte*, p. 211,
concerning *minhah* for the afternoon prayer, we may consider
whether the translators of LXX were not influenced by the
wider meaning conferred on *minhah* by the post-biblical
Hebrew, when it used this word, not only for the oblation,
but for the whole of the offerings pertaining to the

perpetual sacrifice. The phrase *minhath tamid*, which, in any case, is biblical, was used preferably for the evening sacrifice, whereas that in the morning was still called *olath tamid*, and the *minhah*, as a consequence, became later on the prayer of the afternoon in the Synagogal liturgy.

According to S. DANIEL, *Vocabulaire du culte*, pp. 232-234, *'azkarah* is the vegetable offering (the handful of fine flour mixed with oil, as well as all the frankincense) offered on the altar as *'ishsheh* and *reah nihohah*. *'Azkarah*, as a consequence, is a part of *minhah* (or sacrifice). Therefore, *'azkarah* is treated like *'olah*. What is left of the (vegetable) oblation after *'azkarah* has been levied, is given to the priests (unless the sacrifice is offered for the sin of a priest). The nuance, therefore, is not *memorial*, but *remnant, trace, fraction*. In LXX, *'azkarah* is treated as a manner of synonym of *zebah* and of *zikkaron*, and *'azkarah* is translated by *to mnemosunon autes*, "in memory" of *minhah*.

According to S. DANIEL, *Vocabulaire du culte*, pp. 120-130 (ch. QORBAN), *qorban*, a derived of the root qrb is originally a name of action, but it came to mean, instead of the "fact of presenting", "the object which is presented", the "gift", and we find it almost exclusively with this concrete connotation. This object called *qorban* is most often the animal victim or the vegetable offering, brought to the Temple in order to be, properly, a sacrifice; but *qorban* also refers to the products offered in the Temple as levies, concerning which the law prescribes that nothing like honey and fermented things should be brought to the altar; *qorban* is also found in other senses directly connected with worship. Whatever be its applications, *qorban* is translated in Pentateuch with a quasi-perfect regularity, by *doron*. The translators apparently found no difficulty in calling the victim a *doron* even before its immolation, and they did not hesitate before phrases such as those found in Lev. 3:2.8, "he shall put his hand upon the head of his *qorban*" (*to doron*). The translators of Pentateuch can also translate by the same word *doron* the *minhah* and the *lehem*, i.e., the vegetable offering and the shew bread. Some scholars assumed that the choice of *doron* reflected a theological position of the Alexandrians, in which they manifested their conception of a sacrifice as essentially a gift to the Deity (particularly G.B. Gray and L. Moraldi). S. Daniel (p. 125) refuses to take a position with regard to this problem, but she thinks that this translation of *qorban* by *doron*, only manifests the interest of the translators in securing, regardless of any consideration

of etymology, a Greek equivalent which would be quite clear
and whose most applications in current Greek could
correspond to about all those of *qorban* in biblical texts.

Dora, in *Epistle of Jeremiah* (verse 27) manifestly
refers to sacrificial offerings, and is replaced in the
following verses by *thusiai* (verse 28) which refers to
animal offerings only, whereas *dora* probably includes
offerings of vegetable products and of libations as well.
Theodotion seems to preserve *doron* as a translation of
qorban all the more easily because he also preserved *thusia*
to express *minhah* in its religious meaning. But Aquila, who
used *doron* to translate *minhah* in every connotation, was
obliged to find another term for *qorban*, for instance,
prosphora in Lev. 1:2. We know that Symmachus also used
prosphora for the translation of *qorban* in Lev. 1:2, but for
other Hebrew terms elsewhere.

30. R. de VAUX, *Les sacrifices de l'Ancien Testament*,
Cahiers de la Revue Biblique, Paris, Gabalda, 1964, p. 40
(English translation, *Studies in Old Testament Sacrifice*,
Cardiff University of Wales Press, 1964, 120p.).

31. Concerning the revenues of the Temple and clergy, see
R. de Vaux, *Les Institutions de l'Ancien Testament*, Le Cerf,
Paris, 1958, 2 vol. (abbreviated, *Institutions*) vol. II, ch.
VIII, "Le sacerdoce apres l'Exil," pp. 274-277.

Concerning *Spec. Leg.* I,152, where the Law prescribes
that the offerings be brought to the Temple and then taken
from there by the priests, see S. DANIEL, "La Halacha,"
Philon d'Alexandrie, CNRS, p. 230.

32. A.F. RAINEY, "The Order of Sacrifices in Old Testament
Ritual Texts," *Biblica* 51, 1970, pp. 485-498, distinguishes,
following B.A. Levine, between "prescriptive" and "descriptive" texts, and raises the question of whether the order of
the sacrifices reflected in Levine's biblical sections which
are from administrative origin (Numb. 7 and 28-29), was the
order actually adopted in the daily practice of an Israelite
sanctuary. The proceeding seems to have been, on every
feast day, to make the sin offering before the burnt-
offering or the sacrifice of peace. And this conclusion is
very important for the determination of the religious
meaning of the sacrifice of peace. According to the ritual,
therefore, it can be said that atonement comes first; then,
consecration; finally, communion.

33. R. de VAUX, *Sacrifices*, *op. cit.*, p. 36.

34. *Le Lévitique*, *La Sainte Bible*, Le Cerf, Paris, 1958, Introd., p. 11.

35. M. HARL explains the Philonic notion and the Greek sources of the Divider Logos (*Heres*, pp. 62-102; see also her note, p. 72, on the Logos as holding the contraries together, *Les oeuvres* 15). She finds a Biblical origin for the notion of the Divider Logos in the sacrificial knife, pp. 82 *ff*., which, in our opinion, is well attested in thanksgiving, where many distinctions are necessary so that nothing worth mentioning would be forgotten, and nothing doubtful would be ascribed to God.

36. Concerning the addition of salt to the incense offering on the shew bread table, according to *Spec. Leg.* I,175, see S. DANIEL, "La Halacha," *op. cit.*, p. 223.

37. From the earliest texts after the time of Homer, *thusia* is the most common word for every kind of sacrifice which is not burnt-offering, i.e., where only part of the victim is consecrated on the altar, the rest being eaten by the faithful in a banquet. The other testimonies in our possession for this concrete use of *thusia* seem to refer only to animal victims, but LXX attests the possibility of using it also for vegetable offerings. See S. DANIEL, *Recherches sur le vocabulaire du culte dans la LXX*, Paris, 1966, p. 210.

38. S. DANIEL, "La Halacha," *op. cit.*, p. 235.

39. Concerning the *lehem* and shew-bread, see also S. DANIEL, *Vocabulaire du culte*, p. 130-153.

40. A. PELLETIER, *Supplément au Dictionnaire de la Bible*, VI, pp. 965-976, quote p. 973.

41. P. 112.

42. E. COTHENET, *Supp. au Dict. de la Bible*, VI, especially cols. 1315-1325.

43. H. CAZELLES, *Le Lévitique*, *La Sainte Bible*, p. 12.

44. E. COTHENET, "Parfums dans la Bible," *Suppl. au Dict. de la Bible*, VI, col. 1321.

45. *The Mishna*, Danby, pp. 93-98.

46. J.L. MCKENZIE, *Dictionary of the Bible*, "First-Fruits," p. 279.

47. MCKENZIE, First-Born, *ibid.*, p. 278.

48. H.J. KRAUS, *Worship in Israel*, p. 45, for instance, concerning the Pasch.

49. R.K. YERKES, *Sacrifice*, p. 104, makes an observation about the Greek *thusia* which we can retain in order to explain the extension of the meaning of *aparche* to a part of the sacrifice and not only to the first-fruits. "During the prayer, the officiant cut some hair from the neck of the victim and cast it into the fire. While this act is not specifically mentioned at every *thusia* in Homer, its mention in conventional language is frequent enough to warrant the assumption that it was a regular part of the rite. The customary word to describe it is *aparchomai*, which is the technical word for offering first-fruits and also for commencing libations. The noun *aparche* is used by Euripides to indicate the beginning of a *thusia*".

Concerning the exegesis of Numb. 28:2, see S. DANIEL, *Vocabulaire du culte*, p. 188-189. The phrase *reah nihoah* (*eis osmen euodias*) is a final clause. These forms of sacrifices are destined to please God, not to give Him calm and rest.

50. These laws are Ex. 13:11-13 (the consecration of every first-born male of the cattle); Ex. 22:28-30 (the first-born of men and cattle); Ex. 23:4-20 (the first-fruits of the harvest; the obligation for every adult male to appear three times a year before the Lord); Ex. 30:11-16 (the half-shekel given by every Israelite for his redemption); Lev. 2:14-16 (the first-fruits of cereals and the offering of fine flour); Lev. 3:3-5 (the fat and the lobe of the liver of a sacrifice of salvation); Lev. 23:19 (the feast of the sheaf among the feasts coming at the same time); Lev. 27:32 (the tithes of the cattle); Numb. 3:12-13 (the Levites taken as ransom for the first-born of Israel); Numb. 15:19-20 (the first loaf); Numb. 18:15-20 (the redemption of the first-born); Numb. 26:1-2 (the basket); Numb. 28:2 (the first-fruits brought for the feasts); Numb. 28:26 (the leavened loaf of Pentecost).

51. First-fruits and *eucharistia* are also associated in *Mos*. I,253; *Spec. Leg*. I,138;144;152;184&185; II,134;171; *Sacr*. 52; *Q.G*. I,60-64.

52. I. HEINEMANN, *Philons griechische und Judische Bildung*, 1962, pp. 142-144.

53.   *Ibid.*, pp. 106-110.

54.   PLUTARCH, *De tranquillitate animae*, 477 *c*, 20.

55.   Note on *Spec. Leg.* II, 42, *Philo*, Loeb, vol. VII, p. 334.

56.   Concerning the number of sacrifices offered for the feast of First-Fruits, according to *Spec. Leg.* I, 184, and for the feast of Atonement, according to *Spec. Leg.* I, 188, see S. DANIEL, "La Halacha", *Philon d'Alexandrie*, CNRS, p. 231.   See also A.F. RAINEY, "The Order of Sacrifices in Old Testament Ritual Texts", *Biblica* 51, 1970,   pp. 492-493, and R.K. YERKES, *Sacrifice*, pp. 141-142.

57.   HEINEMANN, *Bildung*, pp. 110-119.

58.   P. 132 fff; 164 fff.

59.   R. de VAUX, *Institutions*, II, ch. 16, "Le Sabbat," p. 378.

60.   HEINEMANN, *Bildung*, pp. 120-121.

61.   R. de VAUX, *Les sacrifices de l'Ancien Testament*, Gabalda, Paris, 1964, p. 25.

62.   HEINEMANN, *Bildung*, pp. 121-124.

63.   R. de VAUX, *Sacrifices*, pp. 23-25.

64.   P. 79.

65.   HEINEMANN, *Bildung*, pp. 124-128.

66.   *Philo* VII, on *Spec. Leg.* II, 163, note A, pp. 406-407.

67.   JAUBERT, *Alliance*, p. 57.

68.   *Ibid.*, pp. 398-399.

69.   Concerning the priesthood of the nation of Israel, see V. NIKIPROWETZKY, *De Decalogo*, complementary note on *Dec.* 159, pp. 160-161, *Les oeuvres* 23.

70.   JAUBERT, *Alliance*, p. 282.

71.   JOSEPHUS, *Ant.* III,X,5, or 248-251 in the Loeb.

72. Concerning the Chaburoth, see particulary Gregory DIX,
The Shape of the Liturgy, London, 1945, pp. 50-70; Johachim
JEREMIAS, *The Eucharistic Words of Jesus*, N.Y. 1964, pp. 29
ff.; Jacob NEUSNER, "Chaburoth," *HTR* 53, 1960.

73. V. NIKIPROWETZKY, "Les Suppliants chez Philon," *REJ*,
1963, p. 275.

74. HEINEMANN, *Bildung*, pp. 128-130.

75. R. de VAUX, *Institutions*, pp. 494-495.

76. HEINEMANN, *Bildung*, p. 131.

77. P. 62.

78. P. 85.

79. Note of F.H. COLSON on *Spec. Leg.* II,214, p. 440.

80. MCKENZIE, "Feast of Tabernacles", *Dictionary of the
Bible*, pp. 863-864.

81. HEINEMANN, *Bildung*, pp. 17-19.

82. For instance, *Virt.* 221; *Som.* I,77-78; *Dec.* 61-66;
Spec. Leg., I,19-21.

83. For instance, *Cher.* 94; *Deter.* 21; *Deus* 102-123.

84. V. NIKIPROWETZKY, "Les Suppliants chez Philon," *REJ*,
1963.

85. S. DANIEL, *Le vocabulaire du culte dans la LXX*, ch.
III, "La notion de service," p. 55-117. The notion of
"service", with *'abad* and the substantive *'abodah* (service,
slave, bondage), in the profane sense, is translated by
ergazesthai, doulos, ergon. In the religious sense *'abad*
means "to worship", and *'abodah* means the celebration of
rites or a general attitude of dependence and submission
toward God. They are translated by *latreuein* or by
douleuein. In the sense of a religious, but not priestly,
service, in Exodus, the phrase "to serve the Lord" always
refers to the celebration of sacrificial rites; *'abodah*
three times means the Paschal sacrifice; in Deuteronomy, "to
serve the Lord" is not any longer exclusively connected with
the accomplishment of Ritual, but also means reverence
towards God or the cult of idols. In the priestly service,
'abodah (leitourgia) means the office of priests and

Levites.   In Exodus, it means the taking up and the taking
down of the Tabernacle. In Numbers, where the duties of the
latter are described in all their diversity, the translators
use either the terms which commonly express the idea of
working in profane language (*ergazesthai* and *ergon*), or the
compound words *leitourgein* and *leitourgia*, which, at least,
in that Version, belong to religious language.   The verb
sabah and the substantive *sebah* can similarly refer to the
army, to war, or to the office of the Levites, and are
translated by *leitourgein, leitourgia*, and sometimes simply
by *poiein*. The root *sharath*, which is less used than *'abad*,
is also connected with the idea of "service". It is used in
the Piel, and the participle can also refer to a person.
When *sharath* is used for religious service, that of the
Levites or of the priests, it is translated with a remarkable uniformity, and the equivalent chosen for it is
leitourgia.   For the translators of Pentateuch, *leitourgein*
is strictly reserved to the exercise of worship by the
ministers consecrated in view of this service.   It is never
used for a religious "service" coming from a layman.
Neither is it used for any other function which could be
entrusted to the priests, even when they are entrusted with
it for the reason that they are priests.   On the contrary,
latreuein is never used in reference to priestly service.

        For the Greeks, *leitourgia* means a public duty, which
can be the cult of the gods (cf. Aristotle, *Pol*. 1330 *a* 13).
In Israel, the public duty of the service of God is
entrusted to the priests and Levites, and the translators
refer to it by *leitourgein, leitourgia* in its religious
sense attested before them.   The verb *therapeuein* is used
for the worship of idols in Epistle of Jeremiah (verses 25
and 28), and, in Judith (11:17), can express the devotion of
the heroine to the God of Israel. It is also found, with the
sense ascribed to *leitourgein*, in the section where the
Old Tobiah recalls how he has always fulfilled his religious
duties, particularly the payment of the tithes "to the sons
of Levi who serve (*therapeuein*) in Jerusalem" (1:7).
Therapeuein and *therapeia*, which were used for the care of
human beings, children, the sick, etc., are used for the
service of the gods as early as the first texts of the
Apocrypha (= deutero-canonical books), and, since then, have
always belonged to the vocabulary of religion. *Therapeutes*,
a derived, already attested to in Plato in the sense of a
"faithful", "worshiper", of a god, was, as we know, very
frequent in the late Greek.   The exceptional use of
threskeuein or *therapeuein*, instead of *latreuein* or
leitourgein, shows that the authors or the translators of
the Apocrypha (the deutero-canonical books), in spite of the

great influence which the vocabulary of the canonical books
exercised on them, readily exploited as well the possibili-
ties of the language of their own time.

86. The function of the high priest is described in Sirach
45:14-22, which mentions the unction, covenant, priesthood,
daily sacrifices, the blessing over the people, the incense-
offering, the income taken from the first-fruits, from the
sacrifices, finally, God as his portion of inheritance. See
also, *ibid*., 50:1-24, concerning priest Simon and the
blessing.

87. However, concerning the primacy of the interior worship
among the pagans, see the selection of great texts given by
A. JAUBERT, *Alliance*, note 72, p. 399. We quote, for
instance, Isocrates, *To Nicocles* 20 (ed. Teubner, p. 18),
"Fulfill thy duties towards the gods as our forefathers
taught thee, but believe that the finest sacrifice, the
noblest gesture of deference, is to prove thyself the best
and the most righteous of men". See also the discussion of
E. Bréhier (*Idées*, pp. 226-229) on interior life in the
Greeks, the Jews, and Philo. Moral life has become the
chief element of the true worship.

88. See the note of V. NIKIPROWETZKY on the term
thérapeute and its semantic background, in "Les Suppliants
chez Philon d'Alexandrie," p. 265. See also F. DAUMAS,
Introduction to *De contemplativa vita*, pp. 15-17, *Les
oeuvres* 29.

89. Concerning the Levites and servants of the Temple, and
their functions, in Philo and in the practice of the Temple,
see I. HEINEMANN, *Bildung*, pp. 27-28. For a more general
historical understanding, see what R. TOURNAY says
concerning the blessing of the tribe of Levi in "Le psaume
et les bénédictions de Moïse," *Revue Biblique* 65, 1958, pp.
194-195. Only with the development, he says, of the second
temple which reached its climax in the time of the Chronist
(about 300 B.C.), did the Levitical group come to be
particularly specialized in psalmody and chant; but
precisely, this psalmody and chant present a character
essentially didactic and parenetic.

Since Philo comments on Pentateuch exclusively, we
understand that he says nothing at all concerning the function of the Levites in sacred music.

See also S. DANIEL, note on *Spec. Leg*. I,156, "La
Halacha," in *Philon d'Alexandrie*, CNRS, p. 236.

90. F.H. Colson suggests that Philo sometimes used another version of LXX, concerning *didomi soi auton doton* (I *Sam.* 1:28), about *Deus* 6 (*Philo* III, p. 483). Philo develops on this text his idea that God gives man to man, which is the basis for the eucharistic offering of the self to God.

91. NIKIPROWETZKY, "Les Suppliants chez Philon," pp. 265-278.

92. DE JONGE, *The Testament of the Twelve Patriarchs,* Assen, 1953, pp. 48-49.

93. LEDOGAR, *Acknowledgment,* p. 97.

94. *Leg. Al.* III,11; *Som.* II,74; *Spec. Leg.* I,171; *Her.* 200; *Q.E.* II,71.

95. P. 49.

96. JAUBERT, *Alliance,* pp. 399-400.

97. WOLFSON, *Philo,* II, pp. 237-252.

98. *Ibid.,* pp. 246-247.

99. HEINEMANN, *Bildung,* pp. 66 & 472.

100. WOLFSON, *Philo* II, pp. 247-248.

101. *Ibid.,* p. 248, note 60.

102. For a resume of the question of the psalms of thanksgiving according to H. Gunkel, see Hermann GUNKEL, *The Psalms,* p. 17-18 (translated by Thomas M. Horner, Facet Books, Fortress Press, Philadelphia 1967, from the second edition *Gegenwart,* 1927-1931). See also, concerning the psalms of private thanksgiving, Sigmund MOWINKEL, *The Psalms in Israel's Worship* (English transl. by D.R. Ap. Thomas, Oxford 1967), vol. II, pp. 31-43, and H.J. KRAUS, *Worship in Israel* (English transl. by G. Buswell, Oxford, 1966), pp. 213-226.

103. WESTERMANN, *The Jerome Commentary,* "Psalms," p. 571.

104. R.E. MURPHY, *Ibid.,* pp. 573-574.

105. E. LIPINSKI, "Macarismes et Psaumes de congratulation," *Revue Biblique* 75, 1968, pp. 321-367.

106. *Sacr.* 63; *Agr.* 79; *Som.* II,268-271; *Her.* 14-16; *Congr.* 92-96.

107. Concerning hymnology and liturgical dance, see F. DAUMAS, *De vita contemplativa*, note 1 and 3 on *Cont.* 33 and 35, p. 142-143, *Le oeuvres* 29. Concerning the method of composition of ancient hymns, see the bibliography given by A.-J. FESTUGIERE, *La Révélation*, II, *Le Dieu cosmique*, note 3, p. 313, and the resume on this literary genus given p. 313 *ff* about the Hymn of Cleanthes.

108. JAUBERT, *Alliance*, pp. 168-170, and p. 176.

FOOTNOTES TO CH. III

1. Among the pagan parallels to the Philonic cosmic *eucharistia*, and probably among its sources, there is the famous hymn to Zeus of Cleanthes. We refer to the detailed commentary of this hymn given by A.-J. FESTUGIERE, in *La Révélation* II, *Le Dieu cosmique*, pp. 310-325. Many of the ideas reappear in Philo. Every man must sing to Zeus, from whom all originate, who is the author of all life, the God whom the Universe obeys. Zeus directs the Universal Logos who runs through all beings. Without Zeus, nothing can be done in the five parts of the world, except for the evil accomplished by the wicked who disobey the Divine Law of the Universe. Zeus is also a Saviour, the giver of every good thing, who rescues men from ignorance and confers on them right judgment. Therefore, we must honor him in singing his mighty deeds, "since there is no higher privilege for man and for gods than to sing always and fittingly the Universal Law". Let us notice in this hymn the terms expressing praise: *psosaudan* (verse 3); *hymnein* (verses 37 and 39); *time* (C.J. de VOGEL, *Greek Philosophy* III, n. 943). Festugière continues his development (*Le Dieu cosmique*, pp. 325-332) on the cosmic religion in the Stoics, and on Aratos' religious feelings regarding the world (pp. 332-340). Aratos' cosmic poem, *Phainomena* had become so classical that Paul quotes it in his speech in Athens. Aratos praises Zeus for the earth and seasons, for the beauty of the sky in a clear night, for the providence of the Father who feeds us and watches over us in every thing because we are of his own race.

2. WOLFSON, *Philo* I, pp. 57-66.

3. *Ibid.*, pp. 66-68.

4. *Ibid.*, pp. 73-85.

5. J. DANIELOU, *Philon d'Alexandrie*, 1957, pp. 129-138.

6. See Jean PEPIN, *Mythe et Allégorie*, Paris, 1958, the section on "Philon et les 'physiciens'," pp. 239-242. *Ibid.*, pp. 242-244 on cosmic allegory in Josephus.

7. *Abr.* 99; *Jos.* 151; *Leg. Al.* I,159; *Her.* 280; *Q.G.* III, 11.

8. *Q.G.* II,1,2,3; *Leg. Al.* II,9-11; *Spec. Leg.* I,271, etc.

9. Cf. *Flac.* 123; also the cosmic poem of Aristobulus quoted by Eusebius of Cesarea, *Praep. Ev.* XIII,12; see also the prayers of Book VII of *Apostolic Constitutions*, in E.R. GOODENOUGH, *By Light Light*, ch. XI, and Louis BOUYER, *Eucharist*, ch. 5, pp. 127-135.

10. See *Bible de Jerusalem*, note 1 on Wisdom 18:9: the author figures the first Pasch according to the image of the Pasch as it was celebrated in recent times, which included the Hallel, Ps. 113-118.

11. Concerning the vesture of the high-priest, although without the cosmic symbolism, see Sirach 45:6-13, and also *Letter of Aristeas*, 96-99.

12. See LEDOGAR, *Acknowledgment*, pp. 99-104, concerning the use of *eucharistia* in the Greek later books of the Old Testament, and pp. 90-94 concerning the use of *eucharistia* in the Hellenistic world independently from Philo.

13. *Plant.* 126-129, and the story of the Muses in Hesiod, *Theogony* 50 ff. For the identification of the superior intelligences with the "souls" of the heavenly bodies from the time of Plato, see WOLFSON, *Philo* I, pp. 360-366. According to Wolfson, Philo does not consider the stars as living beings (p. 365). It seems, though, that Wolfson's demonstration, which relies on the notion of "life", would turn to a positive conclusion if he considered the notion of "heaven", i.e., the superior substance, which is rational, kindred to the human mind, and of which all heavenly beings consist.

14. Concerning the music of the spheres in *Mos.* II,103 (the canticle of Moses at his death), see P. BOYANCE, *Etudes sur le Songe of Scipion*, 1936, pp. 97-98, and, of the same, "Les Muses et l'harmonie des sphères," *Mélanges Grat*, Paros 1946,

t.I, pp. 3-16, and the note of M. HARL on the notion of the harmony of the universe in Philo, in *Heres*, note 1, pp. 69-70, *Les oeuvres* 15. *Timaeus* (36 *c-d*, 40) provides the essential data concerning the music of the heavenly spheres, but Philo confers on them a very definite religious orientation (cf. M. ALEXANDRE, "La culture profane chez Philon," *Philon d'Alexandrie*, CNRS, 1967, p. 122).

15. *Pros ton deuteron theon, hos estin ekeinou logos*, according to the Greek fragment preserved by Eusebius, *Praep. Ev.* VII, 13, cf. R. MARAY, *Philo*, Suppl. II (Loeb), p. 203, n. 62 on *Gen.* 9:6.

16. Concerning the various hierarchies of the Philonic powers, see E.R. GOODENOUGH, *By Light Light*, pp. 23-47, who does not believe in a distinct existence of the powers: they are conventional aspects of the divine light-stream, but nothing else. They are functional distinctions of the unique divine power, but not personal distinctions (*ibid.*, p. 26).

17. M. HARL explains the Philonic notion and the Greek sources of the Divider Logos (*Heres*, p. 62-102. See also her note p. 72 concerning the Logos as a conciler of opposites (*Les oeuvres* 15). She finds a biblical origin for the notion of the Divider Logos in the sacrificial knife (pp. 82 *ff*), which, in our opinion, is well attested to in thanksgiving.

18. Concerning the symbolism of the vesture of the high-priest, see F.H. COLSON, *Philo* VI (Loeb), complementary note on *Mos.* II,117-135, p. 609, and E. BREHIER, *Les idées philosophiques et religieuses de Philon d'Alexandrie*, pp. 99-100.

19. P. 104.

20. Concerning the Logos in Philo and the spiritual worship in the soul, in relation to the three temples (the Universe, the Temple of Jerusalem, and the soul), see A. JAUBERT, *Alliance*, pp. 486-489. See also M. HARL, *Heres*, pp. 135-137 (*Les oeuvres* 15). Concerning the Logos more precisely as a cosmic priest in Philo, in relation to Aaron and the high-priest of the Temple of Jerusalem, see A. JAUBERT, *Alliance*, pp. 483-486.

21. Concerning the assimilation of the high-priest to the universe, as figuring a lower, although very valuable, form of worship, see E.R. GOODENOUGH, *By Light Light*, p. 106.

22. See App. A. Greek Frg. on Ex. Book II, n. 68, commenting on Ex. 25:21 *b*, F.H. COLSON, *Philo*, Suppl. II (Loeb), pp. 255-256 (*Q.E.* II,51-68).

23. Concerning the Logos as the "place" of the Intelligible world, and the term "place" as a divine name in Judaism, see WOLFSON, *Philo*, I, pp. 246-247.

24. See M. ALEXANDRE, *De congressu*, note 1, p. 110, on *Congr*. 8 (*Les oeuvres* 16). The central branch of the candlestick is oriented toward God (Lev. 24:4), and, according to Philo (*Spec. Leg.* I,296) figures virtue or wisdom raising towards God unceasing thanks.

25. Concerning the decade in relation to the first-fruits, see M. ALEXANDRE, *De congressu*, note on *Congr*. 97-98, p. 75, *Les oeuvres* 16. The theme of the first-fruits is central in the disgression on the decade. It is connected with the themes of dedication, consecration, thanksgiving for the divine gifts of praise. See also *ibid.*, pp. 242-244, the note on the Philonic speculations concerning the decade.

26. Concerning the notion of theology, understood as research and defense of the true notion of God, appearing in Plato and Aristotle, and taken up again by each of the following Greek systems, see W. JAEGER, *Theology of the Early Greek Philosophers*, p. 4. See also, concerning *theologia* as contemplation in Plato, Aristotle, Plutarch, A.-J. FESTUGIERE, *La Révélation* II, *Le Dieu cosmique*, Appendix, "Pour l'histoire du mot theologia," pp. 598-605.

27. Concerning Philo's discussion of biblical anthropomorphism, let us notice with W. JAEGER, *The Theology of the Early Greek Philosophers*, pp. 42-50, the origin of the Philonic solution in Aristophanes and its climax in Euripides. God is not like a mortal. With regards to Him, we must use the criterion of the *theoprepes*, "what befits God".

28. F.H. COLSON, *Philo* IV (Loeb), p. 574, explains, about *Her*. 246, the position of the great schools of philosophy concerning the creation of the world. Particularly, what Philo says concerning the unity of the Universe is almost entirely a quotation from *Timaeus* 41 *b*. The same F.H. Colson (*Philo* I, Loeb, p. 476) identifies the opponents of the five dogmas of Philo according to *Op*. 170-171.

29. WOLFSON, *Philo* I, pp. 164-200.

30.   For that purpose, he relies on *Op*. 170-172;   *Spec. Leg*.
I,327-344; *Dec*. 15; *Mos*. II,12;14; *Prob*. 80; *Som*. II,283.

31.   Sometimes Philo condemns the art of the   Sophists, and
sometimes he finds it relevant or even good.   For the discussion of this problem, see Alain MICHEL, "Quelques aspects
de la rhétorique chez Philon," *Philon d'Alexandrie*, CNRS,
1967, pp. 81-101, particularly pp. 83-85, and M. ALEXANDRE,
"La culture profane chez Philon," *ibid*., p. 113.

32.   Concerning Egyptian atheism according to Philo and
others, see WOLFSON, *Philo* I, pp.   29-32.   Concerning the
Egyptian king as *ho nous philosomatikos*, see   GOODENOUGH, *By
Light Light*, pp. 139-140.

33.   Concerning the rejection of the doctrine of Epicurus,
particularly by the Jews, see J.G. KAHN, note on *Conf*. 109,
De confusione, pp. 171-172, *Les oeuvres* 13.

34.   Those who are discarded from the Assembly.   See E.R.
GOODENOUGH, *By Light Light*, pp. 124-125.

35.   Concerning the   notion of creation in Philo,   the terms
which   he   uses: *ktistes*,   *technites*,   *demiourgos*,
kosmoplastein, *gennan*, *poietes*, and the problem of creation
ex nihilo, see M. HARL, *Heres*, note 1, p. 64, *Les oeuvres*
15.   About this last problem, see A.-J. FESTUGIERE, *La
Révélation* IV, *Le Dieu inconnu et la Gnose*, pp.   33-34 for
the position of Plato and Aristotle; and E.   BREHIER, *Idées*,
pp. 80-82 for those of Philo in relation to Plato.

36.   Concerning the "policeman-God" in the Greeks, see W.
JAEGER, *Theology of the Early Greek Philosophers*, pp. 186-
190, particularly the fragment of Critias' *Sisyphus* quoted
p. 187 (Greek text in Vogel, *Greek philosophy* I, n. 95).
Cf. H.A. WOLFSON, *Philo* II, p. 167.

37.   Philo extends the meaning of *ek pornes* to the son of
the adulterous woman, just as LXX, which represents a position more strict than the position of the Hebrew of Deut.
23:3.   See S. DANIEL, "La Halacha," note on *Spec. Leg*. I,
326, *Philon d'Alexandrie*, CNRS, p. 224.

38.   E. BREHIER (*Idées*, pp. 164-169) tries to identify the
teaching which Philo criticizes under the name of the
Chaldeans. He notes that Philo answers it with the analysis
of the philosophical itinerary of Abraham. M. ALEXANDRE, *De
congressu*, note 1, pp.   138-139, *Les oeuvres* 16, writes,
"Philo's attacks against the "Chaldaic opinion" reaches far

beyond the world of Astrologists: against all the currents
of the cosmic religion, Philo is affirming the transcendence
and the creative power of the unique God". J. PEPIN finds
out the teaching of the Chaldeans in the *De philosophia* of
the young Aristotle, which teaches the self-motion of the
Universe and the deity of the ether, a teaching echoed later
on by the Stoic Allegorists (*Théologie cosmique et théologie
chrétienne*, PUF, Paris, 1964, abbreviated, *Théologie
cosmique*, pp. 286-291.

39. E. BREHIER (*Idées*, pp. 200-205) recognizes in the
impossibility of knowing the divine essence, according to
Philo, in spite of his fundamental intellectualism, a kind
of anti-Stoic scepticism, which excites the soul to a
perpetual search for this infinite object. Ecstasy consists
in this pursuit.

40. Concerning Philo's use of the Skeptical "tropes" of
Aenesidemus, see F.H. COLSON, *Philo* III, (Loeb), appendices,
on *Ebr*. 175-193, pp. 506-508; VI, appendices, on *Jos*. 125-
147, pp. 601-602. See E. BREHIER (*Idées*, pp. 210-216).
Brehier, then, discusses Philo's usage of Scepticism in his
itinerary toward faith. However, we think that Philo rather
uses Scepticism as a purification of the mind and a preparation for listening to the voice of God, than as a component
of the very edifice of faith itself.

41. Concerning the knowledge of God through revelation,
when God makes Himself heard by man, and not simply known
through the "proof from the deeds of God", see H.A. WOLFSON,
Philo II, p. 189.

42. Concerning Abraham's migration and the Philonic
ecstasy, first, out of the body, and, second, out of the
self, concerning its Platonic aspects and its biblical
expression, see M. HARL, *Heres*, Introduction, pp. 27-30, *Les
oeuvres* 15.

43. Concerning the similarity between the heaven and the
intellect, and concerning the motion of the soul as the
imitation of the regularity and of the stability of the
sphere of the fixed stars, in order to discover beyond the
heavens the transcendent God Who is the pilot of the
Universe, see M. HARL, *Heres*, Introduction, pp. 90-102, *Les
oeuvres* 15. Her whole introduction is very enlightening.
However, we think that we should distinguish more strongly
the various lines of Philo's reasonings, particularly the
notion of substance (the ether is the most sublime substance), the Forms or *logoi*, individual beings, and the

powers which are, as it were, several expressions of the divine face looking at men.

44. Concerning the notion in Judaism of the migration of the souls, and of the world as a temporary residence where we should not establish ourselves, see J.G. KAHN, *De confusione*, note 7 on *Conf*. 82, pp. 161-162, *Les oeuvres* 13. M. Harl recognizes in the word *hebraios* the meaning of "migrant", and refers to Erich FASCHER, "Abraham, physiologos und philos theou," in *Mullus*, Fest. Klauser, 1964, pp. 111-124 (*Heres*, note 3, pp. 47-48, *Les oeuvres* 15).

45. J. PEPIN, *Théologie Cosmique*, pp. 490-491.

46. See Werner JAEGER, *Aristotle*, *Fundamentals of the History of his Development*, Oxford Univ. Press, 2d ed., 1948 (1962), translation by R. Robinson from the first German edition of 1923), ch. VI, pp. 124-166. See Anton Hermann CHROUST, "A Cosmological Proof for the Existence of God in Aristotle's Lost Dialogue *On Philosophy*," in *The New Scholasticism*, XL, Oct. 4th, 1966, pp. 447-463; "The Doctrine of the Soul in Aristotle's Lost Dialogue *On Philosophy*," *ibid*. XLII,3, Summer, 1968, pp. 364-373. More generally, for the fragments of Aristotle's *De philosophia*, see Mario UNTERSTEINER, *Aristotele Della filosofia*, Introduzione, Testo, Traduzione e Commento esegetico, Edizioni di Storia e Letteratura, Roma 1963, 312p. (*Temi e Testi* 10).

47. F.H. Colson, about *Som*. II,233, raises the problem of the contradiction between *Op*. 7 and *Aet*. 19 concerning the destructibility of the world, and finds an answer in *Her*. 246: the Creator can, indeed, destroy it, but will never actually do it (*Philo*, Loeb, vol. VI, p. 610).

48. FESTUGIERE, *Le Dieu cosmique*, pp. 79-90.

49. *Ibid*., p. 104.

50. *Ibid*., p. 151.

51. Concerning the world as the temple of God, the ethereal substance of the heavenly beings, and the soul as a "heavenly plant" with a vocation of harmony with the Cosmos, according to the *De philosophia* of the young Aristotle, see A.-J. FESTUGIERE, *La Révélation* II, *Le Dieu cosmique*, pp. 233-259. In Stoicism, the materiality of the system of the world is affirmed, and ethics proposes to achieve this

cosmic harmony, but in a materialistic system (*ibid.*, p. 260 ff). More strictly moral with Zeno, more scholarly and dialectical with Chrysippus, Stoicism takes on, with Cleanthes, a religious character properly speaking, and even mystical (*ibid.*, p. 310). When, after a gap of one and a half century (from the death of Chrysippus, 206 B.C., to the *Dream of Scipio*, 54 B.C.), we observe the renewal of the religion of the world, in the time of Cicero, and probably of *De mundo*, this religion certainly preserves a scientific aspect, but does not depend any longer on a particular system of philosophy. This characteristic will last until Hermetism and Plotinus, and, beyond them, until the last philosophers of Athens and Alexandria. We are confronted here, actually, with a dogma of paganism: the tenets that the world is beautiful, that it is a mighty deed worthy of adoration and love, since, being itself an anti-god, it manifests the reason and providence of the Deity which manages it. It is the predominance of religious dogmatism and of philosphical eclectism, with some anti-Christian tendancies (*ibid.*, p. 343).

52. The proof from the structure of the world (*Spec. Leg.* I, 33-40; cf. *Leg. Al.* III, 97-99), is paralleled in the Stoics, see S.V.F. II, 1099-1020, particularly Cicero, *De nat. deorum* II,16-17; III,26; cf. also *Tusculanes*, I,68; *Pro Milone* 83,84, and *Zen. Mem.* I,4.

53. FESTUGIERE, *Le Dieu cosmique*, pp. 219-260.

54. *Ibid.*, pp. 260-280.

55. *Ibid.*, pp. 506-510.

56. The antithesis *hyparxis-ousia* seems to be, in Philo, as in the pagan authors where we find it, a commonplace. We can not even say that it implies necessarily the idea of transcendence. The cosmic God is also *aphanes*: we do not see Him, but we see that He exists. However, Philo's God is certainly transcendent, and this not only because Philo's theology is inspired by the Bible, whose God is distinct from the world which He created, but also because, with the Platonic (*Timaeus*) and Stoic teaching on the Cosmic God, Philo combines other teachings of Neopythagorean and Platonic origin, which imply the transcendence, and even the unknowableness of the First Principle. Cf. A.-J. FESTUGIERE, *La Révélation* IV, *Le Dieu inconnu et la Gnose*, p. 17.

57. J. PEPIN, *Théologie cosmique*, pp. 250-291.

58. *Ibid.*, p. 273.

59. *Ibid.*, p. 274.

60. *Ibid.*, pp. 262-263.

61. *Ibid.*, p. 519.

62. *Ibid.*, p. 521.

63. Concerning the ether, as the substance of the heavens and of the human mind, the quintessence, the substance of the stars and of the highest heavenly sphere which encompasses all others, in relation to Philo and to the philosophical sources of this notion, see J. PEPIN, *Théologie cosmique*, p. 241; 490 (according to Cicero, *The Dream of Scipio* 4, 17); 536 (complementary note). It is the teaching of the young Aristotle, beyond the Stoics.

According to J. Pépin (*Théologie cosmique*, p. 340), the theological elaboration of the notion of creative power (*poetike dynamis*) and its connection with the texts of Scripture can certainly be ascribed to Philo as their author, but the formula itself, as applied similarly to the problem of the formation of the Universe, was known in the Greek tradition: it appears twice in the *Sophist* of Plato in reference to the Cause turning non-being into being (265 *b*; 269 *b*), in Aristotle, though only concerning elements or bodies of sense-perception, for instance, *De Caelo* I,7, 275 *b* 5, in Theophrastes, *Physic opinion*. frg. 3 (cf. notes 6 and 7, *Theologie cosmique*, p. 340).

64. WOLFSON, *Philo* I, p. 293.

65. Concerning the transcendence of God and the theory of the double monad (the One being sometimes superior to, sometimes identical with, the Monad) in Philo, in the Neo-Pythagoreans, and in Plato in *Parmenides* (141 *e* 7-142 *a* 7) and in *Letter* VII, see A.-J. FESTUGIERE, *La Révélation* IV, *Le Dieu inconnu et la Gnose*, pp. 19-25; 84-91.

66. The teaching that God is self-sufficient is found in the Greeks: Euripides, Xenophon, Menedemus in Diogenes. In Plato, the Good, and, in Aristotle, God, is self-sufficient. See H.A. WOLFSON, *Philo* I, note 45, p. 172.

67. Plato, *Protagoras* 322 *a*; *Laws* IV,716 *c*; *Tehetetus* 151 *e*, etc.; Aristotle, *Metaphysics* X,1053 *a* -1053 *b*; Diogenes

Laertius IX, 51. C.J. de Vogel gives the chief fragments illustrating his thought, *Greek Philosophy* I, pp. 86-92.

68. Diogenes Laertius IX, 51 (Loeb, Clas. Libr.).

69. PLATO, *Protagoras* 322 *a*, transl. E. Hamilton and H. Cairns.

70. Cf. W. JAEGER, *Theology of the Early Greek Philosphers*, p. 176.

71. Ch. Kannengiesser insists on the idea that, in Philo, God is the Cause simple and sovereign, excluding every composition and need which are the characteristics of all created natures, particularly of men. For this reason, God, and not man, owns the absolute power over all things, and can be said to be "the measure of all things". Ch. Kannengiesser places this problem in the ontological perspective ("Philon et les Peres sur la double creation de l'homme," *Philon d'Alexandrie*, CNRS, pp. 282-283).

72. DANIELOU, *Philon*, pp. 57-75.

73. M. ALEXANDRE sees in the Philonic teaching of the kinship between man and the world (especially the heavens) and of the divine sonship of the world, the transposition to the individual man of the biblical theme of the divine sonship of Israel, and she gives sources for these ideas in Greek philosophy (*De congressu*, note 4 on *Congr*. 177, pp. 227-228, *Les Oeuvres* 16).

74. WOLFSON, *Philo* I, p. 293.

75. E. BREHIER (*Idées*, pp. 92-96) shows that the soul, once perfected, does not differ any longer from the transcendent Logos, and is no longer governed by the Logos, because the soul itself is the Logos. However, he gives a Platonic and Stoic explanation which differs from that of Philo, for instance in *Q.E.* II,40. Usually, Philo explains the itinerary of the soul towards God in reference to the divine powers (expressions of the divine face), which the soul successively discovers according to her own dispositions.

76. NIKIPROWETZKY, (*De Decalogo*, complementary note on *Dec*. 176, pp. 164-165, *Les oeuvres* 23) notes that God, in order to punish man, makes use of secondary causes. He can also punish him in a miraculous manner, for instance when He reserves to Himself the three last plagues of Egypt. But God cannot be the cause of evil, whence punishments are

defined as "these goods which imitate evil" (*Fug*. 74).
Concerning the references to this idea in Philo and in
Plato, see *ibid*., p. 128, note 2.

77. Fate, in Plato, takes on an acceptable sense when it is
conceived of as the chain of "secondary causes", if we avoid
conferring on the whole or on the parts of this chain the
absolute power which belongs to God alone. Cf. H.A.
WOLFSON, *Philo* I, pp. 329-330.

78. WOLFSON, *Philo* I, pp. 428-430.

About the notion of *kairos*, its Greek sources, and its
meaning in Philo, see F.H. COLSON, *Philo* VII (Loeb), note
p. 624 on *Spec. Leg*. II,56.

79. About the notion of God as *apoios* in Philo and in the
Greek sources, see E. BREHIER, *Idées*, p. 72, who refers to
Drummond, and H.A. WOLFSON, *Philo* II, pp. 101-110. God does
not belong to any class of beings, and is superior to all
existing things. Bréhier sees the source of this teaching
on the incomparable God in *Deutero-Isaiah*.

80. See Jean DANIELOU, *Philon d'Alexandrie*, Paris, 1958,
pp. 127-128. About Enesidemus, see Brochard, *Les Sceptiques
grecs*, pp. 254-259.

81. See WOLFSON, *Philo* II, p. 216.

82. Among Jewish parallels to the Cosmic *eucharistia* we may
refer to Sirach 42-43. The first book of *Enoch*. 41:7,
offers a parallel to the *eucharistia* of the heavens and
stars.

83. E. BREHIER, *Idées*, pp. 69-82.

84. At Qumran also cosmic praise is known, for instance,
"Hymns" X, pp. 182-183; XVIII, p. 200 (G. VERMES, *The Dead
Sea Scrolls in English*, Penguin Books, 1973). The members
of the community of Qumran worship God the Creator and
Providence of the universe. But do they do so in the name
of all humanity, in the manner of universal priesthood? A.
Jaubert answers (*Alliance*, p. 175): "We could have
concluded that, as in other circles of Judaism, there was a
universal mediatory function of the believer's priesthood,
and, therefore, of the community who has entered into the
Covenant of the sons of Sadoc. But the text of *Benedictions*
(I QS *b* III,28) is actually very isolated: the people of
Qumran do not seem to have been interested in "mediation"

for mankind in the sense of "salvation" provided to men
classified in the category of the "impious." But in other
regards, the cosmic function of the priesthood flourished in
Qumran under the aspect of praise and of illumination."
(*ibid.*, pp. 178-179).

FOOTNOTES TO CH. IV

1. R. ARNALDEZ, "La dialectique des sentiments chez
Philon," (*Philon*, CNRS, pp. 299-330), and *De virtutibus*,
Introduction, particularly pp. 20-21, *Les oeuvres* 26, notes,
concerning Islamic mysticism, "On the second highest degree
of mystical ascent, man is the lover, and God is the object
of the love. But, on the highest degree, the soul realizes
that, actually, in the display of her deep love, she is the
object of the love, and God is the Lover". This observation
leads Arnaldez to discover in Philo a similar theory of the
"dialectical reversal of sentiments". In the progress of
spiritual life, sentiments metamorphose, and reach their
perfection when they join in God their cause, root and
truth. In this sense, faith is "saved" when man gives up
"trusting himself", and is able to "humiliate himself"
before the Benefactor God. In this degree, God takes the
initiative in moral choice. On the contrary, when man
(Cain) thinks that he can accomplish by himself his own
salvation, relying on his own free will, actually, he
confines himself to self-love and is found abandoned by God.
The key of the metamorphosis is the theory of the participation in the virtues of God, rather than the birth of the
virtues in the soul. With good reason, R. Arnaldez sees in
this a dynamic system, dealing with "values", rather than a
philosophy of corporeal and incorporeal essences. In this
system, man is a pure subject, whose primaeval error
consisted in uttering Descartes' *Cogito*, i.e., in saying, "I
am", "I think", "I feel", etc., instead of discovering his
liberative and salvative passivity with regards to God. The
ponos (effort) is required, but is ultimately condemned to
fail because it implies a contradiction, since success comes
from God and consists of a perfect participation in the
divine power. All our sentiments: joy, hope, sadness,
fear, are "dialectical" in the same manner, and liable to
evolve in the right or the wrong direction. Concerning the
virtue of humanity (in *De virtutibus*, pp. 20-21), R.
Arnaldez shows that the true unity among men, as the other
sentiments, is ultimately the work of God, and can exist
only through the common love of men, especially of leaders,
for the Creator and Father of the Universe. R. Arnaldez
emphasizes the necessity, in the life of virtue, of both

disappropriation and participation: we would say, of the
eucharistic spirit.   However, the basis of this theory is
Platonic: the participation in the Forms or higher realities is more rich than the simple intellectual assimilation
understood in the Aristotelian or modern sense of the word.
It carries along the "heart" and deeds, and relies on the
experienced   certitude of the metaphysical   reality of
spiritual values.

2. DANIELOU, *Philon*, p. 116.

3. *Ibid.*, p. 103.

4. P. 249, note 1.   E.R. GOODENOUGH (*By Light Light*,
pp. 279-282) compares the poem of Orpheus quoted by
Aristobulus and preserved by Eusebius (*Praep. Ev.* XIII,12)
to the original preserved in the *Testamenta* of Orpheus (cf.
Lucien CERFAUX, "Influence des Mystères sur le Judaisme
alexandrin avant Philon," *Museon* 37, 1924, pp. 36-48).   He
notes that the Jews, long before Philo (following Schurer,
Goodenough proposes 200 years), had already started to
transform their Jewish notion of Wisdom into the mystical
doctrine of *Sophia* understood as a stream of divine light.
With that purpose, Aristobulus repeats and corrects the poem
of Orpheus. In the time of Philo, the Jews were far beyond
this stage of assimilation, and did not care any more for
the teachings of Orpheus or of Isis.   According to
Goodenough (*ibid.*, pp. 282-289), *Sibylline Oracles* also
depend heavily on Orphic sources for their mystical aspects.
Goodenough tries to prove the Orphic dependence of Philo's
teaching, and deals with his findings in a way which seems
too onesided.   He does the same with Ezekiel the poet,
Artapan (*ibid.*, pp. 289-293), and with the *Oratio ad Graecos*
of Pseudo-Justin (*ibid.*, pp. 298-305).

5. DANIELOU, *Philon*, p. 117.

6. LARCHER, *Etudes sur le Livre de la Sagesse*, Etudes
Bibliques, Paris, 1969, pp. 151-178.

7. H. LEWY, *Sobria ebrietas*, pp. 63-66.

8. E.R. GOODENOUGH (*By Light Light*, pp. 269-277) discusses
the speculations of Wisdom of Solomon on the role of the
Wisdom who pre-exists the world. Certainly, his theory of a
double mystery in Philo: that of Aaron based on the
contemplation of the world according to the cosmic symbolism
of the vesture of the high-priest, of the incense offering,
and of the furniture of the temple, on the one hand, and, on

the other, the mysteries of Logos-Sophia, the male-female
principle, which reflects Orphic, Persian and Isiac speculations, is very artificial, because it supposes the
existence, in the Judaism of the Diaspora, of a cult with
mysteries and initiations, etc., of the type of the
Hellenistic mysteries, and a too close dependance on
theosophic sects. Goodenough developed these theories in a
time when the enthusiasm for the study of mystery religions
reached its climax. It is true, though, that Philo bases
his mysticism on this twofold initation, and, particularly
for the second, that he plays on the figure of *Sophia*
assimilated with the holy wives of the Patriarchs, divinely
pregnant, begetting for man, daughter of God, pre-existing
the world, and creative, source of immortality and of
perfection. But Philo does not actually teach a double
mystery. Through the contemplation of the cosmos,
especially of the heavens, we reach the Creator on the
summit of the world and of man. This is Cosmic theology,
nothing more, and the revelation concluding this search for
God is simply the experience of the living God, for which
Dialectics cannot substitute. Therefore, it is not a
mystery properly speaking, and Philo does not present the
revelation granted to Abraham as a mystery.

With the relations between the perfect man and Sophia,
we enter a different world of thought, and the question is
no longer about contemplation or even creation. We leave
the domain of Cosmic theology, and enter that of the
theology of grace. The language now is that of mysteries
with their arcana, for the simple reason that the divine
generation of virtue is expressed in the vocabulary of the
human generation and in the symbolism of the wives of the
Patriarchs according to the peculiar and sometimes odd
situations which characterize their conjugal life. These
teachings have no relevance for those who have not reached
yet in their own life the corresponding level of purification and of interior life. The proof of it is that they
mock this so-called intrusion of sexuality in these speculations, and find themselves quite satisfied with the
triviality of the literal meaning of these sections. However, this language is, for Philo as for the majority of
mystics, the most appropriate, and, furthermore, it is
biblical. We know the speculations on Eve, on the Bride of
Song of Songs, on the adulterous wife of Hosea, on the
Church as the Bride of Christ in Paul.

In Philo, the originality is perhaps less in the fact
that he speculates on the wives of the Patriarchs, which
seems to be quite acceptable in a Judaism for which the

essentials of Scripture are the Pentateuch, but the fact
that he uses for the individuals and for interior life these
biblical images commonly used for the people of Israel.
Therefore, the true mystery of Sophia in the life of the
perfect man is a theology of grace. Here the role of the
Logos is limited, and apparently confined to the problem of
knowledge, of intercession, of purification and adoration.
I do not see that he plays the part of a male, except
through virilizing discipline. On the contrary, Wisdom
takes on several forms. She is barren together with Sarah
when Abraham is still in need of Sophistic culture figured
by Hagar and Ismael. She begets with Sarah when Hagar,
barren in wisdom, is discarded, and when Generic Virtue,
made pregnant by God and not by man, dwells with Abraham
with her divine power and her promise of immortality. She
is fertile and without eclipse in Isaac from his birth, in
the figures of his mother Sarah and of his wife Rebecca.
She is conflicting in Jacob the Ascetic with the pleasure of
the senses and its powerful attraction figured by Rachel,
but, although hated together with Leah, she alone is fruitful of the true goods. Other wives, such as those of Moses,
are also figures of Wisdom.

Goodenough, on our opinion, pushes too far the
synthesis of Wisdom as a Creative agent, and her role in the
life of virtue or in the theology of grace. Creative Wisdom
is attested to, indeed, in Philo, where it is uneasy, but
necessary to distinguish her role from that of the Logos.
Wolfson identifies them with good reasons, but unduly, since
in Philo Logos and Wisdom have their respective biblical
setting, and consequently a character of their own. The
same is true with the *pneuma*. It would be interesting, but
this would lead us too far, to study without too much
prejudice the term *sophia* in Philo, and, in particular, to
make a clear distinction between, on the one hand, the
biblical sources where it is found, and, on the other, its
role in the context, as a creative agent in a Cosmic
theology, or as a pedagogical agent in a theology of grace.
These two aspects find support in the book of Proverbs which
Philo cites, and in Wisdom of Solomon, which he may know,
although we cannot affirm that he uses it. For this reason,
we treated this book as a parallel and not as a source of
Philo.

Goodenough, in the section to which we are referring,
gives an interesting study of the speculations of Wisdom of
Solomon on Wisdom and particularly on her pedagogical
aspect. With good reason, he depicts her as immaterial, the
source of a stream of immaterial light, as a legislative

power making of Solomon a living law.   She operates in him
through teaching and grace, and establishes him in his
particular character as she does for the other heroes of the
Bible.   Because of her highest aspects (Wis. 7:15-8:1),   we
understand that she can be the cooperator of God in the
works of creation, and, for this reason, qualified for her
role of pedagogue of men.   However, in Wisdom of Solomon,
Wisdom does not appear as the wife of man, what she is in
Philo definitely.   When Goodenough sees Wisdom as a female
principle both in Wisdom of Solomon and in Philo, in the
manner of Orphism, of Isis, and of the powers of Mithra, he
is too unprecise.

9. P. 251, note 1.   A. JAUBERT notices in *Letter of
Aristeas* "The first outlines of what we can call in Philo a
theology of grace" (*Alliance*, p. 327).

10. P. 254, note 1. Concerning the idea of divine grace as
a divine radiance falling on the soul with the energy of a
stream, read the whole book of E.R. GOODENOUGH, *By Light
Light*, remembering that the author reduces too much divine
grace to the figure of light, which he poses as the basic
schematic representation of the system of Philo.

11. We mention two studies on divine light, that by E.R.
GOODENOUGH, *By Light Light*, which is well represented by its
title, and that by Franz-Norbert KLEIN, *Die Lichttermino-
logie bei Philon von Alexandrien und in den Hermenischen
Schriften*, E.J. Brill, Leiden, 1962, pp. 11-79.

12.   JAUBERT, *Alliance*, pp. 379-447, see p. 438.

13.   P. 109, 121, 131, 154.

14. Read Richard BAER, *Philo's use of the Categories male
and female*, Brill, Leiden, 1970, particularly pp. 40 *ff*, and
51-64.

15. On the contrary, the Patriarch's second wives and
concubines figure the lower goods which are a preparation
for virtue.

16. Concerning Isaac, who was born from a womb which was
unable to bring forth life (*Cher*. 8), see F.H. COLSON, *Philo
II* (Loeb), pp. 481-482.

17. *The Shepherd of Hermas*, Vis. I,2-4; III,18(10).

18. *De Josepho, Les oeuvres* 21, Introduction, p. 35.

19. The practice of the virtues of active life is a
necessary preparation for those who want to adopt contemplative life. Philo compares these two forms of life to the
years of active service of the priests of the Temple, and to
their years of retirement, respectively (Numb. 4:3 *f*; *Fuga*
34:38). His position can be compared to that of Antiochus
of Ascalon, who also supports the theory of inborn virtues,
and the threefold division of the goods, and who criticizes
those who renounce political life in order to care for
philosophy only. Antiochus offers a positive evaluation of
political life, and, generally, accepts the teachings of a
temporal Peripatetism. See E. BREHIER, *Idées*, pp. 259-261.

20. The figure of Tamar is idealized by the Rabbis in
spite of her intercourse with Judah. See F.H. COLSON, *Philo*
VIII (Loeb), p. 450, note on *Virt*. 221.

21. Cf. daily sacrifices, p. 70; Spiritual sacrifice,
p. 85.

22. The manna is a food of wisdom. See M. ALEXANDRE, *De
congressu*, notes 3 and 4, pp. 224-225, *Les oeuvres* 16. See
also P. BEAUCHAMP, "La cosmologie religieuse de Philon et la
lecture de l'Exode par le Livre de la Sagesse: le thème de
la manne," *Philon d'Alexandrie*, CNRS, pp. 207-218.

23. FESTUGIERE, *Le Dieu cosmique*, p. 129; cf. *Her*. 96-99.

24. BREHIER, *Idées*, pp. 255-256, notes 8-10.

25. FESTUGIERE, *Le Dieu cosmique*, pp. 310-335.

26. WOLFSON, *Philo* I, pp. 223-224.

27. *Ibid*., pp. 286-289.

28. Philo quotes Prov. 8:22 in *Ebr*. 31 ("God created me
first of all His works and founded me before the ages").
Philo reads *ektesato* = "obtained me", instead of *ektise* =
"created me" of LXX. In this he is closer to the Hebrew
kanah. Aquila, Symmachus and Theodotion, like Philo, read
ektesato. See F.H. COLSON, *Philo* III (Loeb), note on *Ebr*.
31, p. 501.

Concerning the Divine Logos with regard to the Jewish
speculations on Wisdom and particularly on the title
protogonos and on the theme of the Image, see J.G. KAHN, *De*

confusione, complementary note on *Conf*. 146, pp. 176-182, *Les oeuvres* 13.

29. E.R. GOODENOUGH (*By Light Light*, pp. 43-44) criticizes E. Bréhier's explanation of the Philonic powers as deriving from Stoic notions. But Bréhier also seems unprecise concerning their nature. He writes, "The divine powers are not distinct from the Forms; the incorporeal patterns, therefore, are considered as active causes, and, in return, powers are considered as Form" (*Idées*, p. 156; cf. p. 152). Philo, indeed, endowes the Forms with energy, but we must distinguish more definitely than Bréhier between archetypes, divine powers, angels, the souls of the stars, the souls living in the air, and the souls of men.

   M. HARL ("Cosmologie grecque," *Philon d'Alexandrie*, CNRS, p. 200) notes the concurrence of the two schemes of the Philonic powers, the one under the *Logos*, and the other under *Theos* and *Kyrios*, both of them including creation. However, we do not think that these two-schemes should be combined, because their meaning is different, the former referring to the theory of knowledge and perhaps to the question of praise, and the second, to the progress and the correction of the soul.

30. BREHIER, *Idées*, pp. 144-151.

31. M. ALEXANDRE (*De congressu*, note 1 on *Congr*. 38, p. 132, *Les oeuvres* 16) compares the quasi-personification of the Graces in Philo to the Stoic exegesis of the *Charites*. See also E. BREHIER, *Idées*, p. 38, 108 and 148. See particularly, Pierre BOYANCE, "Echo des exégèses de la mythologie grecque chez Philon," *Philon d'Alexandrie*, CNRS, pp. 178-183. Concerning the Philonic theory of the powers in relation to Hermetism and to the Greek tradition, see A.-J. FESTUGIERE, *La Révélation* III, *Les doctrines de l'âme*, p. 165. The Hermetist does not borrow from Philo this theory, which does not present in his teaching the Jewish features which we find in Philo, but he finds a sufficient basis for it in paganism.

32. WOLFSON, *Philo* II, p. 41.

33. *De divinatione* I,1-3; II,1-4, cf. BREHIER, *Idées*, p. 186.

34. *Phoedrus*, 244 *d-e*; 245 *a*; 249 *b*, cf. WOLFSON, *Philo* II, p. 14.

35. WOLFSON, *Philo* II, pp. 1-72; H. LEWY, *Sobria ebrietas*, *passim*.

36. BREHIER, *Idées*, pp. 119-120.

37. GOODENOUGH, *By Light Light*, p. 161.

38. *Ibid.*, p. 163.

39. FESTUGIERE, *Le Dieu inconnu et la gnose*, p. 48.

40. FESTUGIERE, *Le Dieu cosmique*, p. 549.

41. BREHIER, *Idées*, p. 120.

42. FESTUGIERE, *Le Dieu inconnu de la gnose*, p. 224. For a parallel in the *Hermetic Corpus* to the role of God in the regeneration of the soul and the development of virtue, *ibid.*, pp. 246-257.

43. M. ALEXANDRE, *De Congressu*, *Les oeuvres* 16, Introd., p. 74.

44. There is no soul completely deprived of the seed of virtue. Concerning this idea in profane literature and at Qumran, see V. NIKIPROWETZKY, "L'Elenchos," *Philon d'Alexandrie*, CNRS, 1967, p. 259, note 3. Concerning the "seed of the heart" in Judaism, see *ibid.*, pp. 267-273.

45. For the biblical symbolism of the rootedness of the righteous in divine wisdom, see M. ALEXANDRE, *De congressu*, complementary note on *Congr.* 56, pp. 239-240, *Les oeuvres* 16. In her introduction (*ibid.*, pp. 73-74, note 4), M. Alexandre explains the Philonic idea of the soul made pregnant by God and of the part of divine Wisdom in this impregnation, through the symbolism of the wives of the Patriarchs. She shows that this idea has, indeed, Greek sources, but also Jewish and biblical sources, seeing that, for instance, Prov. 8:22 is quoted in *Ebr.* 31; Jer. 3:4 is quoted in *Cher.* 49-51, and perhaps Wis. 8:2.9.16. Concerning 'ever-virgin' Wisdom (*aeiparthenos*), *ibid.*, complementary note on *Congr.* 7, pp. 235-236.

46. W. VOELKER shows the dependence of virtue on God, and Platonism as the explanation of this biblical teaching (*Fortschritt und Vollendung bei Philo von Alexandrien*, *Eine Studie zur Geschichte der Frommigkeit*, Leipzig 1938, abbreviated, *Fortschritt*, pp. 215-217.

47. W. VOELKER, *Fortschritt*, pp. 143;200;205, shows that the Philonic piety, particularly thanksgiving, is definitely Jewish and not Greek, on the basis of the doctrine of God as Creator, and he refers to the same judgment in E. Schwartz, *Aporien*, p. 539, A.3.

48. BREHIER, *Idées*, p. 272.

Concerning the three ways of Patriarchs in the Greeks, see W. VOELKER, *Fortschritt*, p. 154-155. For the different positions of the Greeks on the origin of virtue in relation to these ways, see E. BREHIER, *Idées*, pp. 272-281. Concerning *theia eutuchia* in Aristotle, see A.-J. FESTUGIERE, *La Révélation* IV, *Le Dieu inconnu et la Gnose*, pp. 251-252, and 315.

49. FESTUGIERE, *Le Dieu cosmique*, p. 151.

50. J. DANIELOU, *Philon d'Alexandrie*, pp. 57-75.

51. P. 123.

52. The contrast between heavenly and earthly virtue (*Congr*. 8) is inspired by *Phoedrus* 247 *d-e*, describing the (super-) celestial place where are found the intelligible realities, Justice, Temperance or Wisdom, Science, Beauty. It transposes into philosophical terms the speculations of Judaism on the pre-existing and creative Wisdom (Prov. 8; Wis. 7:25 *f*; 9:9-18; Sirach 1:1-20 and 24). The distinction between special and generic virtues is formulated in the vocabulary of Aristotelian logics. See M. ALEXANDRE, *De congressu*, complementary note on *Congr*. 2, p. 234, *Les oeuvres* 16.

53. BREHIER, *Idées*, pp. 259-260; DANIELOU, *Philon*, pp. 57-75.

For the doctrine of the three kinds of goods in Aristotle, *Nic. Eth*. I, 10098 *b*; *Pol*. 1233 *ff*; and in the Stoics, SVF III, 136.

54. Concerning the guardians of Plato, see *Rep*. 416; 539 *e*; 540 *a-c*; *Critias* 112 *b-e*. For the parallel between the guardians of Plato and the Philonic teaching of the necessity of active life as a preparation for contemplative retirement, see V. NIKIPROWETZKY, *De Decalogo*, complementary note on *Dec*. 108, pp. 155-157, *Les oeuvres* 23. V. Nikiprowetzky has the Therapeutae particularly in mind in

this Philonic criticism of an untimely haste to join
contemplative life.

55. *Introduction to Philo Judaeus*, Oxford, 1962, p. 63.

56. WOLFSON (*Philo* II, pp. 262-264) compares the position
of Philo to that of Plato, Aristotle, the Stoics and the
Jews, particularly the Essenes, concerning the predominance
of contemplative life over active life, and conversely.
Philo follows the Stoics concerning the duties of active
life.

57. Regarding the divine filiation of Isaac, the figure of
joy, E.R. GOODENOUGH (*By Light Light*, p. 235) notes that the
Greeks used to consider happiness not as a fruit of virtue
properly, but as a divine thing and as a gift of God.
Aristotle insists on this idea strongly (*Nic. Eth.* 1,9,1).
Concerning the association between virtue and joy, cf.
Cicero, *Tusc. Disp.*, V,43, "semper sapiens beatus est".
Concerning joy as an elevation of the soul contrasted with
the emotion of pleasure, see S.V.F. III,431-432.

58. Moral conscience and repentance are a work of God in
the soul, and depend on the divine mercy. See W. VOELKER,
Fortschritt, pp. 94,97,100.

Concerning the precedence of piety among the virtues in
Philo, see W. VOELKER, *ibid.*, pp. 224-225.

Paul SCHUBERT, *Form and Function of the Pauline
Thanksgiving*, pp. 205-206, notes that *eucharistia* is a "Neo-
Stoic" term, since it is completely absent from SVF and
appears for the first time in Andronicus in the first
century B.C., where it is catalogued between piety and
holiness among the virtues.

59. Concerning the contrast between *living* and *living well*
in the Greeks (Plato, Aristotle, Polybius), and references
in Philo, see M. ALEXANDRE, *De congressu*, note on *Congr.* 33,
p. 128, *Les oeuvres* 16.

60. *Quis rerum*, Les Oeuvres 15, pp. 188-189, note 4.

61. M. ALEXANDRE (*De congressu*, complementary note on
Congr. 161, pp. 256-257, *Les oeuvres* 16) gives the Roman,
Greek, and Philonic sources for the doctrine of *ponos*.

Concerning the exchange of a sheep for a donkey, which
figures the painstaking in study and its profit for the soul,

see F.H. Colson, *Philo* II (Loeb), note on *Post*. 95, pp. 449-500. See also *Philo* III (Loeb), note on *Deus* 97, p. 481. Moral effort is never taken in vain (cf. *Sacr*. 113-117).

About the redemption of the first-born of all impure domestic animal, see S. DANIEL, "La Halacha," note on *Spec. Leg*. I,135, in *Philon d'Alexandrie*, CNRS, p. 230.

Concerning the four passions, their references in Philo and the parallels in the Greeks, see V. NIKIPROWETZKY, *De Decalogo*, complementary note on *Dec*. 142, p. 158-159, *Les oeuvres* 23. About their nature in Philo (passions are not judgments, as in Chrysippus, but the natural activity of the irrational part of the soul), see M. ALEXANDRE, *De congressu*, note 4 on *Congr*. 81, pp. 159-160, *Les oeuvres* 16.

62. BREHIER, *Idées*, pp. 270-271.

63. Does Philo depend on the Cynics ?   E. Bréhier answers positively (*Idées*, pp. 261-264), following WENDLAND, *Philo und die kynisch-stoische Diatribe*, Berlin 1895. Alain Michel confutes this view and shows that the moralism and the devices reminiscent of Cynicism in Philo appear in the Platonists, the Peripatetics and the Stoics as well as in the Cynics. We know that Heinemann insists very much on the idea of a Cynic source of Philo.

E. Bréhier (*Idées*, p. 255) writes, "In the picture of the wise man (*sophos, spoudaios, asteios*), Philo adopts the famous Stoic paradoxes. A list of them is found in the treatise *Sobr*. 56-58. A special treatise is destined to show that the wise man alone is free. However, although these paradoxes occur frequently in his writings, Philo very rarely troubles to justify them. Philo's thought was shaped in a milieu where Stoicism was the common and, in some regards, classical, philosophy. The justification which sometimes he gives for these paradoxes tends to spiritualize them. See (*ibid*., notes 6 and 8), respectively the list of these paradoxes in Philo, and the way he spiritualizes some of them.

64. The notion of sacrifice in Philo does not grant a place to suffering, either in ascetical effort, or in expiation, for the reason what suffering is imperfect and human, and cannot in any way be a participation in divine things. See A. JAUBERT, *Alliance*, p. 493.

65. Concerning the meaning of *oudeneia* in Philo in comparison with the Greek and biblical parallels, see M.

HARL, *Heres*, note 3, pp. 25-26, *Les oeuvres* 15.   Let us add
that it is not enough for the soul to feel "very small" in
order to be bolder in the dialogue with God. Humility is to
be seen in a wider context, including the maturation of the
soul through skepticism, which dissuades man from his
pretention to be the measure of all things, and even of
knowing himself.

66.   Concerning the characteristics of the proud man (*Virt*.
350) and of the lover of vain glory (*Virt*. 173), see the
references to profane literature given by M. ALEXANDRE, *De
congressu*, note 1 on *Congr*. 127, p. 194, *Les oeuvres* 16.
About *ogkos* (puffing up in pride), see, *ibid*., note 3; about
oiesis, which is the more radical form of pride, see, *ibid*.,
note 2 on *Congr*. 138, pp. 200-201; about *philautia*, see,
ibid., complementary note on *Congr*. 130, p. 247. Concerning
typhos (puffing up leading to vain opinion), see V.
NIKIPROWETZKY, *De Decalogo*, note 1 on *Dec*. 4, p. 40, *Les
oeuvres* 23; F.H. COLSON, *Philo* VIII (Loeb), note on *Virt*.
17, pp. 440-441, and M. ALEXANDRE, *Congressu*, p. 256.

67.   Concerning the symbolism of the colours of the stones,
and the respective characteristics of Judah and of Issachar,
see W. VOELKER, *Fortschritt*, pp. 310-311.

68.   The two books *De Somniis* particularly reflect Philo's
concern for preventing the form of impiety which threatens
the ascetic advanced in virtue.   For instance, *Som*. I, 130-
132 on the numbness of Jacob's hip; (Gen. 32:25); I *Som*. 158
on the vision of the ladder of Jacob; *Som*. I,211-212 about
the "ashy-sprinkled animals" (Gen. 31:10), which figure the
nothingness of men; and particularly *Som*. II,19-30, which
includes many of these figures.   Let us notice among them
the symbolism of Joseph's sheaf, the law of Lev. 19:9
forbidding to gather that which remains of the reaping;
Deut. 1:17 on the judgment which belongs to God alone and
the circumcision of the proud pretention.   We may add to
this list *Som*. III,69 about the hand which touched the
genitals (Deut. 25:11-12); *Som*. II,75 about the obligation
to offer handfulls of ears as first-fruits according to Lev.
23:10; and *Q.G*. IV,100, where Rebecca, who lowers herself in
order to draw water, is exalted.

69.   BREHIER, *Idées*, p. 298.

70.   DANIELOU, *Philon d'Alexandrie*, p. 92.

71.   JAUBERT, *Alliance*, p. 419.

72. WOLFSON, *Philo* II, p. 288.

73. R. LE DEAUT, *Liturgie juive et Nouveau Testament*, Institut Biblique Pontifical, Rome, 1965, p. 62.

74. FESTUGIERE, *Les doctrines de l'âme*, p. 94. The *Hermetic Corpus*, particularly *Asclepius* and *Poimandres*, makes a large and significant use of *eucharistia, eulogia, hymnos*, and offers an interesting parallel to Philo's doctrine of grace, of thanksgiving, and of the spiritual sacrifice of praise, cf. for instance, *Poimandres* XIII, 17-22, and Stobeus Frg. XXIII, 56. We turn the reader to a succinct inquiry, "L'Eucharistie dans le Corpus Hermétique" given as appendix in our French edition, J. LAPORTE, *La doctrine eucharistique chez Philon d'Alexandrie*, Paris 1972, pp. 247-264.

75. There is a theology of grace underlying ancient Jewish prayers, for instance, the *Shema*, the *Eighteen Benedictions*, and the *Tahanun*, cf. K. HRUBY, "Quelques notes sur le *Tahanun* et la place de la prière individuelle dans la liturgie synagogale", *L'Orient Chrétien* IX, pp. 75-104. Concerning the prayers contained in Books VII and VIII of *Apostolic Constitutions*, which contain elements of cosmic praise and a theology of grace, cf. E.R. Goodenough, *By Light Light*, pp. 306-336, and L. BOUYER, *Eucharist*, pp. 119-135.

76. At Qumran also it is easy to find a theology of grace (inspiration in prayer, conversion of the heart, forgiveness of sins, divine help in good deeds and perseverance) and of justification (Deuteronomic theology of the Covenant) with a warning against relying on merit. For this last point, see "Hymns" IV, 7 (G. VERMES, *The Dead Sea Scrolls in English*, pp. 163-164).

ABBREVIATIONS FOR THE WRITINGS OF PHILO

Abr.	De Abrahamo.
Aet.	De aeternitate mundi.
Agr.	De agricultura.
Alex.	Alexander.
Cher.	De Cherubim.
Conf.	De confusione linguarum.
Congr.	De congressu eruditionis et gratia.
Cont.	De vita contemplaiva.
Dec.	De Decalogo.
Deter.	Quod deterius potiori insidiari soleat.
Deus.	Quod Deus sit immutabilis.
Ebr.	De ebrietate.
Flac.	In Flaccum.
Fug.	De fuga et inventione.
Gig.	De gigantibus.
Her.	Quis rerum divinarum heres sit.
Hypoth.	Hypothetica (Apologia pro Iudaeis).
Jos.	De Josepho.
Legat.	Legatio ad Caium.
Leg.Al.	Legum allegoriae.
Migr.	De migratione Abrahami.
Mos.	De vita Mosis.
Mut.	De mutatione nominum.
Op.	De opificio mundi.
Plant.	De plantatione.
Post.	De posteritate Caini.
Praem.	De praemiis et poenis, de exsecrationibus.
Prob.	Quod omnis probus liber sit.
Prov.	De Providentia.
Q.G.	Quaestiones et solutiones in Genesim.
Q.E.	Quaestiones et solutiones in Exodum.
Sacr.	De sacrificiis Abelis et Caini.
Sobr.	De sobrietate.
Som.	De somniis.
Spec. Leg.	De specialibus legibus.
Virt.	De virtutibus.

BIBLIOGRAPHY

LIST OF QUOTED STUDIES:

Philo with an English translation by F.H. COLSON & G.H. WHITAKER, in ten volumes and two supplementary volumes, The Loeb Classical Library.

Les oeuvres de Philon d'Alexandrie, published under the patronage of the University of Lyons, by Roger ARNALDEZ, Jean POUILLOUX et Claude MONDESERT, Editions Le Cerf, Paris, 1961 ff. (abbreviated: *Les oeuvres*).

Philo of Alexandria, Colloques nationaux du Centre de la Recherche scientifique, Lyon, 11-15 septembre 1966, Editions of CNRS, 1967 (abbreviated: *Philon d'Alexandrie, CNRS*).

M. ALEXANDRE, "La culture profane chez Philon, "*Philon d'Alexandrie, CNRS*, pp. 105-131.

---*De Congressu, Les oeuvres* 16.

R. ARNALDEZ, *Introduction générale*, et *De opificio, Les oeuvres* 1.

---*De virtutibus, Les oeuvres* 26.
---*De mutatione, Les oeuvres* 18.
----"La dialectique des sentiments chez Philon," *Philon d'Alexandrie*, CNRS, pp. 299-333.

J.-P. AUDET, "Esquisse historique du genre littéraire de la bénédiction juive et de l'eucharistie chrétienne," *Revue Biblique* 65, 1958, pp. 371-399.

----*La Didachè, Instructions des Apôtres*, Etudes Bibliques, Gabalda, Paris 1958, 500p.

R. BAER, *Philo's use of the Categories Male and Female*, Brill, Leiden 1970, 116p.

J.M. BAUMGARTEN, "Sacrifice and Worship among the Jewish Sectarians of the Dead Sea Scrolls," *H.T.R.* 46, 1953.

P. BEAUCHAMP, "La cosmologie religieuse de Philon et la lecture de l'Exode par le Livre de la Sagesse," *Philon d'Alexandrie*, CNRS, pp. 207-221.

E.J. BICKERMANN, "Bénédiction et prière," *Revue Biblique* 69, 1962, pp. 524-532.

G. BORNKAMM, "Lobpreis, Bekenntnis und Opfer," *Apophoreta, Festschrift fur Ernst Haenchen*, Verlag A. Topelmann, Berlin 1964, 299p.

L. BOUYER, *Eucharist, Theology and Spirituality of the Eucharistic Prayer*, University of Notre Dame Press, transl. C.U. Quinn, 1968, 484p.

E. BREHIER, *Les idées philosophiques et religieuses de Philon d'Alexandrie*, Etudes de Philosophie Médiévale, 2d ed. Vrin, Paris 1925, 336p.

V. BROCHARD, *Les Sceptiques grecs*, Bibliothèque d'Histoire de la Philosophie, Vrin, Paris, 2d ed. repr. 1959, 432p.

H. CAZELLES, "L'Anaphore et l'Ancien Testament," *Eucharisties d'Orient et d'Occident*, Lex Orandi 46, ed. B. Botte et al., Paris 1970, pp. 11-21.

----*Le Lévitique, La Sainte Bible*, Le Cerf, Paris, 1958.

A.H. CHROUST, "A Cosmological Proof for the Existence of God in Aristotle's Lost Dialogue *On Philosophy*," *The New Scholasticism*, XL 4 oct. 1966, pp. 447-463, "The Doctrine of the Soul in Aristotle's Lost Dialogue *On Philosophy, ibid.*, XLII, 3, 1968, pp. 364-373.

E. COTHENET, "Parfums," *Suppl. Dict. de la Bible*, vol. 6.

S. DANIEL, "La Halacha de Philon selon le premier livre des *Lois Spéciales*," *Philon d'Alexandrie*, CNRS, p. 221-243; *Recherches sur le vocabulaire du culte dans la Septante*, Librarie Klincksieck, Paris, 1966, 428p.

J. DANIELOU, *Philon d'Alexandrie*, Librarie Artheme Fayard, Paris 1957, 220p.

F. DAUMAS, *De vita contemplativa, Les oeuvres* 29.

R. Le DEAUT, *Liturgie juive et Nouveau Testament*, Institut Biblique Pontifical, Rome 1965, 90p.

N. DEMBITZ, "Gomel," *The Jewish Encyclopedia* V, p. 40.

G. DIX, *The Shape of the Liturgy*, Adam & Charles Black, London 2d ed. 1945.

I. DURHAM, "Shalom and the Presence of God," *Proclamation and presence, Old Testament Essays in Honour of Gwyne Henton Davies*, Richmond, Virginia, 1970, pp. 272-293.

A.-J. FESTUGIERE, *La révélation d'Hermes Trismégiste*, Etudes Bibliques, Gabalda, Paris.
   I. *L'astrologie et les sciences occultes,* 1950, 440p.
   II. *Le Dieu cosmique,* 1949, 610p.
   III. *Les doctrines de l'âme,* 1953, 313p.
   IV. *Le Dieu inconnu et la gnose,* 1964, 315p.

L. FINKELSTEIN, "The Birkat Ha-Mazon," *JQR* 19, 1928-29, p. 211-262.

----"The Development of the Amidah," *JQR* 16, 1925-26.

A. GONZALEZ, "Prière dans l'Ancien Testament," *Suppl. Dict. de la Bible,* fasc. 44.

GONZELMANN, "Eucharistein," *TWNT* (English ed.), IX, 7, pp. 399-401.

E.R. GOODENOUGH, *By Light Light, The Mystic Gospel of Hellenistic Judaism,* Yale Univ. Press, 1935, 427p.

----*An Introduction to Philo Judaeus,* Blackwell, Oxford 1962, 167p.

J. GUILLET, "Le langage spontané de la bénédiction dans l'Ancient Testament," *RSR* 57, 1969, pp. 163-204.

H. GUNKEL, *The Psalms,* transl. Thomas M. Horner, Facet Books, Fortress Press, Philadelphia, 1967.

P. HAAG, "Pâques d'après la Mishna," *Suppl. Dict. de la Bible,* vol. 6.

L. HALKIN, *La supplication d'action de grâces chez les Romains,* Bibl. Fac. Phil. & Lettres 128, Belles Lettres, Paris, 1953, 136p.

M. HARL, "Cosmologie grecque et représentations juives chez Philon d'Alexandrie." *Philon d'Alexandrie,* CNRS, pp. 189-207.

----*Heres, Les oeuvres* 15.

I. HEINEMANN, *Philons Griechische und Judische Bildung,* Darmstadt, 1962, 606p. (abbreviated: *Bildung*)

"Hermes Trismegistus," *Hermetica. The Ancient Greek and Latin Writings which contain religious or philosophical teachings ascribed to Hermes Trismegistus,* ed., tr. by Walter Scott, vol. I, Introd., Text and Translation, Oxford, at the Clarendon Press, 1924, 550p.

F.J.A. HORT & J.O.F. MURRAY," Eucharistia-eucharistein," *JTS* 3, 1902, pp. 594-598.

K. HRUBY, "Quelques notes sur le *Tahanum* et la place de la prière individuelle dans la liturgie synagogale," *l'Orient Syrien,* IX, 1964, pp. 75-104.

----"Les heures de prière dans le judaïsme à l'époque de Jésus," *La prière des heures,* Lex Orandi 35, Le Cerf, Paris

----"L'action de grâces dans la liturgie juive," *Eucharisties d'Orient et l'Occident,* Lex Orandi 46, Le Cerf, Paris 1970.

----"La notion de *Berakhah* dans la tradition et son caractère anamnétique," *Questions liturgiques* 2, 1971, pp. 155-170 (Louvain).

The Jerome Biblical Commentary, ed. by R.E. Brown, J.A. Fitzmyer & R.E. Murphy, Prentice Hall 1968.

J.G. KAHN, *De confusione, Les oeuvres* 13.

C. KANNENGIESSER, "Philon et les Pères sur la double création de l'homme." *Philon d'Alexandrie,* CNRS, pp. 277-299.

F.-N. KLEIN, *Die Lichterminologie bei Philon von Alexandrien und in den Hermetischen Schriften,* E.J. Brill, Leiden 1962, 232p.

K. KOHLER, "Benedictions," *The Jewish Encyclopedia* III, pp. 10-12.

W. JAEGER, *The Theology of the Early Greek Philosophers,* The Gifford Lectures, 1936, Clarendon Press, Oxford, 1947, 259p.

----*Early Christianity and Greek Paideia,* Harvard Univ. Press, 2d ed., 1965, 154p.

----*Aristotle, Fundamentals of the History of his Development,* transl. R. Robinson, Oxford, Univ. Press, 2d ed., 1948
(1962), 475p. (First German ed., 1923).

A. JAUBERT, *La notion d'Alliance dans le judaisme aux abords
de l'ère chrétienne,* Le Seuil, Paris, 1963, 542p.

H.J. KRAUS, *Worship in Israel, A cultic History of the Old
Testament,* transl. G. Buswell, Blackwell, Oxford, 1966,
245p.

C. LARCHER, *Etudes sur le Livre de la Sagesse,* Etudes
Bibliques Gabalda, Paris, 1969, 442p.

R.J. LEDOGAR, *Acknowledgment, Praise-verbs in the early
Greek Anaphora,* Herder, Rome, 1968, 190p.

H. LEWY, *Sobria ebrietas, Untersuchungen zur Geschichte der
antiken Mystik,* A. Topelmann, Giessen, 1929, 175p.

E. LIPINSKY, "Macarisme et Psaumes de congratulation," *Revue
Biblique* 75, 1968, pp. 321-367.

J.L. MCKENZIE, *Dictionary of the Bible,* The Bruce Publ.
Comp. Milwaukee, 1965, 954p.

A. MEASSON, *De sacrificiis, Les oeuvres* 4.

A. MICHEL, "Quelques aspects de la rhétorique chez Philon
d'Alexandrie," *Philon d'Alexandrie,* CNRS, pp. 81-105.

O. MICHEL, "Homologein," *TWNT (Theol. Dict. of the N.T.)* V,
pp. 199-220.

The Mishna, Transl. by Herbert DANBY, Oxford, Univ. Press,
1933.

S. MOWINKEL, *The Psalms in Israel's Worship,* trans. by D.R.
Ap. THOMAS, 2 vol. 246p. & 303p., Blackwell, Oxford, 1967.

R.E. MURPHY, Review of Frank Crusemann, Studien zur
Formgeschichte von Hymnus und Danklied in Israel, *The
Catholic Biblical Quarterly (CBQ)* 33, 1971, pp. 250-251.

V. NIKIPROWETZKY, *De Decalogo, Les oeuvres* 23.

----"Les suppliants chez Philon d'Alexandrie," *REJ*, 1963.

A. Pelletier, "Pains de proposition," *Suppl. Dict. de la Bible*, vol. 6, pp. 965-976.

----*Lettre d'Aristée à Philocrate*, SCH, Le Cerf,Paris, 1962.

J. PEPIN, *Mythe et Allégorie, Les origines grecques et les contestations judéo-chrétiennes*, Aubier, Paris, 1958, 522p.

----*Theologie cosmique et théologie chrétienne*, PUF, 1964, 600p.

A.F. RAINEY, "The Order of Sacrifices in Old Testament Ritual Texts," *Biblica* 51, 1970, pp. 485-498.

J. ROBINSON, "Die Hodajot-Formel in Gebet und Hymnus des Fruchristentums," *Apophoreta, Festschrift fur E. Haenchen*, A. Topelmann, Berlin, 1964, 194-235.

T. SCHERMANN, "Eucharistia und eucharistein in ihrem Bedeutungsvandel bis 200 n. Chr.," *Philologus* 69, 1910, pp. 375-410.

P. SCHUBERT, *Form and Function of the Pauline Thanksgiving*, Topelman, Berlin 1939, 185p. We refer to it in the ms., Diss. Philosophy, Univ. of Chicago, Ill., 1935, ms.

M.J. SCHWARTZ, "L'Egypte de Philon," *Philon d'Alexandrie*, CNRS, pp. 35-45.

E. Mary SMALLWOOD, *Philonis Alexandrini Legatio ad Gaium*, E.J. Brill, Leiden, 1961, 330p.

R. TOURNAY, "Le psaume et les bénédictions de Moise (Deut. 33), *Revue Biblique* 65, 1968, pp. 181-213.

M. UNTERSTEINER, *Aristotele, Della Filosofia, Temi e Testi* 10, Roma 1963, Ed. di Storia e Let., Roma, 1963, 311p.

R. DE VAUX, *Studies in Old Testament Sacrifice*, Cardiff, Univ. of Wales Press, 1964, 120p.

----*Institutions del'Ancien Testament, 2 vol. Paris 1960.*

W. VOELKER, *Fortschritt und Vollendung bei Philo von Alexandrien, Eine Studie zur Geschichte der Frommigkeit*, Texte und Untersuchunden, 49, I, Leipzig, 1938, 350p.

G. VERMES, *The Dead Sea Scrolls in English*, Penguin Books, 1968, 258p.

H.A. WOLFSON, *Philo*. 2 vol., Harvard Univ. Press, 4d ed. 1968, 462 & 531p.

R.K. YERKES, *Sacrifice in Greek and Roman Religions and Early Judaism*, Adam & Charles Black, London, 1953, 270p.

COMPLEMENT OF BIBLIOGRAPHY

P. ANDRIESSEN, "L'Eucharistie dans l'Epitre aux Hébreux," *Nouvelle Revue Theologique* 94, 3 March 1972, pp. 269-277.

Y. ASKHENASY, "Célébration de la Pâque Juive," *Questions Liturgiques* 52, 2, April 1971, pp. 141-154.

B. M. BOKSER, *Philo's Description of Jewish Practices*, Center for Hermeneutical Studies in Hellenistic and Modern Culture, Berkeley 1977, 27p.

P. BORGEN, *Bread from Heaven. An Exegetical Study of the Concept of Manna in the Gospel of John and in the Writings of Philo*, Leiden, 1965.

A. BOULEY, *From Freedom to Formula. The Evolution of the Eucharistic Prayer from Oral Improvisation to Written Texts*, Catholic Univ. of America 1981, 302p. (Cf. Bibliography pp. 265-282).

H. CAZELLES, "Eucharistie, Bénédiction et Sacrifice dans l'Ancien Testament," *La Maison-Dieu* 123, 1975, pp. 7-28.

G. CUMING, *He Gave Thanks. An Introduction to the Eucharistic Prayer*, Grove Books Bramcote Notts, 45 p.

R.J. DALY, *Christian Sacrifice. Studies in Christian Antiquity*, Catholic Univ. of America 1978, 586p.

D. DELASSUS, *Le Thème de la Pâque chez Philon d'Alexandrie*, Mémoire de maitrise, Univ. of Lille III, 1972.

C. GIRAUDO, *La Struttura letteraria della Preghiera Eucharistica, Saggio sulla genesi leteraria di una forma*. Analecta Biblica, 92. Rome, Biblical Institute Press, 1981, 387p.

K. HRUBY, "La "Birkat Ha-Mazon," la prière d'action de grâces après le repas," *Mélanges B. Botte,* Mt.-César 1972, pp. 205-222.

J. JEREMIAS, *The Eucharist Words of Jesus*, N.Y. 1966, 278p.

J. LAPORTE, "Philo in the Tradition of Biblical Wisdom Litérature," *Aspects of Wisdom in Judaism and Early Christianity,* ed. R.L. Wilken, Notre Dame 1975, pp. 103-142.

L. LIES, *Wort und Eucharistie bei Origenes,* Innsbruck 1978, 363p.

Burton L. MACK, Imitatio Moses. Patterns of Cosmology and Soteriology in the Hellenistic Synagogue," *Studia Philonica* 1972, pp. 22-55.

----"Logos and Sophia. Untersuchungen zur Weissheits- theologie im hellenistischen Judentum," *SUNT* 10, 1973.

H. B. MEYER, "Das Werden der literarischen Structur des Hochgebetes," *Zeitschrift fur Katholische Theologie* 105, 2, 1983, pp. 184-202.

V. NIKIPROWETZKY, "La spiritualisation des sacrifices et le culte sacrificial au temple de Jérusalem chez Philon d'Alexandrie," *Semitica* 17, 1967, pp. 97-116.

----*Le commentaire de l'Ecriture chez Philon D'Alexandrie,* Lille 1974.

----"Le *De vita contemplativa* revisité," *Sagesse et Religion,* Colloque de Strasbourg 1976, Paris PUF pp. 105-121.

Ch. PERROT, "Le repas du Seigneur," *Maison-Dieu* 123, 3, 1975, pp. 29-48.

S. SANDMEL, "Virtue and Reward in Philo," *Essays in Old Testament Ethics. In Memoriam J. Philip Hyatt,* ed. J.L. Grenshaw, J.T. Willis, N.Y. 1974, pp. 215-223.

T.J. TALLEY, "From Berakah to Eucharistia: A Reopening Question," *Worship* 50, 2, March 1976, pp. 115-137.

J. VIDAL, *Le thème d'Adam chez Philon d'Alexandrie,* Mémoire de maitrise, Univ. of Paris IV, 1971.

D.S. WINSTON, "Philo's Theory of Cosmogony," *Religion Syncretism in Antiquity: Conversation with Geo. Widengren*, ed. B.A. Pearson, Missoula 1975, pp.157-171.

INDICES

I

SCRIPTURE

Genesis			Exodus	
2,12	173		2,21	154
4,1-2	148		3,12	44
17-25	156		12	74
5,8	45		12,14	79
8,12-18	22		13,1-2	44,45,156
9,6	100		8	79
26	30		11-16	44,70
12,2-3	30		15,1-20	18,26,27,82,97
13,9	78		17,15	37
14,22-23	26,35		18,9-15	51,74
15,8-10	35,44		19,1	83
17,1	115		21,11	44
3	35		5-6	45,156
18	41		22,6-14	44,155
18,1-15	35,115,126		23,10	156
19,26	46		19	44,70,156
30-38	122		25b	54
24,26	31,50		25,1-2	44,156
31	31		27,30-32	156
67	151		28,17-18	174
25,1-2	44		29,31-42	61,65,156
27,38	41		30,11-16	44
29,31	164,171		34	113
35	32,33,173		32	91
30,1-3	152		34,26	70
18	174			
31,10-13	46		Leviticus	
32,25	46		1	63,64
38,26	133		3-17	156
49,8	31,32,33		4	64
15	174			

255

Leviticus (cont.)

2,1-3	156
8-9	66
13	66
14	40,67,156
14-16	66
3	23
3	157
16	149
6,12-15	65
13	67
7	23
12-15	23,56
8,24-30	92
11,3-8	42
17,11	64
19,9	146
24	44,70,156
22,29	56
23,1-17	43,65,70,80,146
18-19	23
27,1-8	25
28	45
30-33	44,72

Numbers

3,12-13	91
41	44
5,2-4	122
6,14-18	23,46
21-22	40,45,155
10,10	23
12,1	154
15,1-12	65
7	59
18-20	65
18,12-18	70
24,5-9	65
25,1	91
27,1-11	27
30-33	44
28,2-8	44,45,61,74,156
29	44
29,12	39,87
30	25
31,28	45
39-40	26,177

Deuteronomy

1,17	175
4,6-7	43
5,2-4	121
6,10-13	155
7,13	23
18	16,104
8,8	175
11-18	40,43
12-20	155
17-18	14,21,22
9,5-6	178
14	21,29
21	16,104
11,18-21	42,104
14,6	43
15,17-21	43
16,20-22	46,93
17,18	155
21,15-17	170
22,8	175
23,1-9	21
2-4	121
18-19	156
21	40,156
22-23	45
25,11-12	46
26,1-10	26,44,45,70,88
29	44
27,1-11	26
28,29	44
29,12-36	87
39	87
32,1-43	27
33,2-5	60

Proverbs

3,19-20	102
8,22	164
11,16	16
16,21	24

Psalms

19	18
23	26
30	26
36	26
38	69
0	69

Psalms (cont.)
79   26
94   26
100   56
118   87
141   69,94

I Samuel
1,11   46,92
2,30   19

II Chronicals
15,10   84

II Maccabees
1,11   16
10,7   16
12,31-32   84

Judith
8,25   16

Esther
8,12   16

Sirach
24,33   16
37,11   16

Isaiah
66,3   69

Ezekiel
45,18-25   184

Hosea
1,3   63

II

FIGURATIVE BIBLICAL PERSONS &
PERSONS OF THE ANCIENT WORLD

Aaron, 92, 94.
Abel, 4, 36, 120, 133, 165.
Abraham, 30, 31, 35, 37, 39, 50, 53, 106, 115, 123, 149,
    150, 156, 184.
Adam, 119, 147.
Alexander, 100.
Besaleel, 110.
Cain, 4, 36, 119, 120, 131, 148, 150, 165, 173, 175, 176,
    183.
Enoch, 148, 150.
Essau, 154.
Essenes, 74, 84, 141.
Eve, 147.
Hagar, 149, 165, 166, 167.
Hannah, 154.
Isaac, 33, 37, 39, 74, 150, 167, 169, 170.
Ismael, 149.
Israel, 35, 170.
Issachar, 33, 173, 174, 175.
Jacob, 33, 152, 154, 170, 175.
Jethro, 50.
Joseph, 35, 153.
Judah, 4, 27, 31, 33, 34, 35, 60, 153, 156, 173, 174, 175.
Laban, 31, 35.
Leah, 32, 33, 152, 153, 165, 170, 173.
Levi, 22, 91, 181.
Miriam, 50, 78, 82.
Moses, 37, 78, 82, 108, 110, 118, 119, 130, 134, 147, 154,
    160.
Noah, 108.
Pharaoh, 120.
Rachel, 152, 153, 165, 170.
Rebecca, 31, 151, 165, 167.
Samuel, 92, 154.
Sarah, 76, 149, 150, 161, 166, 167.
Sem, 31, 108.
Seth, 108, 156.
Tamar, 33, 154.
Terah, 174.
The High Priest, 34, 39, 69, 81, 90, 103, 104, 105, 108,
    109, 110, 111, 173, 181.
The Muses, 39, 43, 75, 94, 107, 181.
Therapeutae, 50, 74, 82, 84, 93, 96, 100, 101, 141.

III

ANCIENT AUTHORS

Aratos, 218.
Aristeas, 3, 4, 16, 95, 103, 106, 142, 143, 157, 184.
Aristobule, 100, 142.
Aristotle, 4, 59, 116, 125, 126, 129, 130, 131, 134, 135,
    158, 165, 168, 170, 183.
Book of Jubilees, 83, 84.
Cicero, 15, 125, 160, 168.
Cleanthes, 4, 27, 158, 182.
Clement of Alexandria, 175.
Apostolic Constitutions, 182.
Hermetic Corpus, 94, 95, 163, 164, 167, 177.
Cynics, 73, 74, 76, 78, 85, 87, 128, 158, 165, 171.
Diogenes Laertius, 132.
Enesidemus, 135.
Epicurus, 125.
Heraclitus, 123, 125.
Hesiod, 27, 128, 130.
Josephus, 68, 104, 110, 81.
Origen, 150, 176.
Plato, 3, 21, 63, 90, 91, 102, 107, 119, 122, 125, 126, 128,
    130, 131, 132, 134, 136, 150, 158, 160, 163, 165, 167.
Plutarch, 161, 162, 164.
Protagoras, 4, 120, 131, 132, 148, 183.
Qumran, 3, 22, 50, 56, 84, 87, 88, 97.
Shepherd of Hermes, 152.
Stoics, 123, 125, 128, 129, 133, 135, 158, 160, 168.
Testaments of the Twelve Patriarchs, 81.
Wisdom, 3, 16, 102, 103, 110, 142, 164.
Xenophon, 9, 170, 171.

IV

MODERN AUTHORS

Alexandre, M., 108, 112, 113, 115, 120, 123, 134, 159, 164,
    167, 170, 174.
Arnaldez, R., 141, 229.
Audet, J. P., 17, 20, 25, 49, 50, 51, 52, 53, 55.
Baer, R., 147.
Baumgarten, J. M., 49.
Beauchamp, P., 157.
Bickerman, E. J., 20.
Bornkamm, G., 17, 21, 24.
Bouyer, L., 102, 178.

Brehier, E., 1, 2, 3, 12, 90, 110, 121, 123, 134, 135, 154,
    158, 160, 161, 163, 164, 165, 168, 171, 172, 176.
Cazelles, H., 2, 24, 49, 52, 55, 56, 57, 59, 64, 70.
Chroust, A. H., 126.
Colson, F. H., 53, 74, 80, 81, 87, 92, 110, 111, 118, 119,
    123, 127, 135, 154, 159, 174.
Cothenet, E., 69.
Daniel, S., 17, 23, 24, 40, 58, 63, 65, 75, 90, 91, 122,
    171.
Danielou, J., 1, 2, 101, 125, 142, 167, 176.
Daumas, F., 91, 97.
Deaux, R. Le, 177.
Dembitz, N., 20.
Durham, I., 23.
Festugiere, A.-J., 2, 3, 90, 100, 115, 121, 125, 128, 129,
    131, 158, 162, 163, 164, 166, 177, 178.
Finkelstein, L., 49, 62.
Gonzales, A., 20.
Goodenough, E. R., 1, 2, 49, 102, 110, 119, 121, 142, 145,
    151, 153, 159, 162, 164, 178.
Guillet, J., 17, 20, 41, 53.
Gunkel, H., 96.
Halkin, L., 8, 14.
Harl, M., 65, 110, 121, 123, 159, 170, 173.
Heinemann, I., 1, 73, 74, 76, 78, 79, 80, 83, 85, 96, 125.
Hort, F. J. A. and J. O. F. Murray, 1.
Hruby, K., 2, 17, 29, 49, 53, 61, 62, 63, 178.
Jaeger, W., 117, 122, 132.
Jaubert, A., 2, 81, 90, 94, 95, 97, 144, 145, 146, 172, 177.
Jeremias, J., 24.
Kahn, J. G., 120, 123, 159.
Kannengiesser, C., 132.
Kohler, K., 19, 49.
Kraus, H. J., 71, 93.
Laporte, J., 153, 241.
Lardner, C., 142.
Ledogar, R. J., 1, 8, 9, 14, 16, 21, 22, 38, 52, 62, 63, 94,
    104.
Lewy, H., 142, 160.
Lipinsky, E., 2, 50, 51, 97.
McKenzie, J. L., 70, 71, 87.
Michel, A., 17, 21, 120.
Mowinkel, S., 18, 96.
Murphy, R. E., 97.
Nikiprowetzky, V., 81, 83, 89, 91, 93, 134, 160, 169, 173.
Pelletier, A., 68.
Pepin, J., 2, 3, 101, 125, 126, 129, 123, 131.
Rainey, A. F., 64, 75.
Robinson, J., 17, 21, 22, 34.

Schermann, T., 1, 8, 9, 37.
Schubert, P., 1, 8, 10, 49, 170.
Tournay, R., 91.
Vaux, R. de, 64, 76, 78, 79, 80, 83.
Volker, W., 164, 165, 170, 174.
Westerman, 96.
Wolfson, H. A., 1, 32, 95, 96, 97, 100, 108, 111, 120, 122,
    125, 131, 134, 135, 136, 158, 160, 169, 177.
Yerkes, R. K., 10, 17, 26, 29, 63, 71, 75, 119.

STUDIES IN THE BIBLE AND EARLY CHRISTIANITY

1. Hugh M. Humphrey, **A Bibliography for the Gospel of Mark, 1954-1980**

2. Rolland Wolfe, **The Twelve Religions of the Bible**

3. Jean LaPorte, *Eucharistia* in Philo

4. Peter Gorday, **Principles of Patristic Exegesis: Romans 9-11 in Origen, John Chrysostom, and Augustine**